Zulu Conquered

'First came the trader, then the missionary
and then the red soldier.'

*A remark attributed to King Cetshwayo kaMpande
of the amaZulu, 1879*

A British concept of dealing with Zululand, 1879

Zulu Conquered

The March of the Red Soldiers
1828–1884

Ron Lock

Frontline Books, London

For my Grandson,
Cameron Laatz
Who died too young.

Zulu Conquered: The March of the Red Soldiers, 1828–1884

This edition published in 2010 by Frontline Books,
an imprint of Pen & Sword Books Limited,
47 Church Street, Barnsley, S. Yorkshire, S70 2AS
www.frontline-books.com, email info@frontline-books.com

Copyright © Pen & Sword Books Ltd, 2010

ISBN: 978-1-84832-564-7

A CIP data record for this title is available from the British Library.

For more information on our books, please visit www.frontline-books.com, email
info@frontline-books.com or write to us at the above address.

Typeset by JCS Publishing Services Ltd, www.jcs-publishing.co.uk

Printed and bound in the UK by CPI Mackays, Chatham ME5 8TD

Contents

Illustrations

Plate Section (between pages 118 and 119)

Acknowledgements

My thanks again to Elizabeth Bodill for the patience in coping with many revisions of this book. My thanks are also due to Miriam Vigar for reading the draft manuscript and contributing constructive suggestions; to Peter Quantrill, my co-author on other projects, for valued observations; to Michael Leventhal of Frontline Books for his continual interest and encouragement; John Young for his generosity in supplying the jacket illustration; the staff of the Killie Campbell Library (now called The Campbell Collection); and likewise the Africana Museum, Johannesburg; to Arthur Konigkramer of AMAFA and, last but not least, my graciously long-suffering wife in the midst of rooms strewn with books and papers whilst moving house.

Chapter 1

First Come the Traders

'First came the trader, then the missionary, then the red soldier.' Such was the remark attributed to Cetshwayo kaMpande, king of the Zulu nation, as he attempted to grasp the implications of an ultimatum that the British High Commissioner for southern Africa had served upon him in December 1878. It was an ultimatum so outrageous in what it demanded, that it was quite clear it had been designed to be totally beyond the compliance of the Zulu king. Now there would be war: Cetshwayo's army, medieval in terms of weapons, versus the red soldiers of Queen Victoria, armed with the breech-loading rifle.

Although the Zulu, who call themselves the People of Heaven, had held sway in south-eastern Africa ever since King Shaka had forged numerous Nguni clans into a single realm, they had only encountered white men some fifty years earlier. Now, in less than a man's lifetime, the red soldiers were coming to enforce the White Queen's rule.

For centuries there had been rare appearances of Europeans along this south-eastern coast of Zululand but they had been castaways, the survivors of tragic shipwrecks. Perhaps the first white men to set eyes on the rolling green hills and forested valleys, fringed with a shoreline of crashing breakers, were Vasco Da Gama and his Portuguese sailors. They did not set foot ashore – in fact, for the next 300 years no one would deliberately do so – but Da Gama nevertheless gave the land a European name, Natal, having sighted it on Christmas Day 1497.

Tides and winds ensured that unseaworthy ships, or ships with incompetent crews, were wrecked on a particular 500-mile-long stretch of the South African coast. It was as if a magnet drew the ships ashore there instead of elsewhere on a coastline over 2,000 miles in length.

Many of the passengers and crew survived the numerous shipwrecks and got ashore – some desperately injured but many unscathed. However, all were as one in their desperate plight. Their only hope of succour and rescue was to reach the Portuguese base of Lourenço Marques, no more than a toehold on the African coast but blessed with a natural harbour, if little else, where Portuguese ships called at infrequent intervals.

The Nguni/Zulu people, far to the north, were amongst the last of the tribes to witness the tragic human remnants of the shipwrecks. By the time the survivors reached Nguni territory their numbers would have been decimated again and again by injury, murder, cannibalism, disease, starvation and despair. As few reached so far north, records of encounters with the Nguni/Zulu are rare; the survivors of the *San Alberto*, wrecked in 1593, were most likely the first white men to encounter them.

The *San Alberto* castaways also recorded that as they made their way further north, so the local people became increasingly friendly. On crossing the 'Uchugla River' – the present-day Thukela – the Nguni/Zulu became so impressed with the fervour the Portuguese displayed

1. Cetshwayo kaMpande, king of the amaZulu

during their religious devotions that they naively joined in with great abandon and rejoicing, 'kissing and embracing the Portuguese' and 'treating them with the utmost familiarity'. The Portuguese also found that mutual beard-stroking – an affable form of greeting that they had encountered during their march north – was also practised by the Nguni/Zulu.

In 1755 a handful of Englishmen, the first of what would become a massive invasion of Britons over the next 200 years, was thrown upon the shores of Zululand. Unlike the Portuguese ships that had met disaster on the return journey from India, the *Doddington*, a British East Indiaman, was wrecked on its outward voyage, three months after setting sail from England. She went aground near Algoa Bay (present-day Port Elizabeth) and so quickly did she sink that only twenty-three of the total ship's company of almost 300 men and women survived.

Sixty years later, in preparation of a survey of the coast between Port Natal and Delagoa Bay, three ships of the Royal Navy dropped anchor off what is now Zululand. In 1819 Shaka, the illegitimate son of Senzangakhona, the ruler of the Zulu clan, had defeated the numerically superior Ndwandwe army of Chief Zwide kaLanga. It was the first of many victories that Shaka would win with a ruthlessness of purpose that, within a few short years, would establish the kingdom of the Zulu. Shaka saw to it that what had been an insignificant Nguni clan, would become the Zulu nation. He introduced a new form of warfare: instead of the opposing sides standing back, throwing spears at each other, Shaka invented a short, broad-bladed stabbing spear – similar to the Roman sword of ancient times – that was to be used hand-to-hand and thus retained. It was never to be thrown, on pain of death. The Zulus named this weapon '*iklwa*', derived from the sucking sound made when the blade was withdrawn from a victim, but the Europeans used the term 'assegai' for both this and the lighter throwing spear.

As clans were conquered one after the other, the captured youths were formed into age-group regiments. Thus the defeated clans lost their former identities and became 'Zulu'. On one occasion Shaka was taken to task by an old comrade in arms who asked how it was that a warrior of a newly-conquered clan could be given rapid promotion in the Zulu army. He replied: 'A man who fights in the Zulu army becomes a Zulu as if he had been born a Zulu.' Shaka ruled over a kingdom that stretched from the borders of Swaziland and Mozambique, south for 450 miles and inland as far as the Drakensberg Mountains.

In 1822 Captain William Fitzwilliam Owen, RN, with the crews of his three Royal Navy ships HMS *Leven*, *Barracouta* and *Cockburn*, appeared to be unaware of the momentous upheaval that was taking place in the green hills beyond the pounding breakers. No doubt he was more concerned with the decimation of his officers and men. Having been assailed by swarms of mosquitoes along the Mozambique coast, men were dying of malaria at an alarming rate. Captain Owen was to lament that there was hardly a landmark named by the survey south of Delagoa Bay that did not record the fate of some crew member. The one exception was Point Durnford, named after the young officer who had delineated it. But even his name bore connotations of ill omen, for the young officer's nephew, Colonel Anthony Durnford to be, would be killed by the Zulus fifty-seven years later at the Battle of Isandlwana. The only contact that the sailors had with the Zulu people was a sharp skirmish with one Soshangene, a renegade Zulu commander who, having fallen foul of Shaka, had left the Zulu kingdom with some of his warriors and was now freebooting in Mozambique. One of Owen's officers, Captain Lechmere RN, described Soshangene as 'wearing full military attire with a crane feather headdress atop his shaven head, monk style, and with a false beard made from oxtail hair' (here again the Zulu fascination with beards). Captain Lechmere's description was the first of fully-fledged Zulu warriors:

> . . . tall, robust, and warlike, in their persons open, frank, and pleasing in their manners with a certain appearance of independence in their carriage . . . , infinitely above the natives of Lourenço Marques . . . their appearance was warlike, and had a striking affect as the extensive line moved through the various windings of the path. The grass being wet, they were observed taking particular care to keep their shields above it, as the damp would render them unserviceable; the spears attached to them, being thus elevated, were often seen glittering in the sun above the brow of the hill.

A fine description and one that any British redcoat would recognise half a century later as being that of a Zulu warrior. Although Soshangene appeared to be friendly, one night he led an attack on a survey party, but was sent packing in disarray by a volley of naval musketry. Thus, it would seem, the first British engagement with the Zulus was fought by bluejackets rather than by redcoats.

Captain Owen, and what remained of his decimated crews, finally sailed south to Cape Town to replenish stores and recruit more men and it was not long before he was again heading for Zululand to complete his survey. Calling in at Algoa Bay, he made the acquaintance of two ex-Royal Navy officers, Francis George Farewell and James Saunders King, both of whom had been forced to retire from the Navy due to the end of the Napoleonic Wars. They were now, like Owen, headed for Zululand, not to survey the coast but in two chartered ships, the *Salisbury* and the *Julia*, to make contact with the powerful and mysterious King Shaka, of whom much was spoken but of whom little was known. It was Farewell's belief that all the gold and ivory that was exported by the Portuguese from Lourenço Marques originated in Shaka's kingdom. To fulfil their purpose, Farewell and King required an interpreter and it was their good fortune that Captain Owen had just such a man – Jacob, a former convict of mixed blood who was, perhaps, due to return to jail. In any event, Jacob, willing or otherwise, went aboard the *Salisbury*, the first step in a long and eventful journey that would raise him from the status of felon to that of interpreter and advisor to the Zulu monarch: a most influential position.

On reaching Zululand they found every attempt to anchor and row a boat ashore thwarted by the crashing surf. During the final attempt to land, the ship's boat was overturned, the cargo lost, three men drowned, and several more were marooned for five weeks. However, Jacob, who was amongst the landing party, was not to be found when rescue came: he had departed inland to his destiny with Shaka.

Turning their vessels south, Farewell and King decided to try their luck at what became known as Port Natal (known later still as Durban), a fine harbour, the only one for hundreds of miles in either direction, but a haven that was guarded by a sandbar across its entrance. The *Salisbury* stood just off shore being of too deep a draft to cross the bar, while the *Julia* managed to enter harbour at high tide. So the traders' enthusiasm, despite the dangers and hardships, soared.

Back in Algoa Bay, Farewell and King, now believing a rumour that the Zulu king's great cattle kraal was fenced entirely of elephant tusks, obtained financial backing from the local merchants for a more ambitious expedition. Amongst the recruits was an Englishman of effervescent disposition by the name of Henry Francis Fynn and, although only twenty-one, a trader and traveller of considerable experience. He would purchase all the commodities that the expedition would offer in trade for ivory and gold, it being firmly believed that gold was to be had in abundance. It was decided to send Fynn on ahead, with twenty-five men aboard the little *Julia*.

Again the vessel was successful in crossing the bar, and on 10 March 1824 Fynn and others went ashore to make contact with the local inhabitants, spending a fearful night being attacked by 'wolves' (wild dogs or hyenas?) that persistently dragged away every item of bedding and clothing that they could fasten their teeth to. Having travelled twelve miles (to probably present-day Umhloti), Fynn was taking a rest when his attention was drawn to a frightening spectacle. Coming along the beach, seemingly following in Fynn's tracks was a massive force of warriors:

> I immediately concluded they had come in pursuit of me after having already destroyed the party I had left building. The bush along the beach was dense and, as I was sure they had seen me, flight appeared inadvisable. On the approach of the head of the column I was struck with astonishment at their appearance, for it was sufficient to terrify. Evidently they were equally surprised at mine, and looked at me with a kind of horror. The leaders talked much among themselves, but at length passed on along the beach. This dense mass of natives continued to pass by me until sunset, all staring at me with amazement, none interfering with me.

For many days Fynn and his followers stayed in the nearby village of a local Zulu headman while news was sent to Shaka that the white visitor awaited his permission to proceed. Word came that Fynn must wait and that, in the meantime, he would be attended by an officer named Msigali and twenty warriors. When Msigali arrived Fynn was appalled at his evil appearance and wanted to get rid of him at all costs. He wrote: 'There was something so frightfully forbidding in this man's countenance that in addition to the conviction that one of his duties was to spy and report on my every action, I felt he looked as much like a murderer as it was possible to infer from his countenance.'

Word also came to Fynn that Farewell had arrived at Port Natal aboard another chartered vessel, the *Antelope*, bringing with him eight horses, the first to be seen by the Zulu people. Fynn immediately returned to Port Natal and shortly thereafter news came that the visitors had permission to proceed on the 200-mile journey to Shaka's capital. During their travels Fynn and Farewell were struck by the cleanliness and order that prevailed.

It took Fynn and his party two weeks to reach Shaka's residence at Dukuza (present-day Stanger) which they first saw from a distance of fifteen miles. When closer Fynn estimated that the capital was two miles in circumference and that there were 80,000 warriors, all dressed in war attire, on parade. Before meeting Shaka he was requested to gallop around the perimeter of the capital and then again, accompanied by the rest of the party who were mounted. Finally, leaving their mounts behind, Farewell, Fynn and their companions were ushered into the royal enclosure where eventually, from the midst of many Zulu dignitaries,

2. Henry Francis Fynn, the first white man to visit the Zulu Kingdom, later became a confidant of King Shaka. (*KZN Archives, Pietermaritzburg*)

Shaka revealed himself and the white men were formally presented with elephant tusks. Then, at a gesture from the Zulu monarch, the whole mass of warriors fell back, making way for their king. What followed must have been an awe-inspiring spectacle, the like of which no white man had ever seen and few would ever see again.

Despite Fynn's apparent composure, he and his companions must have been gripped with apprehension. During their journey from the coast it had become abundantly clear that human life was accorded little value and that their fate depended solely on Shaka's whim: a smashed skull and instant death could be the result of royal displeasure.

Fynn continued in his diary:

A portion of each of these [regiments] rushed to the river and the surrounding hills, while the remainder, forming themselves into a circle, commenced dancing with Shaka in their midst. It was a most exciting scene, surprising to us, who could not have imagined that a nation termed 'savages' could be so disciplined and kept in order.

Regiments of girls, headed by officers of their own sex, then entered the centre of the arena to the number of 8,000 – 10,000, each holding a slight staff in her hand. They joined in the dance, which continued for about two hours.

The King came up to us and told us not be afraid of his people, who were now coming up to us in small divisions, each division driving cattle before it. The men were singing and dancing and whilst so doing advancing and receding even as one sees the surf do on a seashore.

The following morning the white men were ordered to the royal presence where they witnessed Shaka, surrounded by 200 people, being attired for the day. His headdress was a circlet of otter skin adorned with scarlet feathers of the lourie bird and a single crane feather, over two feet long. A servant held a war shield above the king's head, sheltering him from the sun. Ornaments protruded from his earlobes, which had been cut and stretched to hold them; around his shoulders hung tresses of monkey and genet skins, twisted into the shape of animal tails; tufts of white ox-tail decorated his arms and legs; about his waist was a kilt of twisted monkey tails; he was armed with a white ox-hide shield and stabbing spear.

Shortly after their arrival, the formal presentation of Farewell's gifts occurred. This was the first time that white men had approached the Zulu people as traders, and on somewhat of an equal footing, rather than as castaways seeking succour. Farewell and Fynn's gifts to the king were opulent, and had been well chosen: every description of beads to be had; woollen blankets; brass bars; sheets of copper and a variety of animals including cats and dogs. However, the king betrayed no sign of appreciation.

After a week had passed at the king's great kraal, the white men decided to return to Port Natal and their anchored vessels. However, on hearing of their intention Shaka refused to let Fynn go, insisting that he remain behind. Farewell was full of apprehension and greatly distressed at having to impart this news to Fynn, who had not been present when Shaka had issued his decree, yet, Fynn, far from being anguished at the news was happy to remain and learn more about these intriguing people and their king.

In a good mood, Shaka presented Fynn with five elephant tusks and promised to send his soldiers to hunt for more ivory: the first of the traders to encounter the Zulu people were off to a good start, mainly due to the rapport that Fynn had established with Shaka. Yet, had Shaka the slightest premonition of the part these traders and others who would follow, would play in the downfall of his nation, he would have been justified in destroying them on the spot. Fynn himself provides a cameo of the traders' involvement in the demise of the Zulu Empire as fifty years later, Lieutenant General Lord Chelmsford, at the head of a column of 15,000 soldiers, would especially request that Fynn's son, also Henry Francis, be attached to his staff as advisor and interpreter.

Shaka was as good as his word and shortly sent his soldiers scouting for elephant and it is an indication of the multitude of game that roamed Zululand at the time that a herd was encountered within an hour or so's march from the capital. The soldiers, rather than attack the herd, sent word back in order that the white men could join in the sport. Now Fynn was in trouble, for during his verbal sparring with Shaka the previous evening, he had extolled the power and superiority of the white man's firearms yet the only weapons he had to hand were some old muskets and fowling pieces suitable for little else than bringing down a duck in flight. Fynn's attempts to explain the technical limitations of his weapons and the need for a gun of larger calibre were greeted with derision. It was obvious that if Fynn was to retain any esteem – even his life – he would have to sally forth and do his best. So, gathering together a little force of half a dozen sailors who had volunteered to remain behind at Dukuza, Fynn set off to do battle with the elephants followed by Shaka and a throng of jeering warriors. Shortly, the scouts up ahead called for silence and, lest the herd should take off and deprive the king of gloating over the white man's humiliation, the assembly proceeded with the utmost stealth – Fynn in the lead with the rumbling of the great beasts' stomachs giving a guide to their exact location.

Fynn, after due consideration, decided the only thing he could do was to advance his men in line abreast and at his whispered command, all fire at once, scattering the herd every which way and bearing the mocking levity that would inevitably follow. Standing like the tattered remnants of a military piquet, Fynn and his men, at forty yards, fired a volley and a great tusker fell dead with a thud that shook the ground. Shaka and his warriors, with a derisive howl frozen on their lips, stood staring at the fallen beast, while the equally astonished Fynn doing his best to appear that the demise of the tusker was no more than it should have been. It was as though they expected it to jump up at any moment. Finally Fynn went forward and with some difficulty traced the cause of death: a musket ball, fired by a sailor who previously had neither seen an elephant nor fired a musket, had penetrated the ear straight into the brain.

By evening, Shaka had recovered his composure and proceeded to elaborate the many advantages nature had bestowed on the Zulu people, citing for instance how superior a black skin was to a white one which was so ugly it was kept covered by clothes. And despite the sensational killing of the elephant, Shaka was in no doubt that if it came to a pitched battle between his warriors and European soldiers with muskets, his men would inevitably win. He argued that when a shield was dipped in water previous to an attack, it would deflect a musket ball and, as the solder attempted to reload, his warriors would close; and should the soldiers attempt to run, his warriors, fleet of foot, would inevitably overtake and destroy them. It was not only the King's conjecture of what the result would be if his warriors did battle with the red soldiers, it was, unbeknown to either Shaka or Fynn, an accurate foretelling of the Battle of Isandlwana, fifty-six years in the future.

Fynn spent much of his time reading – perhaps compiling a store of knowledge with which to confound the king in future. Then one evening as dusk approached, he made his way to the great kraal where Shaka was dancing with his warriors. (These were not dance routines given over to frivolous pleasure, but extremely athletic and disciplined movements designed as exercise for war.) Flaming bundles of dried reeds illuminated the spectacle but hardly had Fynn arrived than there was a sudden cry from the midst of the throng followed by confusion and instant darkness as the torches were extinguished. Shaka had been stabbed, the assegai passing through his left arm, on through his ribs and up under his left breast. Fynn was in imminent danger. The attempt on the king's life could well have been construed by the gathering as the work of Fynn, the white wizard – it could well have been deliberately planned to appear so. Fynn eventually found Shaka lying in a hut surrounded by some of his ministers. His own doctor had also arrived.

The night had become a turmoil of anguish, fear and revenge as the whole population vied with one another in performing exhibitions of hysterical remorse. Those unable to express grief – for instance those who could no longer produce tears of sorrow – were immediately put to death. Later it was discovered that the would-be assassins were a small raiding party from Shaka's rival, King Zwide of the amaNdwandwe. Two regiments were immediately stood-to and despatched on the trail of the raiders. By noon the warriors had returned, bringing with them the bodies of three men, the supposed assassins.

During the days of the king's recovery Farewell, accompanied by another trader, a Mr Davis, had arrived at the royal kraal, bringing gifts for the king. However, from what transpired the gifts were clearly items of barter. Fynn usually provides a detailed description of the items presented to Shaka, but on this occasion he was silent – perhaps too embarrassed to mention what Farewell and Company were offering in exchange for 2,500 square miles of prime African real estate, rich in grazing, fertile of soil, teeming with animals bearing valuable hides and ivory and the finest harbour between the Cape and Delagoa Bay. Not a bad deal in exchange for beads, blankets, brass bangles and the like. If Shaka didn't realise what he was doing, the white men certainly did. And, for what it was worth – and as it turned out later, very little – it was all tied up in a legal contract, prepared in advance by Farewell and Company, that is quite remarkable, and worth reading in full:

> I, Inguos Shaka, King of the Zulus and of the country of Natal, as well as the whole of the land from Natal to Delagoa Bay, which I have inherited from my father, for myself and heirs, do hereby, on the seventh day of August in the year of our Lord eighteen hundred and twenty four, and in the presence of my chiefs and of my own free will, and in consideration of divers goods received – grant, make over and sell unto F.G. Farewell and Company, the entire and full possession in perpetuity to themselves, heirs and executors, of the Port or Harbour of Natal, known by the name of 'Bubolongo,' together with the Islands therein and surrounding country, as herein described, viz: The whole of the neck of land or peninsula in the south-west entrance, and all the country ten miles to the southern side of Port Natal, as pointed out, and extending along the sea coast to the northward and eastward as far as the river known by the native name 'Gumgelote,' and now called 'Farewell's River,' being about twenty-five miles of sea coast to the north-east of Port Natal, together with all the country inland as far as the nation called by the Zulus 'Gowagnewkos,' extending about one hundred miles backward from the sea shore, with all rights to the rivers, woods, mines, and articles of all denominations contained therein, the said land and appurtenances to be from this date for the sole use of said Farewell and Company, their heirs and executors, and to be by them disposed of in any manner they think best calculated for their interests, free from any molestation or hindrance from myself or subjects. In witness thereof, I have placed my hand, being fully aware that the so doing is intended to bind me to all the articles and conditions that I, of my own free will and consent, do hereby in the presence of the undermentioned witnesses, acknowledge to have fully consented and agreed to on behalf of F.G. Farewell as aforesaid, and perfectly understand all the purport of this document, the same having been carefully explained to me by my interpreter, Clambamaruze, and in the presence of two interpreters, Coliat and Frederick, before the said F.G. Farewell, whom I hereby acknowledge as the Chief of the said country, with full power and authority over such natives that like to remain there after this public grant, promising to supply him with cattle and corn, when required, sufficient for his consumption, as a reward for his kind attention to me in my illness from a wound.
>
> SHAKA, his X mark.
King of the Zulus.

Thus Farewell and Company, within a few months, had acquired thousands of square miles of the Zulu kingdom ... well, temporarily at any rate.

A few days later, back at Port Natal, the traders celebrated their good fortune by firing a salute of twenty rounds and declaring that possession had been taken in the name of His Britannic Majesty King George IV. However, Zwide, the rival king who had instigated the attack on Shaka's life, had still to be dealt with. An army of four regiments, totalling 7,000 warriors, was assembled, each regiment complete with its own individual uniform and regalia: headdresses of otter skin, crane and eagle feathers; kilts of genet skins; ox-hide shields of different regimental colours – white, red-spotted, black and grey; trappings of ox tails covering the chest and shoulders. Each man carried a club (knobkerrie) and a single stabbing spear – no cowardly throwing spears, it will be noted: 'They held their shields down at the left side – and, at a distance, very much resembled a body of cavalry. The first and third divisions marched off making a shrill noise, while the second and fourth made a dreadful howl.'

3. Fully equipped for war, a warrior carries his large shield, spear and knobkerrie. (*Local History Museum, Durban*)

Chapter 2

The White Warriors

Eventually Fynn could come and go as he pleased, and he decided to explore to the south, into the amaPondo country of King Faku. Nine months later, laden with ivory, he eventually reappeared at Port Natal. A description of his arrival by Nathaniel Isaacs, a newcomer to the port and also a dedicated diarist, relates that Fynn was barefoot, wearing a crownless straw hat and clothed in skins, all his European garments having perished long since. He was also accompanied by over one hundred amaPondo followers who would not leave his side.

Much had happened at Port Natal during Fynn's absence: other ships had called in and more trader/adventurers had landed; the *Julia*, on a return sailing to the Cape had vanished *en route*, no trace of her ever being found and James King, the former captain of the *Salisbury*, had travelled to England in an unsuccessful attempt to persuade the Colonial Office to acquire Port Natal. The British government was, however, interested in trade and suggested that King should return to Zululand and exploit its commercial potential. With a glib tongue, King rounded up a number of speculative investors in London and, having chartered the merchant brig *Mary*, he set sail for the Cape, taking on board an eleven-year-old ship's apprentice by the name of Charles Rawden Maclean, a future author, whose record of his and his companion's adventures is arguably the most accurate and truthful of all those who set pen to paper at Port Natal.

Calling in at St Helena on the return journey to Natal, King also recruited the above-mentioned Nathaniel Isaacs, a Jewish youth of seventeen years who was bored with the social restrictions of the small island and the mundane grind of his job in his uncle's trading store. He craved a life of adventure and would be fortunate in finding thrilling exploits aplenty awaiting him at Port Natal. But in recording his experiences – and many of them were astounding enough without need for embellishment – the truth was not sufficient and he tarnished his tales with exaggeration. A few years later, when down on his luck and contemplating the publication of his diaries, Isaacs wrote to Fynn, who was also thinking of appearing in print, suggesting that Fynn should make the Zulu monarchs '. . . as bloodthirsty as you can and endeavour to give an estimate of the number of people they murdered during their reign, and also describe the frivolous crimes people lose their lives for. It all tends to swell up the work and make it interesting.' Therefore Isaacs' descriptions, and by implication those of Fynn also, of his encounters with the Zulu people, and their kings in particular, must be regarded as suspect.

When King approached Port Natal aboard the *Mary*, nothing had been heard of the occupants of the bay for many months and it was believed that, like those of the *Julia*, they had perished. As King sailed close in, a violent storm suddenly erupted, driving the *Mary* onto the now familiar sandbar that blocked the entrance to the harbour. Within a few moments the *Mary* was stuck fast and the pounding seas began their work of destruction. King, his crew and the young Nathaniel Isaacs, clung to the stricken vessel all night but luckily were rescued the next morning.

By this time most of the white inhabitants had taken native wives; they also hunted, fished and took their leisure in the sun. A bountiful and fair exchange, most of them concluded, for the loss of civilisation. One wonders what Shaka, in retrospect, must have thought of the arrangement that he had made and whether or not he regretted having the white men, ever increasing in number, on his doorstep. Shortly after Fynn returned from Pondoland for a second time, Shaka decided to get his money's worth out of his visitors and demanded the presence of every person at the port including the new castaway traders from the *Mary*. They were ordered to assemble complete with their weapons. Shaka was about to go to war again and demanded the support of every man at Port Natal. There was much foot-shuffling and many attempts to plead exemption, but Shaka was adamant and, as Fynn put it, it was quickly realised:

. . . the more we showed willing the better it would be and Shaka, to underline the power he commanded over his own people and the whites alike, pointed out in so many words, that the traders at Port Natal were little better than castaways, marooned on a coast seldom visited by other ships. Furthermore, if the mood took him, he could destroy us all with no one left to tell the tale.

On his return from a successful expedition, Shaka was generous, sharing the spoils amongst all who had taken part. But those accused of cowardice were summarily executed.

But on this occasion the foray planned by Shaka was more than just a raid: it was a full-scale war of conquest and the traders, having arrived early at the main assembly point, witnessed the coming of the various regiments: Fynn's is a unique description of the greatest army that black Africa had ever seen deploying for war – little different, in fact, to the armies of Europe that had assembled, in much the same manner, ten years earlier at Waterloo:

The whole body of men, boys and women amounted, as nearly as we could reckon, to 50,000. All proceeded in close formation, and when looked at from a distance nothing could be seen but a cloud of dust. We had not rested from the time we started, and were parched and almost perishing from thirst, when, coming to a marshy stream, about sunset, the craving to obtain water caused a general and excessive confusion. After the first regiment had passed, the whole of the swamp became nothing but mud, yet this mud was eaten and swallowed with avidity by the following regiments. Several men and boys were trampled to death; and although there was a cry of 'shame' raised by many, and a call to help the victims, everyone was too much occupied to attempt to extricate them.

Shaka's army and the traders marched for a further two days when, shortly after noon, the whole force was formed into a single line across a vast plain driving before them 'hartebeest, rhinoceros, pheasant and partridge in great numbers'.

By the following day their march had brought them close to the enemy who had taken up a position on a fortified mountain. Fynn recorded:

. . . Shaka's forces marched slowly and with much caution, in regiments, each regiment divided into companies, till within twenty yards of the enemy, when they made a halt. Although Shaka's troops had taken up a position so near, the enemy seemed disinclined to move, until Jacob [the interpreter] had fired at them three times. The first and second shots seemed to make no impression for they only hissed and cried in reply: 'That is a dog.' At the third shot, both parties, with a tremendous yell, clashed together, and continued stabbing each other for about three minutes, when both fell back a few paces.

Then the Zulus, having inflicted severe casualties on the enemy, made a final charge:

> ... the shrieks became terrific. The remnants of the enemy's army sought shelter in an adjoining wood, out of which they were being driven. Then began the slaughter of the women and children. They were all put to death, ... from the commencement to the close did not last more than an hour and half. The members of the hostile tribe, including women and children, could not have been less than 40,000. The number of cattle taken was estimated at 60,000.

These figures quoted by Fynn seem to have been subject to gross exaggeration – just as Isaacs had suggested they should be. The very act of exterminating 40,000 people, in as little as ninety minutes – given the means available and the probability of mass escape – is impossible. Charles MacLean, known as John Ross, the young ship's apprentice, heard the first-hand accounts of those returning from the battle and, writing in the *Nautical Magazine* over thirty years later in 1853, set down his version of the battle:

> The enemy fought with great obstinacy and bravery, equal in every respect to the Zulus, but the superior discipline and practice of the latter in war prevailed over the more uninitiated forces of the Sikhunyana. The latter were beaten and almost totally annihilated, no quarter being given or received. The brave fellows, even when wholly discomfited, scorned to seek safety in flight, and even the women stepped into the ranks and filled up the gaps occasioned by their falling husbands. Three thousand men and women of the enemy lay dead on the field, and of more than five thousand Zulu warriors, about half survived to witness the rising sun. To the credit of Shaka, be it said, that on hearing of the gallant defence made by the enemy, he departed from the general rules in Caffrarian

warfare by proclaiming that all of the enemy who had survived and made their escape should be spared and received as his children, and worthy of becoming the companions of Zulu warriors.

The policy of adding these brave men to his band of warriors, to strengthen and promote his success in future schemes of conquest, might be considered as the primary and only motive in the savage chief for exercising this act of mercy, were it not known that courage always had been a sure passport to Shaka's favour and esteem.

As will be seen, both accounts of the battle are similar, but the number of enemy slain range between 3,000 and 40,000 men.

So far much has been said about Zulu men but little about their women, the diarists themselves having found little to say despite the fact that all the white inhabitants – with the exception, as far we know, of Farewell and John Ross – had taken local concubines or wives. Fynn had several wives and, fathering numerous children, would create a sort of Fynn dynasty, many of his descendants – as the current Durban telephone directory will testify – living in and around the area to which he gave his name: 'Fynnlands'. Due to the strict morality of the Zulus, the majority, if not all the traders' native wives would have come from local, subjugated tribes, such as those who inhabited the outlying areas of Port Natal. It is, in fact, John Ross who gives us the first impression of Zulu women even if it were written thirty years after his first encounter.

No doubt the vivacious maidens were consumed with curiosity at the sight of white men. That they really believed them to be beasts born of sea monsters is doubtful as they showed no fear of them: in fact they mischievously sought to satisfy their curiosity, much to the embarrassment of the '*umlungus*' (white men). John Ross described what must have been an embarrassing experience at the hands of the saucy maidens for a boy of eleven:

I observed as we passed along that I was an object of great curiosity to the travellers that we met, and in the villages as we passed along, and I seemed to occupy their undivided attention. A full grown white man had in a measure become familiar to them, but such a little fellow as I was at the time was a new sight for them; hence I became the lion of the party. The women and girls were particularly curious about me, and caused me often to blush from the way in which they inspected and handled me. At first I did not fancy this much, but when I became convinced of the harmlessness of their intentions, I submitted to all their curiosity with as much grace and good humour as I could command.

Whether or not most full-grown white men had indeed become so familiar to the Zulu population as no longer to excite curiosity, such was not the case with prudish seventeen-year-old Nathaniel Isaacs, who travelling to see King Shaka, was confronted near the King's residence by a number of young ladies of the royal household wearing, as a distinction of their position, brass collars around their necks. Isaacs' escort of warriors departed in sudden haste at the sight of these ladies as a sign of respect, and also as a wise precaution. Isaacs, however, considered himself a royal favourite and kept to the path. He described what followed:

> . . . they soon accosted me in the usual manner, that is, 'I see you, give me a pinch of snuff.' In a humorous way they asked me innumerable questions, and said one to another, 'Look at his hands and feet, how pretty they are, – just like ours.' They put up my shirt sleeves, to look at my arms, and uncovered my head to examine my hair, and many other things, which their extreme curiosity urged them to inspect minutely. I tried to get away from them, but they pulled me back again, and asked how many wives I had, and many other ridiculous questions, until I got fatigued with their importunities.

It was not long before Shaka decided to go to war again, demanding the support of the traders who, far from being red soldiers, nevertheless, gave a good account of themselves. Coupled with Fynn's tales of Britannic might, the Zulu king became increasingly curious to have closer contact with white men. Perhaps he even contemplated war to ascertain who was the mightier, his black warriors or the red soldiers of King George.

Chapter 3

Death of King Shaka

In 1827, John Ross became the first of Shaka's white emissaries to set out from Dukuza, the Zulu capital. But Ross was not so much an envoy of the Zulu king as an emissary of his white companions – although his escort, that would ensure the fulfilment of his purpose and safe return, was comprised solely of the king's warriors. An eleven-year-old boy would seem to be a strange choice for the dangerous journey that he was to undertake – especially so as the traders were not short of grown men. Having been marooned for well over half a year, they were in dire need of various necessities but their greatest want was that of medicines.

At the time Ross was most likely resident with Shaka at Dukuza. From the start, the king had been taken by the boy's flaming red hair: 'It appeared that the colour of my hair, which at the time was a brilliant red, had struck him with admiration and astonishment, being no doubt the first of that colour he had ever seen . . . He kept me with him first as a sort of rare pet animal.' There is no doubt that Shaka was amused by the boy and allowed him to take greater liberties than most in and around the royal presence. Years later Ross wrote that Shaka had bestowed upon him '. . . a large amount of genuine kindness and, I must add, a large share of indulgence'.

The traders, having no vessel at the time, were desperate to make overland contact with the Portuguese at Delagoa Bay (present-day Maputo), 300 miles to the north, where they hoped medicines could be obtained. It would be a hazardous undertaking and without a strong escort the traveller would be doomed. Most likely Ross had been chosen because of Shaka's fondness for the boy, the traders assuming the king would provide him with a bodyguard, which indeed he did.

Ross eventually set off with thirty warriors commanded by a chief named Langelibalele (not to be confused with another chief of the same name who was in conflict with the Natal government forty-six years later), whom Ross remembered with great affection.

> When disease and death had thinned the ranks of our crew, and the chance of completing the little vessel we had commenced building, with a view to get back to the civilised world, became exceedingly doubtful, Langelibalele was the name of a chief appointed by King Shaka, who at the time ruled the Zulu nation, to command a party of thirty warriors, charged with the escort of the writer to the Portuguese settlement at Delagoa Bay. Though it was at the time a perilous journey, nobly and faithfully did the chief and his men perform this duty.

However, it was not merely the presence of his escort, it was the fact that they were the envoys of the mighty Shaka whose armies even the Portuguese regarded with trepidation; and Ross's journey was accomplished with great success.

A year or two after Ross' exploit, circumstances at Port Natal necessitated the departure of another diplomatic mission. On this occasion it would proceed south to Algoa Bay, strictly on the king's business. Shaka, like lesser mortals, not only feared dying but, more than most, feared getting old, for advancing years and apparent loss of virility was a death sentence for a warrior king. And, plain for all to see, there were grey hairs in Shaka's beard, the herald of both age and the assassin's spear. Isaacs wrote: 'It will be seen that it is one of the barbarous customs of the Zulus in their choice, or election of their kings, that he must neither have wrinkles nor grey hairs.' On several occasions Shaka had surreptitiously enquired of the white men why it was that amongst them there were many different hair colours; and was it possible for them to choose whatever colour they desired? Later, having been told the truth of the matter, a disgruntled Shaka observed Fynn busily writing with pen and ink and enquired whether or not the markings made by the ink were of a permanent nature. Having been advised that they were, Shaka cast the contents of the inkbottle onto a white ox-hide shield and was bitterly disappointed to find that there was no permanent discoloration. Thereafter, abandoning discretion, he demanded to know whether or not the white men had a solution to his problem. Not realising the seriousness of the king's purpose, Farewell rashly assured him there was a potion that would not only permanently turn grey hair black but, unwittingly, gave Shaka the impression that macassa oil would remove wrinkles and restore youth.

Shaka immediately called for Isaacs, King and Fynn and having received their reluctant assurance that macassa oil would go some way to restoring his hair and vigour, he swore them all to secrecy. From that moment on, at every opportunity, Shaka harassed the traders to find some way of obtaining the magic potion. Now realising that they had unwisely raised the king's expectations and that retribution was bound to follow, the castaways made every effort to deride the qualities of 'Rowlands' Macassa Oil' but the more they protested the more determined the king became. Shaka convinced himself that it was a product reserved for royalty and that it was exclusively used by '*umGeorge*' (George IV). Shaka was determined to possess it.

The apprehensive traders had a tiger by the tail, knowing that there was little likelihood of ever finding macassa oil in Cape Town, even if they were able to get there. However, Shaka knew exactly how to stimulate their endeavour. He set his warriors on a great elephant hunt and produced eighty-six tusks as a down payment and the traders set about the pursuit of macassa oil with renewed vigour.

Shaka now had a dual purpose in sending a deputation to the Cape: first to obtain macassa oil and, in addition, to present an ambassador to the realm of his royal brother *umGeorge*. Fortuitously, a vessel was at hand to convey a deputation south. As usual, Shaka required one of the castaways to remain as hostage and had selected Isaacs for the purpose. But, as Isaacs had been ill for some time, Fynn, who always seemed happy to stay put in Zululand, agreed to remain in Isaacs' stead.

On 10 March 1828, four years to the day since Fynn had first set foot in Zululand, the deputation, including Shaka's ambassador, Chief Sotobe, and other Zulu notables, was ready to sail to Algoa Bay (present day Port Elizabeth). It was an uneventful voyage of four days which, compared with the hazards and duration of an overland journey – several weeks or even months – must have seemed like a miracle to Sotobe and his companions. But on arrival at Algoa Bay, and having appraised the British authorities that the emissaries of Shaka, the mighty Zulu King, were aboard bound for London, there was little reaction.

So, apart from the restriction that Sotobe should not see the garrison defences – an indication that the colonial government was wary of the deputation being spies – their reception had been most satisfactory and they all expected a vessel to arrive any day to convey them to south and on to London. However, they waited in vain. Instead, Major Cloete, a rather sinister figure, made an unannounced appearance, confronted Isaacs and commenced to question everyone. Nor did Cloete have the courtesy to ask Lieutenant King, the leader of the deputation, for the information that he sought but, without pause, kept up his interrogation of Sotobe who became angered and indignant.

The hopes and aspirations of the deputation were doomed; no ship arrived to convey them to Cape Town, let alone to London. At the whim of the Major, they were detained at Algoa Bay for three months, giving the furious chiefs ample time to acquaint themselves with the unimpressive little town, little more than a village in fact, with its paltry facilities and puny defences. Not only were Sotobe and his fellow chiefs furious, they now felt that for the last three years they had been duped by the traders. Where was the might of King George that they had heard so much about? Instead of castles and towers, there were flimsy dwellings; and instead of mighty armies there were but a scattering of soldiers clad in, of all things, red coats that would reveal their position at twenty times the distance that a warrior could cast a spear. Sotobe would carry to Shaka a very different description of the white man's power.

Back at Dukuza, Shaka had become over-impatient to grasp hands in friendship with – as he had been led to believe – the only other monarch in the world equal to him in wealth and might, his royal brother, *umGeorge*. Restlessly, Shaka began to contemplate that it would be but a few weeks' work for his army to scatter the frontier tribes that stood between him and the fulfilment of his vision: the two great kings united. John Ross made mention of Shaka's obsession: 'Shaka had one engrossing idea – that there should only be two kings in the world, King George to be King of the whites and he, Shaka, King of the blacks.'

Having heard no word from his emissaries, Shaka decided to act. Within hours his warriors were marching south, creating panic and consternation, not only amongst the frontier tribes but also amongst the white people beyond the border, causing the military and the

4. A senior chief with his counsellors and guards

settlers of the Cape to join forces against what they believed to be a
Zulu invasion.

But Fynn, having belatedly heard of Shaka's intentions, prevailed
upon him to abandon the invasion. Being ordered to retire, Shaka's
warriors turned the manoeuvre into a gigantic cattle raid, looting an
estimated 10,000 beasts. To complete the chaos, the British army,
finding the frontier tribes armed and ready to do battle with the Zulus,
who were expected to appear at any moment, mistook the tribesmen for
the invaders and fell upon them and, according to Isaacs, 'committed
great havoc and slaughter'.

So when Shaka met his returning emissaries a few days later –
they having been refused further passage to Cape Town – his anger
turned to fury when he learnt that not only had his mission been a
complete failure, worse still, there was no 'Rowlands Macassa Oil' to
be had. Sotobe, fearing for his life, accused the white men of having
hoodwinked Shaka for years, assuring the enraged monarch that the

English were a race of little consequence and that King George was, in fact, the name of a mountain.

Lieutenant King, the erstwhile leader of the mission, fraught with disappointment and an unknown affliction, had been too ill to journey to Shaka's presence, instead it was the unfortunate Isaacs who Shaka believed to be the cause of his displeasure: 'I began to perceive that I stood on the brink of eternity, and that the next look of the savage might be a signal for my death. In this state of horrible suspense I remained three days.'

There is little doubt that the traders were in great jeopardy. Fynn described what happened:

> The description given by the chiefs of their reception differed very much from what Shaka had expected, and they represented everything to the greatest disadvantage to escape being punished by death for not proceeding England. This, would be the deficiency of the so-much expected macassa oil, enraged Shaka against the whole of us, his passion for the present venting itself on Mr Isaacs, whom he endeavoured in every way to insult, accusing Mr King of having plundered his property and bestowing abuse on the whole of us.

However, the monarch's wrath eventually passed but, to bring further disappointment and sadness to all, including Shaka, Lieutenant King died a few days later. It was as if Shaka's mission had achieved only death and disappointment. After Lieutenant King's funeral, Shaka sent for Farewell, Fynn and Isaacs and on arrival at Dukuza expressed his great sorrow and stated that should all the white men ever depart his kingdom, he would have one consolation: 'That a white man [Lieutenant King], and a chief too, lived a long time in my country without molestation from myself or from my people, and that he died a natural death – that will ever be a source of much satisfaction to me.'

Shaka then appointed Isaacs as his chief of the white men and of Natal, and made him a grant of the very same stretch of land that he had made over to Farewell and Company a few years earlier. Fynn makes no mention of Isaacs' good fortune, or perhaps he was unaware that Port Natal had been subjected to a change of ownership. Or perhaps he was too distracted by further deaths that, like a curse, followed that of Lieutenant King. Within weeks of the emissaries' return from Algoa

5. Lt. James Saunders King was buried on the Bluff where his headstone remains to this day. He was a friend of, and respected by, King Shaka. (*Campbell Collection, Durban*)

Bay, Farewell had set out overland for the Cape with the intention of returning with wagonloads of trade goods, but was later murdered in Pondoland by a renegade tribe. In the meantime, a more momentous murder had taken place. The great Shaka had been assassinated by his brother Dingane and his accomplices. Did the mighty monarch perish for the want of a thimbleful of macassa oil?

Chapter 4

Then Come the Missionaries

With the death of Shaka, the traders had to re-appraise their already somewhat precarious position. Although Shaka had the blood of many on his hands he had treated his sponging white visitors with reasonable respect and, as John Ross had noticed, a fair amount of tolerance. What of his assassin, Dingane? It seemed as though Dingane was just as intrigued with the white men as Shaka had been and, like Shaka, was taken in with their tales of British power and might.

Shortly after the successful coup, a deputation of traders wisely tramped north to pay homage to Dingane. Isaacs was not slow in recording his opinion of the new king:

> War and dominion were the ruling passions of Shaka; while women, luxury, and ease, absorbed the whole mind of Dingane. Shaka was the bold and daring monarch of the Zulus, whose name struck a panic amongst the neighbouring tribes; Dingane, on the other hand, is too inert to be feared, and too compliant to be obeyed.... Dingane is certainly impressed with the extra-ordinary idea of the power of a British monarch ...

Isaacs was, however, impressed with the new king's royal bearing:

> ... He is tall, at least six foot in height, and admirably, if not symmetrically, proportioned. He is well featured, and of great muscular power; of a dark brown complexion, approaching to a bronze colour. Nothing can exceed his piercing and penetrating eye, which he rolls in a moment of anger with surprising rapidity, and in the midst of festivities with inconceivable brilliancy. His whole frame seems as if it were knit for war, and every manly exercise; it is flexible, attractive, and firm. He is reserved, even

to the extreme, and in speaking he seems to weigh every word before he utters it, often displaying an impediment in his speech, although he has not any such imperfection, but from a desire to be distinct and to be understood . . . His language is impressive, but more like that of a courtier than a warrior, as he generally discourses on domestic subjects but little about war. He is neither so credulous nor so superstitious as his people, but is very susceptible to any want of respect, when he evinces his displeasure in a tone which cannot be mistaken. He is exceedingly anxious to acquire information, manifests a great desire to be taught himself, and to have his people taught the knowledge of creation; and thus continually expresses a wish to have the missionaries settled amongst them, who, he assures us, shall have encouragement and protection.

At that time there were no missionaries at Port Natal. In fact, Christian zeal was an unlikely virtue amongst the rough hunter/traders. But the missionaries, in their due order of appearance, would surely come, as the Zulu kingdom and its people would find to their cost: first the traders, then the missionaries, and finally and inevitably, the red soldiers.

At the time, Dingane had what amounted to a standing army conservatively estimated at 50,000 warriors. It is probable that Dingane feared his own army and went some way to defuse his warriors' urge to wage war. Shaka had placed a prohibition on marriage, believing that his sex-starved army would fight all the harder to achieve their monarch's approval and permission for the whole regiment to marry forthwith. One of Dingane's first acts on becoming king, therefore, was to abolish the prohibition in the hope that domestic bliss, with a hardworking wife providing sustenance by her labours with a hoe rather than from booty obtained by the husband's assegai, would quell his warriors' martial ardour. However, war had become a way of life and, like all bad habits, was hard to give up. The warriors missed the excitement, the thrill of danger and the elation of conquest; indeed, theirs was an appetite for loot and pillage rather than one for the planting of corn. Isaacs commented: 'With such a body of people encircling the king, and urging him to pursue some warlike object, the Zulu monarch has merely the shadow of power.'

Perhaps Dingane would have been firmer in his resolve to reduce the power of his army were it not for his fear that he might well need it to repel a British invasion from the Cape. Later in his reign Dingane sent John Cane, once Lieutenant Farewell's carpenter and one of the earliest traders, to Cape Town on a diplomatic mission. Cane took with him gifts of ivory from Dingane for the governor of the colony. But Cane's mission, like the earlier one sent by Shaka, was a failure. The British authorities would not let Cane proceed beyond Grahamstown. But on returning to Port Natal Cane did not immediately inform Dingane of his failure nor return the king's ivory. Dingane was so infuriated, believing in some way that Cane had betrayed him, that he ordered all his cattle to be confiscated and Cane driven out of Zululand – the harshest treatment yet awarded to any European by a Zulu monarch.

Jacob the interpreter, ever eager to seize an opportunity to stir up trouble for the traders, implied that Cane had connived with the British in a plan to invade the Zulu kingdom. Furthermore, Jacob brought to Dingane's presence a fugitive from the Cape, a man called Kelimba, who explained to Dingane how at first the traders came, built houses and then forts, all the time taking more land. He then described how the missionaries followed and built their houses (churches) so that they could subdue the people by witchcraft, saying that no less than four kings had recently died in the Cape, their deaths being attributed to missionary sorcery. Jacob also confided to the king that when he was in Grahamstown, he was questioned by the red soldiers as to the state of Zululand: were there lots of cattle? What sort of country was it? Were there roads? Jacob's prophecy, that the white man would soon take all of Zululand, must have been a constant spur to Dingane's doubts and fears that one day the red soldiers would come from the south and conquer his kingdom. Yet, despite British expansion along the Cape/Pondoland border, there was no move against Zululand and Dingane and the traders at Port Natal lived in peaceful co-existence for a number of years.

As the years passed the ownership of the vast territory that Shaka had made over to Farewell and Company, and which Dingane had subsequently given to Isaacs, became vague when Isaacs, Ross and others of the original castaways eventually moved on and left Zululand forever. Although Fynn and Cane remained, they had for the most part set themselves up as chiefs of their own small domains, far from Dingane's capital. It was just as well that none were left who could lay claim to the territory for Dingane would shortly give it to yet another white man.

Once Dingane had expressly wished that a missionary would come to reside in Zululand in order to 'diffuse knowledge amongst his subjects and give him [Dingane] that instruction which he is so anxious to obtain'. In 1835, eleven years after Fynn had first set foot in Zululand, such a man, brimming with religious passion, made his way to Dingane's capital. Allen Gardiner, once an officer in the Royal Navy, had retired early and, after seven years ashore, had determined to become a missionary. He arrived at Table Bay in November 1834 and wasted little time before setting out overland for Port Natal. By February of the following year he had reached Zululand, eager to preach to the Zulu people and their king.

Gardiner was the first of many missionaries that, over the years, would endeavour to convert the Zulu and he would have no more success than those who would follow, bringing with them various interpretations of Christianity. But for the moment Gardiner had a clear field and it would be many years before even a sprinkling of mission stations would begin to dot the hills of Zululand. However, it seems that Dingane was not as keen to receive Christian instruction as he had been some years earlier.

Gardiner had difficulty in getting the purpose of his business across to the king: it was clear it was not that of trade. It helped matters that Dingane had previously heard of the white man's God and of the Good Book that Gardiner referred to frequently. Finally Dingane asked if he and his people could be taught and on being assured that they could, 'seemed to regard the whole as an impossibility'.

Dingane then turned the conversation to gifts and Gardiner was forced to admit that they were still on the road but, to the king's immense delight, described each one in detail. Next, Dingane wished to be told all about the British monarch and how he governed his people. But, it seems, the influence of Jacob still prevailed in Zululand, for the interview over, Gardiner, on leaving the royal presence, was roughly handled by two of Dingane's headmen. Gardiner attributed their animosity to the prophecy that Jacob had once made to Shaka:

. . . That a white man, assuming the character of a teacher or missionary, would arrive amongst them, and obtain permission to build a house; that, shortly after, he would be joined by one or two more white men; and in the course of time, an army would enter his country which would subvert his government, and, eventually, the white people would rule in his stead.

Jacob seemed to have described Gardiner's exact purpose for being at Dingane's capital. Not a comforting thought. Even more disquieting was Gardiner's first experience of a Zulu execution. He had not been long at Dingane's court when he witnessed the sudden apprehension of Goujuana, one of Dingane's royal brothers, a man Gardiner described as one of the most intelligent-looking men he had ever seen and who possessed an open and engaging countenance; an unassuming man who Gardiner had hoped might well be his first convert to Christianity. Goujuana's offence seemed to have been contrived by two of Dingane's powerful *izinduna* (chiefs) who had persuaded the king that Goujuana was plotting against him. More likely his 'offence' was being next in line to the throne. Whatever the reason, Goujuana and his two personal servants were seized and were being hurried through the town to kwaMatiwane, the nearby Hill of Execution, when Gardiner came upon the scene:

> The two servants naturally enough had endeavoured to make their escape; but instead of binding them, they [their captors] determined, as they called it, to take away their strength by throwing them down, . and striking them violently on all parts of the body with sticks – their blows I could distinctly hear. Again they were placed upon their feet, and urged on less rapidly to the fatal spot, near a large euphorbia tree on the brow of the hill, where the whole process was completed by additional blows on the head. Goujuana, I understand, made no resistance, and only requested, as he was led along, that in consideration of his being a king's son, he might be strangled, in lieu of being struck with the knob sticks, which was granted.

Horror-stricken, Gardiner stood transfixed and was still standing thus when the principal executioner strode back into town carrying the brass rings that he had taken from the necks of his victims. 'He advanced directly towards me, and for a second or two, as he was approaching, the thought crossed my mind that I was to be the next victim; but it appeared he was only actuated by curiosity, and after displaying the

6. Capt. Allen Gardiner, RN, would stop at nothing to achieve permission to preach to the Zulu people. (*KZN Archives, Pietermaritzburg*)

brass rings, passed on.' At Dingane's capital such incidents appeared to be of no great moment and there was no pause in the king's pursuit of pleasure. Gardiner's gifts finally arrived, albeit they had suffered on the way due to 'various submersions'. But the gift that Gardiner had correctly anticipated would cause the greatest pleasure arrived unscathed: a red cloak with a long silky nap.

In continuance of the First Fruits Ceremony, held in January to celebrate the annual harvest, it was customary for a great festival to be held at the appearance of the next new moon with the entire population gathering just outside the gates of the town. The king's approach was heralded by a roar of '*Bayete*!', the royal salute, from a thousand throats. But Dingane's physique, once perceived by Isaacs as being that of a warrior king, now resembled the physique of a Falstaff:

> Tall, corpulent and fleshy, with a short neck, and a heavy foot, he was decked out as a harlequin, and, carried away by the excitement of the moment, seemed almost prepared to become one. A correct taste, at least

in these matters, and had his figure been in accord with his equipment, he would have carried the palm in the dance, which he entered into with some zest, and certainly sustained his part with much natural grace, and, for so heavy a man, with no ordinary ease and agility.

Eventually, after being at court for over two months, the longed-for meeting was arranged and Gardiner was able to state his case. Having got into full and zealous stride, he was rudely interrupted by one of the *izinduna* who abruptly told him that they wished no teaching about 'the book' which they could not understand. However, he, Gardiner, would be welcome to stay if he agreed to instruct them in the use of the musket; any other instruction they 'did not care for'.

Bitterly disappointed and with heavy heart Gardiner took his leave of the Zulu capital where the ceremonies and dancing associated with the First Fruits Celebrations were scheduled to continue, off and on, for another month. On his arrival back at Port Natal there was better news. He was presented with a letter from some of the white inhabitants stating that in view of his unfortunate reception by Dingane, they would support a 'missionary establishment' at the Port '. . . whose object would be to inculcate industry and religion . . .'.

A mission station, constructed of wattle and daub, was built at an idyllic location amongst giant shady trees in the hills overlooking the bay. Gardiner named it Berea (the area, which retains this name, is now an expensive residential suburb of Durban). By now the native population of the port numbered an estimated 2,500, all being former subjects of King Dingane who, believing their presence amongst the white man undermined his authority, wanted his runaways returned for trial and punishment. There were hints of retribution if the whites did not hand them over.

At the end of April the constant rumours of Dingane's intention to attack the Port were cause enough for the white inhabitants to call a security meeting:

After some little discussion, on which many plans were advanced, it was unanimously resolved, that as this appeared to be a favourable opportunity, a treaty, based on the following terms, should, if possible, be entered into with Dingane, viz. provided he will guarantee the lives and property of every individual, white and black, now residing at Port Natal;

we, on our part, engage to repel with all our power, and never more to
receive any deserter from his dominions; and immediately to acquaint
him of the circumstance, should any of his people elude our vigilance.

At the same time it was agreed that no runaways should be given
up until some arrangement of this nature had met with Dingane's
sanction.

Gardiner was proposed as the Port's envoy and negotiator, a position
that he accepted with alacrity. Two days later he was on his way,
accompanied by his interpreter, two servants and a hired wagon. The
day following his arrival, Dingane signified his wish to see Gardiner.
Amongst the presents he had brought for the king on this occasion
were a pair of boots and some parcels of beads of a new spotted design.
Dingane was delighted and: 'Observing that the beads were spotted,
he named them the "Ingura" (panther) [leopard] beads, and apparently
much pleased amused himself for some time by arranging them in
various ways.' Dingane suddenly decided to absent himself and before
long a royal servant arrived and took Gardiner outside to where a
concourse of warriors stood surrounding a number of Dingane's seated
indunas. Gardiner was invited to take a seat amongst the ministers and
convinced himself that important business was about to be discussed
but, to the surprise of all, the king suddenly appeared in the most
bizarre attire:

> . . . he had caused his whole body, not excepting his face, to be thickly
> daubed over with red and white clay in spots . . . Thus adorned, a dance and
> a song were the least I expected, but he contented himself with receiving
> the acclamations of 'Byate' . . . and again retired as unaccountably from
> the sight of his wondering subjects, who none of them could devise the
> import of this singular exhibition. All I could collect from them was,
> that it was a new thing, and he had done it because he was the king and
> could do what he pleased. It is not, however, improbable that the sight of
> the spotted beads had put this strange crotchet into his head.

After further delays Gardiner finally succeeded in obtaining another
audience with the king at which gifts were once again presented – some
of a rather peculiar nature: a pair of naval epaulettes, three pairs of ladies'
gilt bracelets, and a picture depicting the Royal Pavilion at Brighton.

Peculiar or not, Dingane was delighted and much admired Gardiner who had decided to impress by wearing his naval full-dress uniform. So in awe was Dingane at Gardiner's appearance that he was momentarily speechless. Gardiner, unaware of the cause of the royal silence and fearing that he might be considered rude, enquired whether the king was waiting for him to speak but Dingane, who seemed transfixed by the splendour of the naval uniform, indicated that he would stare some more before he would say a word.

The meeting was off to a good start and it was in this convivial atmosphere that the missionary and the monarch struck a deal. All runaways/deserters from the Kingdom presently residing at Port Natal would be pardoned and allowed to remain without fear of molestation. However, any future deserters were to be apprehended by the residents of Port Natal, bound and forthwith marched back to Zululand for trial (and almost certain death). In return Dingane agreed to guarantee the lives and property of every person, white and black, residing at the Port. Gardiner would also be free to convert all existing deserters to Christianity. Delighted with his success, Gardiner finally departed for Port Natal – but he had cause to wrestle with his conscience: Dingane, in discussing the runaways already at the Port who, in terms of the treaty, were now exempt from prosecution, had informed Gardiner that there was one man, Makanjana by name, who Dingane particularly wished to be returned, to which Gardiner had reluctantly agreed. On arrival at Port Natal Gardiner instigated a manhunt and after several days Makanjana was apprehended, bound and delivered to Gardiner together with several recent runaways, including a woman, who Gardiner was treaty-bound to return to the King. Within hours, he with his prisoners, was on his way to Dingane.

On reaching the capital, Mgungundlovu, Gardiner found Dingane to be delighted that his runaway subjects had been brought back for trial, in fact he '... appeared in high glee. His women were all singing around him: and on my seating myself, he pointed to me and said that it was on my account this rejoicing was made. I could have burst into tears – it was a most trying situation ... I scarcely dared turn to the right – the countenance of Nonha [the woman prisoner] and her companions was truly distressing. During the long journey of 120 miles they had anticipated a cruel death; and now every instant they expected to be hurried away to execution.' However the execution was stayed – there were other plans for their deaths – and the following day Gardiner did his best to persuade Dingane to pardon them all, but without success.

A couple of days later Gardiner prepared to depart, by which time it was clear that Dingane intended to starve the prisoners to death. However, they were still manacled with Gardiner's handcuffs which he now wished to recover.

> They [the prisoners] were evidently in a state of alarm, supposing that they could only be loosened for the purpose of immediate execution, but the object being explained, they became calm, and soon after returned to their place of confinement.... On leaving town I saw them again, the last thing, recommending them to think much of what had been said to them, and to pray to God through Jesus Christ, as He was able to save their souls, and do them good in another world: they all looked piteously, thanked me, and wished me a pleasant journey.

And so the heinous bargain between the missionary and the monarch was concluded. Dingane had the satisfaction of punishing his defecting subjects while Gardiner no doubt justified himself with the thought that he might well have saved the first Zulu souls even if it were at the expense of their lives.

Back at Port Natal the traders, with a new sense of security as a result of the treaty, decided to lay out the bounds of a new town. However, it was not long before Gardiner was trudging back to Zululand in answer to Dingane's urgent summons.

Despite the presents that Gardiner had as usual brought for the king, he was not given the attention that he normally enjoyed. Eventually he received word that Dingane was too much occupied with overseeing the construction of his new capital and that Gardiner should deal with his *izindunas* instead. Gardiner was soon aware that there was serious trouble afoot. Not only were runaways still receiving sanctuary at Port Natal, young girls were being abducted by white traders and taken away in the white men's wagons. Highly upset, Gardiner insisted on seeing the King, and to impress him, again presented himself in full-dress uniform. The meeting was a success. Gardiner assured Dingane that those guilty of absconding with the girls were not true Englishmen, that they would be reprimanded and the runaways returned. He further assured Dingane that:

> ... the word, which had passed between us, should not fall to the ground; if deserters were found at Port Natal, he might rely upon them being sent back. Dingane then said, that he considered me as Chief of the white people there; and that he should look to me to keep things right. I told him that as far as I was able this should be done, but that beyond persuasion I had no power. His reply was, 'You must have power. I give you all the country called Issibubulungu – You must be chief over all the people there.'

So the same land that Shaka had given to Farewell and Company and had subsequently re-allocated to Isaacs, Dingane now gave to Gardiner. However, it was the last time that a Zulu king would be in a position to bestow the property: within a few months, other white men would take it by force of arms.

Gardiner, delighted with his success and with the acquisition of a territory that could form a new British colony, decided he must set out for the Cape forthwith and thence on to England. His subsequent hazardous overland journey took weeks. He eventually presented his case to an impressed Sir Benjamin D'Urban, Governor of the Cape, who lost no time in communicating with Dingane:

> His Brittanic Majesty's Governor of the Colony of the Cape of Good Hope to the Chief of the Zoolus, Dingane.
>
> I rejoice to hear of the good word which has passed between the Chief and Captain Gardiner and of the Treaty concluded between them for the town and people of Port Natal.
>
> An officer on the part of the King of England, my master, shall speedily be sent to Port Natal, to be in authority there in place of Captain Gardiner, until his return, and to communicate with the Chief, Dingarn, upon all matters concerning the people of Natal. By him I will send to the Chief presents, in token of friendship and good understanding, of which I hereby assure the Chief in the name of the King, my master.
>
> Signed, Benjamin D'Urban,
Governor of the Colony of the Cape of Good Hope.
>
> Given at the Cape of Good Hope, this Fifth day of December, 1835.

(Note that the Governor did not deign to address Dingane as 'King', calling him instead 'Chief', an arrogant mode of address that the British Government would perpetuate in its dealings with all Zulu monarchs). The communication was put aboard the *Dove* which then set sail for Port Natal. A fortnight later, just thirteen months since he first landed at Cape Town, Gardiner sailed for Liverpool. But before he departed he wrote a memorandum extolling the benefits that would arise from Britain's colonisation of 'Victoria', the name that he had bestowed upon the territory. In his memorandum Gardiner maintained that Britain would not need to fear the expense of a full-time military presence of red soldiers. Instead he assured D'Urban that a number of Durban natives, selected for their knowledge of firearms already acquired whilst hunting, could be trained by British NCOs and, he naïvely continued, after three months' training he would have no hesitation in pitting them against the whole Zulu army. At the time, Gardiner's disparaging assessment of the Zulu army's prowess was never put to the test but forty-three years later a British general, equally overconfident and dismissive, echoed Gardiner's proposal and assembled an army, equipped with the latest weaponry, of 15,000 men with which to invade Zululand. Almost 60 per cent of this force were Port Natal (Natal Colony) natives led by white NCOs. The battle that followed on 22 January 1879, of which more later, was one of the worst defeats ever inflicted on a British army.

Just about the time Sir Benjamin had been signing his letter to Dingane, more missionaries, who must have encountered Gardiner on his way south, arrived at Dingane's court. How different they were to the middle-aged, humourless Gardiner. All were American and their leader, George Champion was only twenty-four years of age, his wife a mere nineteen and the others, Aldin Grant, Dr Adams and their wives much the same age.

The Americans encountered far fewer problems than Gardiner ever had and, within no time, in the most primitive conditions, had set up a mission station inside Zululand ten miles north of the Tugela River. Dingane was quite taken with the young people and their children, so much so they were required to visit the king once a month having to walk, or travel by ox wagon, the 200-mile return journey. Perhaps they did not labour the contention that there was a greater king than Dingane. If that were the case it was a different matter with a local chief to whom Champion had preached, only to find that he was accused, a few days later, of being a wizard and responsible for an eclipse and an earthquake that occurred shortly thereafter. Yet, despite illness, death and the most primitive conditions ('At present three cross-legged stools constitute our stock of movable seats. With these and our boxes we are intending to manage until we can get some plain chairs from America'), they continued, steadfast, until they, together with all the other white inhabitants of Natal were, only a few months later, forced to flee.

Chapter 5

Murder of the Voortrekkers

In the mid-seventeenth century the Dutch acquired possessions in the East Indies and by 1662 had established a replenishment station on the southern tip of Africa at the Cape of Good Hope. Soon a hardy population, mainly a mixture of Dutch, German and French, with an additional mixture of Hottentots, Bushmen and slaves imported from the Malay archipelago, had established itself not only in and around the embryo city of Cape Town, but also miles inland, ever seeking new territory and horizons. This heterogeneous population became known as *Boers* (farmers) a white tribe gradually encroaching north and east into Africa. They were a tough, resourceful race leading a frontier existence, often in conflict with wild animals that abounded in the interior and with native tribes into whose territory the Boers steadily encroached. By the early nineteenth century they had fanned out, over a 600-mile front, into what seemed to be a limitless interior. Much to the resentment of the Boers, Britain acquired sovereignty over the Cape and the lands beyond. English was imposed as the only official language whilst Britain's philanthropic attitude towards the native people, at the expense of the Boers, was resented. Britain's abolition of slavery throughout her domains in 1834 was not only cause for great bitterness but as most Boer families were slave owners, it resulted in Boer impoverishment. Although the British government offered compensation to the Boers for the loss of their slaves, Britain, with Machiavellian aplomb, decreed that compensation could only be paid out in London, 6,000 miles and two months' journey away.

By 1836, in a great surge of bitterness, many Boers were ready to leave the land of their birth, to sell all their immovable possessions and, in stout ox-drawn wagons, *trek* (migrate) into the vast unknown to the north, there to establish their own republics and to govern themselves.

However, not only did the Boers disagree with the British Government, they also argued vigorously amongst themselves and although there were 10,000 of them ready to depart in a mass exodus, there was much discussion as to their destination and who would lead them, resulting in various groups heading in different directions.

Most had been aware of Port Natal's existence which, from the exaggerated descriptions of its tropical beauty and potential, had taken on a legendary quality of a country flowing with milk and honey. As early as 1834 a Boer delegation, led by Piet Lafras Uys, arrived at Port Natal with a mandate to meet up with King Dingane and enter into negotiations for a homeland in the sun.

The Uys delegation proceeded into Zululand, guided by Richard King but were halted on the south bank of the Tugela, the river being in flood. However, Uys himself had fallen ill with fever and his younger brother, Johannes, had taken his place. Dingane, well aware through his spy network of their coming, had sent a senior *induna* (chief), with an escort of a hundred warriors, ahead to meet the Boers along the way but, alas, the flooded Tugela separated the two parties. Consequently the best that could be achieved was an agreement in principle that Dingane would be happy to cede the territory (that had been ceded so often before), to Uys and his followers. So, having shouted the essential terms of the negotiation back and forth across the raging Tugela, and having convinced themselves that all too easily had they acquired a slice of paradise, the Uys delegation hastened back to impart the glad tidings to their kin. Whether it was truly Dingane's intention to bestow Port Natal on a people he had yet to meet is another matter.

At the same time other *Voortrekker* groups were sizing up alternative locations of the African interior, some as far as 400 miles north of Port Natal and, as the crow flies, almost 1,000 miles from Cape Town. Barring the path of one such group, led by Sarel Cilliers, was a warrior chief by the name of Mzilikazi. In the time of King Shaka, Mzilikazi had been a regimental commander but had fallen foul of his king. Well aware of the fate that awaited him, Mzilikazi kaMatshobana absconded with his entire regiment and would in time found a nation and kingdom of his own, the Matabele, and in the process acquire a reputation for ferocity which equalled that of Shaka himself. Dingane's regiments had, in the recent past, engaged Mzilikazi in battle and had found their match. During the twenty years that had elapsed since Mzilikazi had defected from the Zulu kingdom, he had through conquest amassed fifty-six regiments of warriors. Then the emigrating Boer convoys entered his domain. Mzilikazi's warriors fell upon the covered wagons, but not before the Boers had formed their convoy into a fighting laager at a place they later called Vegkop. With the wagons chained together, thornbush barriers rammed into the gaps between the wheels and with the women reloading the heavy-calibre flintlock muskets, the men kept the courageous but impetuous warriors at bay. Although they charged again and again, they found the embattled laager to be impregnable and were slaughtered in their hundreds. Then, as the defeated Matabele withdrew, the Boers mounted their already saddled horses and set off in pursuit, shooting the warriors down and turning their defeat into a rout.

The news of Mzilikazi's disastrous encounter struck like a thunderbolt of fear into the hearts of southern Africa's native rulers including the mighty Dingane. Like Shaka before him, Dingane feared the fulfilment of Jacob's prophecy. But if the white man were to deprive him of his realm, Dingane had always assumed that his enemy would be the redcoat English soldiers. Now he had cause to think again. Surely he was about to come face-to-face with the enemy, revealed at last as Boer immigrants. It was as Dingane pondered thus that he received news that another wave of immigrants were poised beyond the Drakensberg Mountains, ready to descend into the Zulu Kingdom. Their leader, Piet Retief, and a few companions were already *en route* to put into effect the treaty terms that had been shouted across the flooded Tugela River three years before.

In the meantime, Allen Gardiner had returned to Africa arriving in Cape Town in March 1837. He had married again during his brief spell in England and was accompanied by his new wife and three children from his previous marriage. He also brought with him the Reverend Francis Owen, of the Church Missionary Society, who would be Gardiner's 'Second-in-Command' in his war with the devil and the saving of Zulu souls. Owen was destined for the front line of battle: he was to take up residence with his family in the heart of Zululand at Mgungundlovu and within hailing distance of Dingane's own abode.

Apart from acquiring a new wife, Gardiner's visit to England had been less than successful. He had hoped to return with administrative power over the population of Port Natal, an authority that would enable him to make arrests and pass sentence for certain crimes. In attempting to achieve such authority he had given evidence in London before a select committee during which he presented the English population at the port as little better than rogues and pirates. The news of his disparaging description preceded him and when he arrived at Port Natal in May, he found himself to be unpopular and resented. Furthermore, during his absence, others had taken over as leaders at the Port, men who were more concerned with their safety than with their salvation.

Their leader, Alexander Biggar, would have been able to claim with some justification that he was the first red soldier to set foot in Natal and, not only a red soldier but a redcoat to boot, albeit that he was now neither, having been cashiered from the 85th Regiment of Foot on a charge of misappropriation of regimental funds. But Biggar was the right sort of swashbuckling man to lead the Port Natal community at that time. In fact, Biggar had been a cavalier type from an early age. Shortly after his fourteenth birthday he had been commissioned as an ensign in his father's regiment, the 85th Foot; four years later, after the regiment had returned to the United Kingdom from Martinique, he was promoted to the rank of Lieutenant and promptly eloped with the local minister's daughter, Mary Straton. The pair were married at Gretna Green. In due course Biggar was promoted to Captain Paymaster of the 85th and, shortly thereafter, the regiment left for Spain where it was engaged in many bloody battles of the Napoleonic Wars thereafter. In 1812, Britain went to war with America and as part of the Light Infantry Brigade, the 85th attacked Washington where, together with other buildings, it burnt the White House and the Navy Yard. But it was a disastrous war for Britain and after two months the invaders were forced to withdraw. Back in England Biggar was held responsible for shortages amounting to £1,300 and court-martialled.

Biggar and his wife Mary, despite the many trials and disruptions their lives must have been fraught with, had no less than thirteen children, ten of whom were daughters. All the girls died, as did one of the sons, and it was with the remaining two boys that Biggar, now the appointed leader of a contingent of twenty-five settlers, landed at the

Cape in 1820. However, constant warfare with the local Xhosa tribe led to his impoverishment and when in 1835 his farm was plundered, he decided to start life again in Natal. Supported by his two sons, Robert and George, he formed the Port Natal Volunteers and, due to the perceived threat from Dingane, set about the construction of a fort that, as we shall hear, was to be the home of the first redcoat occupation of Port Natal. In the meantime Dingane's threat to attack the port was not to be ignored as the traders had taken to harbouring runaways and kidnapping young girls from the Zulu kingdom. The fact that Robert and George had both acquired young Zulu maidens by this method did not help matters.

Apart from earning a living by trading and ivory hunting, the Biggars, it seems, did bring an element of discipline to the otherwise unruly community. Undeterred, however, Gardiner lost no time in departing to state his case with Dingane and to pave the way for the Reverend Owen's arrival.

By this time, Dingane, heartily sick of his greed-driven white neigh-bours, had forbidden all entry to Zululand, causing hunting and trading to cease. He was, however, delighted to see Gardiner and to receive his customary generosity: more gold epaulettes and a silver watch, amongst other things. Port Natal and its future was high on the agenda and it was not long before Gardiner was on his way back with a document, drawn by himself, signed by Dingane and witnessed by three of his senior *izinduna*, all of whom had made their mark, granting to the King of England the territory that had already been bestowed so many times before – more recently it will be remembered to Gardiner himself and later by yelling the terms of its cession to Piet Uys across the raging Tugela.

Gardiner, imagining there to be more to his meeting with the select committee than there had been, believed that the document carrying Dingane's mark would be the foundation of a British Colony. But he was to be doomed to disappointment. In London Lord Glenelg (Secretary of State for War and the Colonies) was penning a dispatch that would damn all Gardiner's hopes and dreams of authority in the land of Port Natal:

They [Her Majesty's Government] are aware, too, of the fact that, without police, a gaol, and a Minister of Justice, the value of such a statute would be comparatively small; but they did not, on this account, deem it right to forego the use of the best obtainable remedy against the lawless conduct of British subjects on the African continent. Captain Gardiner seems to have understood the statute as implying a pledge on behalf of the government to do all that is necessary for giving complete effect to the jurisdiction with which it invests him. It is necessary, therefore, to deny the existence of any such tacit or implied engagement.

His late Majesty disclaimed, in the most direct terms, all right of sovereignty at Port Natal, and all intentions to extend his domain in that direction; and Captain Gardiner was distinctly informed by me that the Government entertained no projects of colonization in that quarter. Port Natal is a foreign land, governed by foreign chiefs, and the Government of this country has neither the right nor the intention to interfere with those chiefs.

So, for the time being, Britain had no wish to acquire Zululand or any part of it.

Five months after his arrival at Port Natal, in an atmosphere of discord and upheaval, the Reverend Owen, his wife, his sister and their Welsh maid, lugging a huge Welsh bible, made their way by wagon to Mgungundlovu with Owen determined to convert and save the souls of all he encountered. He was, however, bound by strict instructions not to involve himself in anything of a secular nature. In particular he was not to enter into any deals with Dingane whereby he would use his influence to have runaways returned to the kingdom: Gardiner's contemptible arrangements with Dingane had received severe criticism in England.

Owen had been chosen by Gardiner as a man cast in his own religious mould and he would have found it difficult to find someone less suited to establish rapport with both the white traders and the Zulus alike. Obsessed with religion and his own righteousness; untiring in his zeal and with a craving to expose sin in all those he encountered, Owen was a very tiresome fellow.

Prior to Owen leaving for Mgungundlovu, the traders at the port would flee at his approach lest he snare them with an impassioned and impromptu sermon. On arrival in Zululand his complex and irrational religious claims became a subject of ridicule and a cause of irritation. The likelihood of a single Zulu convert to Christianity became remote. His attempt to convert Dingane was a disaster. Richard Hulley, a Port Natal trader whom Owen had employed as his interpreter, later recorded the following account:

> The missionary [Owen] after speaking for about half an hour and putting as much gospel truth as he could into his message, was told by the King to stop as he had heard enough. Dingane then said 'I have a few questions to ask you that I may understand. First, do you say there is a God and but one God?' The minister replied: 'Yes.' 'Second, do you say there is a heaven for good people and only one?' Reply: 'Yes': 'Third. Do you say there is a devil?' Reply: 'Yes': 'Four, do you say there is a hell for wicked people?' The minister replied: 'Yes'. Said the King; 'If that is your belief, you are of no use to me or my people; we knew all that before you came to preach to us, I and my people believe that there is only one God – I am that God, we believe there is only one place to which all good people go, that is Zululand – we believe there is one place where all bad people go, there', said he, pointing to a rocky hill in the distance. 'There is hell, where all my wicked people go'. (The king had pointed to the Hill of Slaughter, near his kraal which was white with bones of his victims). Then Dingane added: 'The Chief who lives there is uMatitwani [Matiwane] the head of the Amangwane [amaNgwane]. I put him to death and made him the devil, chief of all wicked people who die. You see then, there are but two chiefs in this country, uMatitwani and myself. I am the Great Chief – the God of the living, and uMatitwani is the Great Chief of the wicked. I have now told you my belief; [Chief Matiwane, of the amaNgwane tribe, had incurred the wrath of the Zulu monarchy some years earlier and, subsequently, believing Dingane willing to forgive him, had journeyed to Mgungundhlovu. There he was cordially received but, later having ordered his eyes to be put out, Dingane executed Matiwane on the hill adjacent to his new capital. Matiwane's was most likely the first execution of any note to take place at Mgungundhlovu and the hill was thereafter called kwaMatiwane and it is still known by that name today.] I do not want you to trouble me again with the fiction of you English people. You can remain in my country as long as you conduct yourselves properly.'

It was the first and last time that Owen was allowed to preach the gospel to the Zulu. But living in hope that Dingane would relent, especially if Owen associated the white man's mysterious accomplishments of writing and drawing with the white man's religion, Owen undertook to teach both skills to whomever – from children to the King. Dingane was particularly fascinated by the way in which news was conveyed by letter and was determined to become literate. He was intrigued when Owen showed him a copy of Gardiner's book, *A Journey Through the Zulu Country*, that had just arrived having being published in London earlier in the year. At first Owen had been apprehensive. Gardiner had drawn a likeness of Dingane in dancing attire which adorned the front piece of the volume but far from being offended, the King was delighted. But Owen's subtle attempt to introduce religion into the conversation, despite reading several passages from Gardiner's journal, 'fell to the floor'. However, the Boer emigrants would soon be calling on Owen's literary skills in order to put their case for a large slice of the Zulu kingdom.

Dingane must have begun to feel overwhelmed by the white man's appeals for land, ivory, concessions and women whilst they offered nothing in return except incomprehensible rhetoric. One of Dingane's greatest desires was to obtain firearms. However, the traders of Port Natal were determined to thwart his aspiration to arm his warriors with European weapons least they should be turned upon themselves. A certain number of firearms had been procured by the Zulu monarchy but most were either useless or had been made so by the traders. In January 1837, the *South African Commercial Trader*, a Cape Colony journal, reported: 'The traders trading with Dingane in guns and powder are becoming rich – but they have hit on a happy expedient of cheating the Chief, who has at last discovered the roguery. They sell him guns, but before delivering them they take either the main spring out of the lock, or some screw, which renders the gun useless.'

Nevertheless, Port Natal traders were becoming alarmed at the number of guns that, one way or the other, were finding their way into Zululand. In November 1836, fourteen traders signed a letter of complaint addressed to the *Grahamstown Journal*:

> . . . Mr Blanckenberg remained at the King's place on the pretext of having important affairs with His Majesty. He shortly afterwards returned to Natal with thirty to forty heads of cattle when it transpired that the greater part of these were the produce of a sale effected by him to Dingane of a new elephant gun. In a few days after his arrival he

forwarded to the King a supply of powder and lead, with a boy to cast the balls, at the King's residence. The great price obtained for the gun induced Messrs. Lake and Isaacs [Could this be Nathaniel Isaacs having returned to Port Natal?] to follow his example. They have since sold to Dingane four elephant guns, with a proportionate supply of ammunition. Mr. R Vigor, on a late journey to the King, also sold a double-barrelled percussion elephant gun for six elephants teeth. Mr. P Kew, who has been trading fourteen guns, has also, according to his own accounts, made Dingane a present of two guns. And there are reports of one or two Hottentots following his example, and of another Hottentot being on the road to Natal to repair six guns belonging to Dingane ...

Dingane, however, wanted an open and regular trade in firearms which, much to his chagrin, most traders were set to deny him. He also complained bitterly about the decimation of his elephants and illegal hunting: 'I have given the whites from the Imslatense [Mhlathuze] River to the Umzimvoobo [Mzimvubu] to shoot in, which is surely large enough [Approximately 30,000 square miles – about the size of Ireland] but if they come and kill all my elephants, where shall I procure ivory to purchase things from them?'

It was thus in the mounting pressure of white demands and encroachment that Dingane received a letter from Piet Retief, with his convoy of no less than a thousand wagons, all assembled at a place called Thaba Nchu, in present day Lesotho, ready to descend the passes of the Drakensberg Mountains into Zululand. Retief believed that he already had a foot in the door of the Kingdom as it was Piet Uys, the *voorloper* (a person who leads or goes ahead) of the convoy, who had negotiated a deal on the banks of the flooded Tugela months earlier.

Retief's letter, dated Port Natal 19 October 1837, had emphasised the Boers' desire to acquire uninhabited land and live in peace as neighbours with the Zulu people. However, Retief made no reference to the location of such an uninhabited place and subtly referred to the recent Boer victory over Mzilikazi. He signed it: ' ... your true friend, Retief, Governor, etc.'

Before dispatching the letter, the Boer leader read it aloud to a gathering of the Port Natal traders who were well aware that the territory Retief had in mind for a Boer Republic was none other than the land of their own occupation, the territory given, via Gardiner, to

the King of England. However, they were more than happy that the
Boers should take it over as clearly it was of no interest to their King or
his government. (The officer that Sir Benjamin D'Urban had promised
to 'speedily be sent to Port Natal' two years earlier had never arrived.)
To make matters clear, fourteen traders signed a letter addressed to Piet
Retief expressing their hope that Boer and Briton would eventually
reside as neighbours. Retief replied: '. . . I do not doubt that the
Almighty, in disposing of events, will ordain that we should be united
for our mutual happiness.' Thus it was more or less agreed – or at least
intended – that Boer and Briton would unite against, one must assume,
the Zulu monarch. Alexander Biggar was as pleased as anyone at the
turn of events and shortly after the Boers had established a republic
they would appoint him '*Landrost*' (mayor or magistrate).

It was not long before Retief and a few companions received Dingane's
consent to proceed to the capital. The majority of the Boers regarded
Retief's mission as so fraught with danger and treachery that he was
begged not to go but to send another, 'from the many who volunteered',
in his place. But Retief would not hear of it. The deputation reached
Mgungundlovu at the beginning of November 1837 and on arrival were
welcomed by two days of spectacular mass dancing displays put on by the
king's regiments. Dingane, more of an impresario than a warrior king, was
at pains to impress. On the great parade ground thousands of warriors
clad in skins and feathers, executed feats of martial dancing, combining
bounds and leaps of astounding agility, their performance accompanied
all the while by an overwhelming din of militant choruses.

Then came the inevitable display of wealth, the parade of thousands
of cattle all of the same colour. The Rev. Owen was present and that
night recorded in his diary: 'He [Dingane] has lately been collecting an
immense herd of oxen from distant parts of the country for no other
conceivable motive than to display his wealth to the Dutch.'

Retief also marvelled at Dingane's 'beautiful habitation' with its many
pillars clad in exquisite beadwork. Finally, on the third day, and with
the Boers duly impressed, Dingane consented to get down to business.
Retief's hopes and expectations came close to being dashed.

Owen was sent for and at Dingane's dictation and Owen's translation,
wrote the following reply to the letter Retief had written from Port
Natal almost two weeks earlier:

To go on now with the request you made for the land. I am quite willing to grant it but first I wish to explain that a great many cattle have been stolen from me from the outskirts of my country by people with clothing, horses and guns. These people told the Zoolus that they were Boers, and that one part was gone to Port Natal and that they (the Zoolus) would see now what would come upon them! It is my wish now that you should shew that you are not guilty of the charge which has been laid against you, as I now believe you to be. It is my request that you should retake my cattle and bring them to me, and if possible send me the thief, and that will take all suspicion away from me, and I will cause you to know that I am your friend. I will then grant your request.

Having read the letter, a dismayed Retief denied the implied charge and suggested instead that a man by the name of Sekonyela, occupying territory high up on the Drakensberg Mountains, could be the culprit as his tribe dressed in European clothes and, furthermore, Zulu cattle had been seen in his possession. Dingane suggested that Sekonyela should be captured together with any guns and horses that he might have.

It was a daunting task. Retief was to retrace his steps for several hundred miles, climb almost 10,000 feet into the Drakensberg Mountains and attempt the recapture of hundreds of cattle from what would surely be a hostile chieftain. With apparent good grace Retief and his companions prepared to depart to accomplish Dingane's bidding. Owen, however, attempted to discourage them, pointing out Dingane's duplicity and that the territory they coveted had already been granted to 'the British Government' and would they, the Boers, if required, in order to take up occupation, become British subjects once again? Retief replied emphatically No. But, as the Boers rode back to Port Natal, Owen's words must have rankled, giving Retief cause to ponder whether or not he was riding on a fool's errand whilst the Zulu king planned some treachery. Foolishly, Retief decided to send a letter threatening retribution should harm befall him and using Mzilikazi's defeat as an example of the Christian God's vengeance:

To Dingane, King of the amaZulus.
Port Natal

. . . Massilicatzi [Mzilikazi], I do not doubt, has fled away, for he must believe that I shall punish him for his improper conduct. Have I not already grounds for complaint in that I have been constrained to kill so many of his nation simply because they executed his cruel orders?

That which just befallen Massilicatzi leads me to believe that the Almighty, the all-knowing God, will not permit him to live much longer. God's great book teaches us that the kings who behave as Massilicatzi has done, are severely punished and that it is not granted to them to live and reign for long; and if you wish to learn more about how God deals with evil kings like these, you can find out from the missionaries who live in your country. You may believe all that these preachers tell you concerning God and his government of the world.

Regarding such matters, I'd advise you to speak frequently with these gentlemen, whose wish it is to preach to you God's work, for they will teach you of how justly God has ruled, and still rules, over all the kings of the earth. . . .

As for the thieves who took your cattle, and what they have said, namely that they were Boers, it was a clever device to induce you to believe that I was a thief, so that they might escape with impunity. I am confident that I shall prove to the King that my people and I are innocent of this crime; Knowing my innocence, I feel that you have imposed upon me a severe obligation which I must fulfil in order to prove that I am not guilty. As for this deed which you require me to perform, accompanied as it is by expense, difficulty and risk to life, I must be answerable to you, to the world and to God, who knows all.

I go now, placing my trust in God, who gives me hope that I shall be able to execute this enterprise in such a manner as to be able to give a satisfactory answer to all. That said, I shall await convincing proof that I am dealing with a King who keeps his word . . .

If Dingane had still been pondering his options when Retief departed to recover the ˉroyal cattle, there can be little doubt that Retief's belligerent and admonishing letter persuaded the Zulu king that the Boers were the white men of Jacob's prophecy and must be dealt with accordingly. Their God and the God of the missionaries being one and the same – yet confusingly different: the one, as continuously described by Gardiner and Owen as being a God of love and forgiveness, and He of the Boers a God of wrath and vengeance: one who rode with his people into battle, sword in hand, to do their bidding. Had not the Boers, aided by Him, recently slaughtered, according to their own boast, 3,000 Matabele!

Yet there may have been another aspect to Dingane's thinking in deciding the fate of the Boers. The British government of the Cape, far from wishing to see the departure of thousands of its best frontier settlers, had done much to discourage the Boer emigration and had declared that they would not only retain the status of British citizens but would be subject to British law no matter where they wandered in Africa below the 25th line of latitude – a demarcation that extended across the continent as far north as present day Swaziland and, at the time hundreds of miles from any British authority. It was legislation impossible to implement but nevertheless designed to foil the establishment of an independent Boer state. It is possible that Gardiner, regarding himself as the local representative of the British government, would have viewed the arrival of the Boers with hostility, their presence thwarting his hopes for the establishment of a British colony. Adulphe Delegorgue (of whom more later), a French scientist-adventurer, who was present in Port Natal at the time and, it must be mentioned, detested the English in general and English missionaries in particular (He described Owen, a Cambridge MA, as 'probably some wretched artisan from England . . . the sort of sorry creature England sometimes uses to propagate her ideas'), maintained that Gardiner and Owen had told Dingane that the Boers had '. . . removed themselves from the authority of their King. They would not behave in this way if they were good subjects. They are tramps who would make dangerous neighbours. They will repay the good you do them with evil.' This is quite plausible as Jane Williams, Owen's maid, later testified: '. . . a kafir [*sic*] messenger from Dingaan [*sic*] came running to us and said we were not to be frightened, that we were King George's children and that the Boers were runaways from him.'

If that were indeed true, Dingane would likely have regarded Retief and his followers as runaways from their monarch – people comparable to his own defecting subjects and deserving of the same fate. He may even have thought that by doing away with them he would find favour with King George. Combined with Dingane's fear of the emigrants' seemingly superhuman fighting ability in defeating Mzilikazi for so little loss to themselves, the fear of their weapons, their horses and of Jacob's prophecy, the missionary's disparaging communications – if indeed such had been made – may just have tipped the scales in

Dingane's decision to exterminate the emigrants, believing it to be necessary before they destroyed him.

All along the passes, high up in the Drakensberg Mountains, a thousand wagons had been waiting, the occupants aware that if Retief was successful in recovering the royal cattle, the promised land, a lush and inviting tropical paradise that lay far below, would be theirs. They had been ordered not to move, not to descend until Retief sent word that the treaty with the Zulu king had been well and truly ratified. But the emigrants had grown weary of waiting in the cold and barren heights. As rumours spread that Retief had been successful in his quest and in capturing Sekonyela, impatience overcame caution and the massive migration down the passes began.

To the Zulu people who inhabited the region, it would have been little different had the invaders been aliens from space. Their appearance, with their great beards and flapping clothing, was particularly frightening; they also rode strange animals that did their bidding and, most terrifying of all, they could kill from a distance with a peculiar-shaped staff that emitted fire and smoke and a noise like thunder in the mountains – the very mountains from which these bizarre beings had appeared. The Zulu clans whose villages and cultivated fields lay in the path of the invaders, fled leaving their crops to be harvested by the aliens. Soon Erasmus Smit, a Boer preacher, was able to boast: 'From the deserted Kaffir villages more than eighty heavy wagon loads [of food] have been brought into the camps, so that through God's guidance we harvest and eat what others have planted . . .' So confident were emigrants that Retief had concluded a deal and an alliance with the Zulu king that Smit further eulogised: 'We thanked our God for hearing our prayers and for the good land which He has given us through all the labour of our Governor [Retief] and the good kindness of Dingane's heart.' Little did Smit know that within days Dingane would decide to destroy them all.

It had taken Retief almost three months to fulfil his quest. He had captured Sekonyela but guessing his fate, had later kindly released him. And instead of saving the booty of firearms and horses for Dingane, Retief had distributed them amongst his own followers. Through his network of spies, all this would have been known to Dingane who had long been preparing for Retief's return to Mgungundlovu. Dingane was well aware that on this occasion it would be no mere diplomatic deputation of a few men as it had been previously but that there now approached a force of white men seventy strong, and as many native followers, all armed and mounted. Either a confrontation or an amicable agreement was inevitable; and, whatever the outcome, Dingane wanted Gardiner as the representative of King George, and John Cane representing the Port Natal Traders, to be present – presumably in the capacities as either witnesses or supporters of his actions. Owen was summoned to write the invitation and Richard Hulley was sent off to Port Natal to deliver it. Dingane, ominously provided Hulley with an escort of twenty warriors: '... ostensibly to carry anything I might have to bring but really to watch my movements, and to learn anything of importance that might arise,' Hulley wrote. But Gardiner, who would normally have leapt at Dingane's invitation, had seen Piet Retief and his armed commando riding north and, as Hulley later remembered, 'declined to be present at the meeting, telling me he did not think it would be safe'.

At sunrise, on 2 February, while Retief was still some way from Mgungundhlovu, Dingane sent for Owen and dictated a letter. Owen recorded in his diary:

The letter was characteristic of the Chief. He said that his heart was now content, because he had got his cattle again: He requested that the Chief of the Boers would send to all his people and order them to come to the capital with him, but without their horses: He promised to gather together all his army to sing and dance in the presence of the Dutch, who he desired would also dance: He said he would give orders that cattle should be slain for them at every place thro' which they passed on their road, and he promised to give a country. I asked how they could come without their horses. He said tell them then that they must bring their horses and dance upon their horses in the middle of the town, that it may be known who can dance best, the Zooloos or the Abalongo, the general term for white people.

Nothing was said about the guns or horses taken from Sekonyela. The Dutch will be too wise to expose themselves in the manner proposed, but I cannot conceive that Dingane meditates any treachery, which, however, he would have the power (if he chose) to exercise toward them, should they venture to come.

The following morning a volley of musket fire announced Retief's arrival. Owen, now full of apprehension, was at home:

Large parties of Zooloos in their war dress were yesterday evening entering the town. This morning when we were at family prayers the unusual sound of muskets was heard from the west; This proved to be the arrival of the Boers who presently entered the town on horseback with their guns in their hands. An immense concourse of Zooloos were present to receive them. The deputation brought with them the cattle which they had recovered from Sekonyela. The Boers immediately showed Dingane the way in which they danced on horseback by making a sham charge at one another making the air resound with their guns. This was something the Zoolu Chief had never witnessed. In their turn the Zooloos exhibited their agility in dancing. About noon I paid a visit to Mr. Retief, who with his party (after the amusement was over) were seated under the Euphorbia trees fronting the gate of the town. The answer he gave to Dingane when he demanded the guns and horses was to shew the messenger his grey hairs and bid him to tell his master that he was not dealing with a child.'

Dingane had been unsuccessful in separating the Boers from their guns and horses but he would try again. In the meantime Retief and his men, tired of the incessant dancing and clamour and anxious to be on their way, pressed Dingane for his signature to the treaty which, written in English, had already been prepared by the Boers. Its content was much the same as the previous treaties that the Zulu monarchs had signed when bequeathing the territory. But Dingane, most likely awaiting the arrival of Gardiner, continued with his spectacle of martial dancing.

Sometime, probably later that day, Dingane having been informed by his spies that neither Gardiner nor John Cane could be expected, decided to proceed without their presence and, still manoeuvring to get possession of the Boer firearms, further decided that the best ruse would be to sign the treaty. Thus he and three senior *izinduna* put their mark to the document which read:

Know all men by this that whereas Pieter Retief, Governor of the Dutch, immigrant South Afrikans, has retaken my cattle which Senkonyela had stolen which cattle he the said Retief now deliver unto me – I Dingane,

King of the Zoolas, do hereby certify and declare that I thought fit to resign, unto him the said Retief and his countrymen (on reward of the case here above mentioned) the place called Port Natal together with all the land annexed, that is to say from Dogeela [Tugela] to the Omsoboebo [Mzimvubu] River westward and from the sea to the north as far as the land may be useful and in my possession which I did by this and give unto them for their everlasting property.

The treaty was signed to the great joy of the Boers and, having thanked Dingane profusely, they obtained his permission to retire to their camp in preparation for a triumphant departure on the morrow.

But there was at least one white person at Mgungundhlovu who knew that the Boers had little time to live. William Wood, a youngster of about twelve years of age who had been brought up amongst the Zulus and spoke their language as fluently as they, had overheard a plan to kill Retief and all his men. This startling news he relayed to Jane Williams, Owen's housemaid, who, perhaps due to the boy's youth, or her own fear, ridiculed him. Nevertheless, there was a feeling of unease

7. Piet Retief was confident he could negotiate a deal with King Dingane but, on Dingane's orders, he and his companions were brutally murdered. (*KZN Archives, Pietermaritzburg*)

amongst the Boers and many wanted to mount up without delay and leave Mgungundhlovu far behind them. But Retief would not hear of it, saying that he trusted Dingane and believed that the Boers had been treated justly. Furthermore, Dingane had requested that the white men delay their departure in order to toast mutual friendship with just one more draught of native beer, to which Retief had agreed. With the treaty safe in his leather pouch, Retief seems to have lost all caution and, instead, to have become overwhelmed with trust in the Zulu king. He even agreed that, as a gesture of respect and friendship, the Boers would leave their guns in camp and would go unarmed to drink their stirrup cup of beer.

The Reverend Owen recorded the events of the following day:

Feb, 6 – A dreadful day in the annals of the mission! My pen shudders to give an account of it. This morning as 1 was sitting in the shade of my wagon reading the Testament, the usual messenger came with hurry and anxiety depicted in his looks. I was sure he was about to pronounce something serious, and what was his commission! Whilst it shewed consideration and kindness in the Zoolu Monarch towards me, it disclosed a horrid instance of perfidy – too horrid to be described – towards the unhappy men who have for these three days been his guests, but are now no more. He sent to tell me not to be frightened as he was going to kill the Boers. This news came like a thunder stroke to myself and to every successive member of my family as they heard it. The reason assigned for this treacherous conduct was that they were going to kill him, that they had come here and he had now learned all their plans. The messenger was anxious for my reply, but what could I say? Fearful on the one hand of seeming to justify the treachery and on the other of exposing myself and family to probable danger if I appeared to take their part. Moreover I could not but feel that it was my duty to appraise the Boers of the intended massacre whilst certain death would have ensured (I apprehended) if I had been detected in giving this information. However, I was released from this dilemma by beholding an awful spectacle! My attention was directed to the bloodstained hill nearby opposite my hut and on the other side of my wagon, which hides it from my view, where all the executions at this fearful spot take place and which was now destined to add sixty more bleeding carcasses to the number of those which had already cried to heaven for vengeance. [The number slain that morning including retainers was closer to 150].

'There (said someone), they are killing the Boers now.' I turned my eyes and behold! An immense multitude on the hill. About nine or ten Zulus to each Boer were dragging their helpless unarmed victims to the fateful spot, where those eyes which awakened this morning to see the cheerful light of day for the last time, are now closed in death. I lay myself down on the ground. [Owen actually fainted.] Mrs and Miss Owen were not more thunderstruck than myself. We each comforted the other. Presently the deed of blood being accomplished the whole multitude returned to the town to meet their sovereign, and as they drew near to him set up a shout which reached the station and continued for some time. Meanwhile, I myself, had been kept from all fear for my personal safety, for I considered the message of Dingane to me as an indication that he had no ill designs against his missionary, especially as the messenger informed (me) that the Boer interpreter, an Englishman from Port Natal was to be preserved. [In the excitement, Tom Halstead, the interpreter, was mistakenly killed.] Nevertheless, fears afterwards obtruded themselves on me, when I saw half a dozen men with shields sitting near a hut, and I began to tremble lest we were to fall the next victims! . . . We then knelt down and I prayed, really not knowing but that in this position we might be called into another world. Such was the effect of the first gust of fear on my mind. I remember the words: 'Call upon me in the day of trouble and I will hear thee.' . . . Dingane's conduct was worthy of a savage as he is. It was base and treacherous, to say the least of it – the offspring of cowardice and fear. Suspicious of his warlike neighbours, jealous of their power, dreading the neighbourhood of their arms, he felt as every savage would have done in like circumstances that these men were his enemies and being unable to attack them openly, he massacred them clandestinely!' [Earlier that morning Owen had conversed with two of Retief's men and recalled that they had spoken kindly of Dingane.] When I asked them what they thought of Dingane, they said he was good: so unsuspicious were they of his intentions. He had promised to assign over to them the whole country between the Tugela and the Umzimvubo Rivers, and this day the paper of transfer was to be signed. My mind has always been filled with the notion that however friendly the two powers had heretofore seem to be, war in the nature of things was inevitable between them.

Yet, despite the horror of what had happened, Owen was able to ponder on what advantage it may provide for his mission. He continued to address his diary:

The hand of God is in this affair, but how it will turn out favourably to
the mission, it is impossible to shew. The Lord direct our course. I have
seen by my glass [telescope] that Dingane has been sitting most of the
morning since this dreadful affair in the centre of his town, an army in
several divisions collected before him. About noon the whole body ran in
the direction from which the Boers came. They are (I cannot allow myself
to doubt) sent to join others who have been ordered to fall unawares on
the main body of the Boers who are encamped at the head of the Tugela,
for to suppose that Dingane should murder this handful and not make
himself sure of the whole number with their guns, horses and cattle,
would be to conceive him capable of egregious folly, as he must know
that the other Boers will avenge the death of their countrymen. Certain
it is as far as human foresight can judge, we shall speedily hear either
of the massacre of the whole company of Boers, or what is scarcely less
terrible of wars and bloodshed, of which there will be no end till either
the Boers or the Zulu nation cease to be.

Owen, his family and Hulley's wife and children spent a terror-filled
day wondering whether, at any moment, they too might be dragged
to kwaMatiwane, there to suffer the same fate as the Boers. However,
the following day Dingane sent a messenger assuring them that as
the people of King George, they would come to no harm and it was
mentioned that young Thomas Halstead, the Englishman that had
accompanied the Boers as their interpreter, had, in the uproar and
confusion, been killed by mistake, which the king greatly regretted. In
the meantime Hulley, having made his abortive visit to Gardiner, had
been delayed for several days on this return journey due to the Tugela
being impassable. It was not until three days after the massacre that he
at last approached Mgungundlovu and was immediately alarmed at the
almost tangible feeling of dread that the silence of the place brought
upon him. Then:

> . . . To the right of the Great Place, in the direction of the execution
> ground. I observed a large flock of vultures hovering over the place of the
> dead. At once I suspected that there had been some evil work going on
> during my absence. Leading my horse I descended the hill. About half
> way down I saw lying by the side of the path the sleeve of a white shirt,
> which had been forcibly torn from the garment; it was partly covered
> with blood. This greatly alarmed me, and I feared lest the mission party

with my family had been put to death. When I reached the king's kraal I rode up to the principal entrance, and from there saw a number of saddles piled one upon the other. I sent a message in to Dingane to give notice of my return; but I was anxious about the safety of my family that without waiting for the messenger to come out I mounted my horse and galloped off on the way to our huts, to see if they were all right.

Hulley eventually found the whole of the missionary party unharmed but hardly had he time to express his joy when a messenger arrived summoning him immediately to the king's presence where he found Dingane in a peevish and dangerous mood, clearly expecting Hulley to condone the massacre on the basis that the Boers had been, or would become, the enemies of both the Zulu and English alike. When Hulley remained impassive and unsupportive, Dingane angrily retorted:

I see that every white man is an enemy to the black; every black an enemy to the white: they do not love each other, and never will. I find fault with the Boers in that they disobeyed my instructions. The chief that I told them to bring to me, they let go. Don't you think I have done a good thing in getting rid of my enemies at one stroke? ... What is it that Captain Gardiner and John Cane had heard that led them to decline coming to the meeting? ... I am sorry that they were not here, as they fully deserved what the Boers received.

Hulley and Owen were aware that their lives teetered on the swing of Dingane's mood and that at any moment they too could be an additional feast for the vultures on kwaMatiwane. But suddenly Dingane's disposition changed. He gave them a pot of beer and sent them home.

The following day Hulley and Owen decided to seek Dingane's permission to return with their families to Port Natal. But the king's mood had changed again. Hulley later recalled the scene:

In reply to our request he said: 'I must take time to think about it. I don't yet understand you. I believe you are as much my enemies as the Boers whom I killed. My people tell me that when the Dutch [Boers] were put to death you [Owen] set up a loud cry. Would you cry for me if I were killed? No, I don't think you would! I was told also that you stood on the front of the wagon with your glass [telescope] in your hand, and that when you saw what was going on you fell down in a faint, and were taken up insensible. No, you cannot be my friends, you are my deadly enemies. If I had done what was proper I should have had you put out of the way at the time I put to death my other enemies.'

Owen protested and cried that Dingane was mistaken. But the king interrupted.

'I want to hear no more of your lies,' said the chief. 'I have had proof that you are my enemy, and I believe it, whatever you may say to the contrary.'

Shaken and consumed with dread, the two white men whispered one to the other the belief that they were about to die. They then fell silent. In the hush that followed they expected Dingane, at any second, by the nod of his head or the raising of a finger, to confirm their immediate and violent death. Then Hulley, with nothing to lose, boldly asked the king how he would explain the killing of the young interpreter, Thomas Halstead, to the English king, Hulley emphasising that Halstead was an Englishman, not a Boer. Hulley prompted that if Halstead's death was indeed a mistake, Dingane would be wise to advise the Cape authorities. The king, taken aback, asked how this was to be done. Hulley replied that he and Owen would write a letter at Dingane's dictation and take it with them. Within an hour, their wagons having been hurriedly packed, Owen and Hulley with their families, still fearful of treachery, headed out of Mgungundhlovu on their way back to Port Natal. Hulley's boldness had saved their lives.

Owen's prediction that Dingane would not stop at the massacre of Retief and his party but would send his regiments to wipe out the rest of the Boers, men, women and children, who were encamped amidst the streams and meadows of the Drakensberg foothills, proved to be prophetic. It was a slaughter more dreadful than that that had taken place on kwaMatiwane a few days earlier. Over 600 men, women and children were put to death, their wagons burnt, cattle taken and their possessions destroyed. Later, the Boers that survived, called the area 'Weenen' – 'weeping', and it is known by that name today.

Dingane had also been correct in his prediction that the English residents of the Port would side with their white Boer kin against him, a black man. As soon as the news of Retief's death reached the ears of the traders going about their business in Zululand, most scampered back to

Port Natal to form a defence. But that enterprising and entrepreneurial body of militia men, the Port Natal Volunteers, took the opportunity not only to retaliate but to line their pockets. Whilst Gardiner and many of the other white inhabitants clambered aboard the schooner *Mary*, which had fortuitously arrived, the Volunteers, led by Alexander Biggar, prepared to sally forth and within a week they were back at the port with hundreds of captured cattle plus as many Zulu women and children who could look to a future of being little better than slaves. Exalted by their success, the Port Natal Volunteers set out to repeat their success. It was a body to be reckoned with: 3,000 Natal Zulus of whom 400 were armed with muskets and had been well trained; the rest carried traditional weapons and all were finely disciplined under their white officers who included a number of the old hands, going back to the first arrivals, such as Richard Wood, John Cane, Charles Blankenberg and, of course, Alexander Biggar.

Bravely, but rashly, this army moved north and on reaching the Tugela its forward skirmishes crossed the river and came in sight of the main Zulu army, approximately 12,000 strong. On reporting this news there was dissent in the traders' camp: John Cane and his supporters were in favour of building a fortification and then luring the Zulu army on to the muskets of the traders' mercenaries. But Biggar was all for immediately crossing the river, taking the Zulus by surprise and putting them to flight. Biggar eventually had his way. Before the trader army, just across the Tugela, lay the Zulu garrison barracks of Ndondakasuka with the main army camping a little distance beyond. Stealthily crossing the Tugela in the darkness, at a drift familiar to many, the traders deployed around the barracks and, at a given signal fired into the flimsy huts, bringing down dozens of warriors as they rose from their sleeping mats, attempting to exit through the waist high doorways. The traders then advanced and set fire to all the huts, completely destroying the barracks.

Elated with this early success the invaders advanced, the musket men forming the front ranks ready to halt, take position and fire at a moment's notice. Biggar must have been reminded of similar moments in Spain and America. The invaders did not have long to wait. Dawn had long since broken but through undulations and broken terrain the advancing Zulus were hard to discern and then, almost suddenly they were there, on top of the traders; now, with caution and stealth abandoned, the warriors were racing across the open ground, to be amongst the first to plunge their stabbing assegais into the enemy. But the traders remained steadfast while the musket men, firing at about one and a half rounds a minute, poured devastating volleys into the Zulu ranks. Legend has it that a deserter from H.M. forces, Robert Joyce, a former redcoat of the 72nd Regiment, played a distinguished role in halting the Zulu charge.

The jubilant trader army then advanced further, mainly to position itself against the threat of the Zulu right horn; Cane and Ogle's companies being in the forefront of this manoeuvre. Indeed, the traders put the Zulus to flight but most likely, fearing a trap, the traders lost their nerve and instead of holding their ground, broke and ran for the river. The Zulus were not slow to react and raced to outflank them, denying the traders the drift crossing, pushing them instead onto and over some cliffs with a drop straight down into the river. The Zulu left horn now charged with great ferocity, forcing the traders back, and disdaining the musket fire that was dropping their companions in heaps, finally got to hand to hand contact with the assegai. The traders were massively outnumbered and driven back; back towards the Tugela where, with the river blocking further retreat, many were surrounded and killed. Robert, the last surviving child of Alexander Biggar, went down fighting and was put to death.

The horns of the Zulu army, that is the wings comprising the fleet-footed younger regiments, sprinted to close the encircling manoeuvre and it was almost over. Many of the Natal Zulus divested themselves of any telltale weaponry or insignia and passed themselves off as Zulu warriors. Those who managed to cross the Tugela, including Biggar, made as fast as they could to Port Natal where they found most of the white inhabitants, including Gardiner and the other missionaries, had sailed away to safety aboard the *Mary*, Allen Gardiner never to return. But Providence was at hand, for hardly had the *Mary* crossed the harbour bar than the *Comet*, another little coaster, completely oblivious of the drama taking place ashore, dropped anchor. The remainder of the white survivors found room aboard, leaving their followers, their black wives and their coloured children, to survive as best they could whilst they, for over a week, sat tight watching the Zulus spread death and destruction a few hundred yards away across the water.

8. Shingana kaMpande, King
Cetshwayo's half-brother, fought
at nDondakusuka, Isandlwana
and Ulundi. (*KZN Archives,
Pietermaritzburg*)

When at last the warriors' rampage came to an end, a few brave souls
rowed ashore to count the cost. Finally, reaching Gardiner's home, they
found it completely despoiled and amongst the ruins vast quantities of
once-valuable books and, smashed beyond repair, the Broadwood piano
that Gardiner had shipped from England at great expense.

Soon the *Comet* also set sail with Owen and his family amongst the
crowd of passengers. He too had reluctantly accepted the futility of
his mission. Another of the fleeing passengers, George Champion, the
young American missionary, later wrote: 'Now, when the Boers settle in
Natal, woe to the natives under their control.' Prophetic words indeed.

It was 4 May 1838. Only fourteen years had elapsed since the first
white traders had sought contact with the Zulu nation and had been
received with hospitality and friendship. However, the sun that had
shone on Zululand prior to the coming of the white man, was now in
decline and it would not be long before the Zulu nation would enter
upon a twilight world of oppression, poverty and defeat. Dingane's

regiments that had been sent to wipe out all the Boers, men, women and children, failed to complete their mission. Those emigrants warned in time of the approaching peril, were able to laager their wagons and fight off the attackers. They were also able to hold on to those vast stretches of Dingane's kingdom that they had already claimed as their own. And so a stand-off developed between the emigrants and the Zulu king whilst each plotted the extinction of the other; the Boers intent on vengeance and securing absolute rule over their promised land.

Word of the merits of the Boer paradise had spread back over the bleak Drakensberg Mountains where there were emigrants aplenty ready to risk all for a stake in 'Natalia', the name by which the Boers referred to the territory they had seized. From amongst the emigrant ranks emerged a charismatic leader, a big flamboyant man who carried a brace of pistols in his belt and from whose hand swung a naval cutlass: As seen by Piet Retief's widow, Andries Pretorius was 'a man sent by God'. He had assembled sixty-four wagons drawn by a thousand oxen. Each wagon had been stripped of everything non-essential until each became a segment of a mobile fortification. At night, or at the approach of an enemy, the oxen would be 'outspanned', that is, unharnessed, and the wagons pushed and pulled into a tight circle. The *disselboom*, or shaft, of each being pushed underneath the back of the wagon in front, and there chained. To prevent an agile enemy entry below the wagon floors or between the wheels, fighting, or wicket gates, made from thorn trees, were secured in place. Thus the whole became a substantial stronghold with oxen and horses tethered in the centre. There were sufficient horses to mount everyone, including the drivers and leaders. By the time Alexander Biggar, with a hundred Port Natal blacks, joined the column (Biggar was intent on avenging the death of his son Robert), Pretorius' army amounted to 687 men armed with a variety of muzzle-loading firearms. And, well-prepared, each man carried a generous supply of powder plus many little cotton sachets each containing a number of lead balls, that would enable the Boers, with one shot, to dispose of several opponents.

Pretorius now sought a confrontation with Dingane's army. Heading towards Mgungundlovu, the Boers, taking strength from worship and prayer, had been in the act of fording the Ncome River, fifty miles from the king's capital, when scouts reported that a massive Zulu army was fast approaching. Pretorius hurried all his wagons back over the river and, on the west bank of the Ncome, between the river and a deep donga (ravine), he formed a laager, the natural barriers forming a moat on two sides. He had stumbled upon what was probably the best natural defensive position in all Zululand.

The Boers sat out the night well aware that a mighty enemy host was close at hand and when in the morning the early mist began to clear, they found the opposing army, 10,000 strong, watching and waiting 450 yards away. The battle that followed was a triumphant victory for the Boers in which they saw the hand of God. In attempting to storm the Boer defences by crossing the Ncome River, hundreds of warriors were shot to death, their blood so discolouring the water that the clash became known as 'The Battle of Blood River'. So numerous were those killed in the pursuit that followed by the mounted Boers, that one of the victors, describing the scene in farming language that his kin would find no difficulty in understanding, stated: 'They [the Zulu dead] lay on the ground like pumpkins on a rich soil that had borne a large crop.'

The Boers turned their victory into a rout, pursuing the defeated warriors for miles, so it is said, shooting them down from the saddle in their hundreds; indeed such was the slaughter that the plain across which the warriors fled became known as the *Intambu* – The Plain of Bones. From the back of a galloping horse, it can be no easy matter to reload an ungainly musket with powder, shot and ramrod, thus the number of Zulu casualties may well be exaggerated.

Several of the combatants recorded the day:

Of that fight nothing remains in my memory except shouting and tumult and lamentations, and a sea of black faces and a dense smoke that rose straight as a plumb-line upwards from the ground. We had scarcely time to throw a handful of powder into the gun and slip a bullet down the barrel, without a moment even to drive it home with the ramrod.

Of the fighting along the donga, Chaplain Cilliers recalled:

A severe fire was opened on them. More than 400 fell in the attack on the ravine [donga]. Then the word of the Lord was fulfilled: 'By one way shall your enemies come, but by the blessings of the Lord shall they fly before your face.' They now offered no further resistance. We were on the

right and left, and they were huddled together. We were animated by
great courage ...

Some 3,000 warriors were slain, or so the Boers claimed, to only
three wounded on the Boer side, one of whom was Pretorius himself,
wounded in the hand. The story goes that Pretorius gave his gun-trained
horse to another man and, in firing at the enemy from a substitute
horse it threw him. As he rose to his feet the warrior thrust at him, the
blade going right through Pretorius' hand; he was saved by a comrade
who shot the warrior dead. Exaggerated enemy casualties make good
propaganda, but there is no doubt about who actually won.

Wishing to follow up their success, the Boers pressed on towards
Mgungundlovu with the intention of taking the capital and torching
it. But Dingane forestalled them. He burnt it down himself and moved
his capital a hundred miles further north amongst terrain less suitable
for horses and wheeled transport.

Across from the smoking capital and the ruins of Owen's mission,
stood the hill of slaughter, kwaMatiwane, and there the Boers found
the bleached remains of their kin who had been slain ten months
before. They also found Retief's leather hunting wallet, still attached
to his skeleton, and within it, in a miraculous state of preservation, the
document ceding Natal to the Boer emigrants. Now there was proof
that Natal was theirs not only by right of conquest but lawfully as well.

They buried the bones of their kin in a communal grave (where they
lie to this day) and then set off in pursuit of Dingane. Near the White
Umfolozi River they encountered the rear guard of the Zulu army and
in the ensuing engagement Alexander Biggar was killed along with
several of his Port Natal Volunteers and five Boers. Dismayed by so
many casualties, but with 5,000 head of captured cattle, the pursuers
decided to call it a day. On their way back they elected to pay homage
to the Englishman, Alexander Biggar, who had fought at their side, and
solemnly named a range of mountains, the Biggarsberg, in his honour.

Unbeknown to Pretorius, much was afoot at Port Natal. The British
had landed. The first of the red soldiers, true to Jacobs' prophecy, had
arrived.

Chapter 6

Then Come the Red Soldiers

There was a new governor in Cape Town. In 1838 Sir Benjamin D'Urban had been succeeded by Sir George Napier who was not only alarmed at the goings on in Zululand but was also not averse to a bit of stealthy empire-building. He had in fact decided that neither the Zulus, the Boers, nor indeed the English traders, had any right of ownership to Port Natal as, in fact, it belonged to Britain. He had recently written to the Colonial Secretary in London:

> The Zulus have no claim to Port Natal other than that which any barbarous nation might pretend to have to any portion of ground which they had once overrun and depopulated, but of which they did not maintain the right of possession. The right of occupancy of Port Natal, if any such right can be said to exist, belongs to the Crown of Great Britain. The few British and other settlers and the emigrant farmers are merely unauthorised intruders on the soil.

In response to that somewhat illogical declaration, Governor Napier had been authorised to send a small expeditionary force to establish order. It fell to the lot of Major Samuel Charters and one hundred officers and men of the 72nd (Duke of Albany's Own Highlanders) Regiment of Foot, to put Port Natal and the territory beyond, under British authority. Napier further explained to the Colonial Secretary that the object of the British occupation would be to bring an end to the fighting between the Boers and the Zulus through the expedient of cutting off the Boer supply of ammunition and gunpowder. It would also prevent the Boers from establishing an independent republic that could be in a position to control the only port on hundreds of miles of coast line.

The British military mission, aboard hired vessels, arrived at Port Natal on 3 December 1838, missing the departure of Pretorius for his expedition against Dingane by just a few days. In the absence of most of the Boer fighting men, there was no resistance to the British landing, the nervous civilians in fact welcoming the presence of the troops.

Major Charters wasted no time in exerting control and when Pretorius and his column returned some weeks later, Pretorius's triumphant ebullience turned to dismay when he saw the Union Jack flying over a new fort that Charters had constructed at the entrance to the harbour. However, Pretorius prudently let things ride for the moment and, with the atmosphere tense, Charters sailed back to Cape Town to report in person, leaving the forty-year-old Captain Henry Jervis, an experienced and highly-capable soldier, to handle the volatile situation.

If peace were to be established between the emigrants and the Zulu kingdom, representatives of both factions would need to come to terms. With this objective in mind, Jervis enlisted the help of Henry Ogle who made contact with Dingane in his capital 170 miles north of the port.

9. Andries Pretorius, the victor of Blood River. According to Boer accounts of the battle, he was the only casualty: a slight wound to the hand. Conversely the Boers claimed to have slain 3,000 Zulus. (*KZN Archives, Pietermaritzburg*)

Dingane immediately responded by appointing Chief Gambutshi as his representative who informed Jervis that Dingane rejoiced at the prospect of peace. However, when Pretorius heard of the negotiations he was furious and demanded that the Boers be privy to, and participate in, all future negotiations. To back up his demands he made mention of 2,000 armed and mounted Boers who were assembling on the other side of the Drakensberg in preparation for settling in Natal.

Finally a meeting was arranged with the Zulu contingent handing over, as a sign of their goodwill, more than 200 horses, being the former property of Piet Retief and his followers. The return of all the captured firearms was also promised.

Jervis proposed the Tongaat River as the boundary between Natal and Zululand but the Boers would not have it, insisting that the Tugela be the dividing line thus giving the emigrants an additional thirty miles of coastline. The Zulu envoys nevertheless agreed and Jervis was able to report the success of his diplomatic negotiations to Governor Napier in the Cape. Yet, had the British been aware of the Boers' desire for revenge, they would have been more cautious: Pretorius, in reference to those 2,000 Boers about to descend the Drakensberg, wrote that they were 'all anxious to give the last deathblow to the now humiliated bloodhound [Dingane], and which he certainly shall not escape'. However, Pretorius, not wishing a confrontation with Britain, wisely bided his time and prepared for the future when, hopefully, the British would have departed. Nevertheless, within months, Pretorius was challenging Captain Jervis in the most threatening manner:

We, the undersigned leaders of the emigrant farmers, party to the late Peace Treaty with the Zulus and others, do hereby solemnly declare that provided the ammunition which was seized by the troops on the occupation of the port is restored to us, it is not our intention to turn our arms against the Zulus, or any other of the native tribes, but to restrict ourselves to measures of self-defence alone, on the territory we now occupy. We positively declare that the peace between us and the surrounding natives is positively certain and will continue as long as they deal with us in a proper manner. We find also in the Cape newspapers proposals for the establishment of a British colony and although we take little notice of what the newspapers say, we have yet to signify to you, should you remain here for that purpose, that we shall never allow one or more persons to establish themselves here without subjecting themselves to the jurisdiction of this community.

And, with the arrival of hundreds more emigrants, Pretorius made additional demands on Dingane who now had his back to the northern boundary of his kingdom. As he could retreat no further without contesting the land of the amaSwazi, the age-old enemies of the Zulus, Dingane decided to summon his army from all corners of the kingdom. But his half-brother, Mpande (who it will be remembered had defeated the Port Natal Volunteers), failed to respond. Mpande, whose territory was the closest to Natal being on the north bank of the Tugela, could see that his domain would be the first battleground in any conflict with the whites. He therefore decided to defect into Natal with all his followers and cattle. The sight of Mpande's 17,000 followers crossing the Tugela put the Natal whites into a froth of panic. When it was realised that they were bent on flight, rather than aggression, many a roguish white man turned his covetous attention to the thousands of cattle that accompanied the defecting prince and his warriors. However, the would-be rustlers were restrained and the Boer *Volksraad* (People's Parliament) gave Mpande and his people sanctuary in return for their avowed treachery towards Dingane.

Mpande's temporary home was now only forty miles north of the port and soon a Boer deputation was on its way to formalise a treaty. Included in the contingent was the young French scientist/ adventurer who has been mentioned earlier, Adulphe Delegorgue, he who had a firm antipathy for the British and a blossoming admiration for the Zulu people – but not before he was an unwilling witness to frightening events that would make him fear for his life. However, high amongst the attributes that he most admired was the beauty of the Zulu maidens. The morning following the Boer contingent's arrival at Mpande's newly-erected village, Delegorgue, an early riser, strolled out to seek the way to the prince's residence and, finding no attendants to ask, trespassed further and further into the royal enclosure until he suddenly stumbled – or rather crawled – into the royal bedchamber:

> Upon mats spread out on the ground, lay ten young girls, their naked bodies firmly rounded and soft as velvet. The limbs of at least six of

them were entwined with those of the king [*sic*], one supported his head upon her body, a living pillow whose breathing induced opium dreams; another bore up his right arm; a third had hold of his left hand and laid her temple upon the broad chest of the brother of Djacka; [Shaka] yet another held his right leg, while the left leg cradled the last one of all.

All were asleep and I, the only watcher, was intending to stay and observe, so that I might describe for you my reader, this charming, dimly lit scene, this picture of the night of an amaZoulou chief, when my companions, the farmers, appeared at the entrance of the hut, demanding audience. I withdrew and told them that Panda was still asleep and that it would be better to wait so as not to upset him.

Delegorgue was able to prevent his companions entering the royal bedchamber and Mpande was left to slumber in peace.

But there was another side to Mpande and the Boers were soon striking a deal with him. The prince and his followers were to join forces against the common enemy, Dingane. The successful outcome of the war yet to be fought, would result in the Boers recognising Mpande as king of the Zulu nation – indeed they would crown him as such –

10. George French Angas was an early traveller/artist at the time when the Zulu army was at the height of its power and magnificence. (*Amafa, Durban*)

in return, the boundary between Zululand and Natalia would not be (as we have already heard) the Tongaat River but, instead, the more northern Tugela. In addition, a strip of coastline, 110 miles long, was to be conceded to them giving access to St Lucia Bay. This, the Boers surmised, would afford them control of all the harbours between the northern Cape and Mozambique thus foiling any further attempts by the Cape Government to bring them under British authority. And Mpande, bolstered by the Boers, would no longer give his allegiance to Dingane and, if not yet a king, Mpande would be a prince and the independent ruler of his people.

The Boers further demanded that three of Mpande's chiefs be created ministers of his realm, that they be privy to the treaty and accountable in the event of any harm befalling Mpande. Two chiefs were immediately nominated but Mpande pondered for some time before naming the third. Finally all three were appraised of the treaty terms and expressed their approval. Well pleased, the new ministers departed to inform the nation that it had been ordered to assemble.

Delegorgue had witnessed these proceedings and, shortly after their conclusion, had wandered away to his wagon to sleep. Hardly had he drifted off when he was awakened by an 'indescribable clamour'.

One of the three new ministers, having arrived at the plain and having addressed the assembled multitude, was now destined to die. It was, it transpired, the third man that Mpande had been so hesitant to nominate, knowing what his fate would be. It was a custom, a ritual of the nation, that on being recognised by his people as their king – or he who would be such – his first act of authority was to condemn to death a person of consequence. The third minister had been the unlucky one destined to perish. That was horrifying enough but the method of his death, that the Boers were about to witness, was doubly horrific. Let Delegorgue continue:

> All those kaffirs who had previously been silent listeners, now took an active part in the bloody altercations. A long undulating serpent of men coiled its way towards a particular spot, where all the fighting sticks were struck downwards and when raised again were tinged with blood. The crowd which clustered about the scene of action were uttering loud confused cries as if to stifle those of the victims and conceal the hideous sight.

It was a man whom they were bludgeoning to death and the man was Panga Zonga, the third of Panda's great headmen, the one who had just accepted responsibility for the life of the chief.

The Boers, unaware that the killing was demanded of Mpande by ancient custom, were appalled. The bloody throng offered the white men a simple explanation that they believed would be understood: 'He was a great rascal and a wizard', they said. 'A man, who under Dingane, had been the cause of many deaths.' It was believed by the multitude that it had carried out an act of justice but the outrage, following so closely on the death of Piet Retief and his followers, filled Delegorgue and his companions with dread and they feared they might be turned upon at any moment. But, keeping a brave face and resisting the temptation to exhibit their fear by flight, they sought Mpande and demanded an explanation:

> He came feigning anger: 4,000 warriors formed a circle about him and he glared with apparent menace at the perpetrators of the murder. In our eyes, Mpande had absolved himself of the crime; his eloquence convinced us of his innocence and only several days later did we learn that this had been his first act of authority: the moment we recognised him as chief of his tribe a man had to die by his orders and the blood of the same man was to be used to anoint his limbs at night while the heart, roasted, was to be presented to him to eat, so that it might fortify his body and quicken his courage.

Delegorgue went on to say that there were those at Port Natal who denied such allegations but, later, after living amongst Mpande's people for ten months, Delegorgue had no doubt that such was the custom. However, for the moment, the Boer delegation were happy to believe what they were told. Delegorgue continued: 'Never before had I seen so great a number of men gathered together. The eloquence of the orators, the exaggerated repetity of their movements, their impassioned speeches, the profusion of their words, the quick, bold gestures, unfamiliar to us Europeans, gestures which were more eloquent than words, all this struck me in a most peculiar way.'

In order to divert their minds from the horror of the killing, Mpande called upon the assembled throng to perform and entertain the white men: 'Suddenly a thousand shrill whistles rent the air, loud enough to split even a kaffir's head. All the warriors had begun running at great speed, fanning out in every direction. When they were about 300 paces from the centre, they suddenly spun around as one man; then, chanting their war cry, these warriors who all looked like devils to me began to charge.'

Now convinced that he was about to suffer a similar fate as Retief, Delegorgue ran for his life but the warriors fanned out, broke ranks and allowed him passage to his wagon where he snatched up his gun ready to fight to the last. But it was not necessary: 'I had completely misunderstood the situation and I had been the more easily misled because I did not know the amaZulu customs. This simulated anger, this sudden advance, this wild stamping, accompanied by the most horrible hissing, was the prelude to a war dance...' Fortunately, just as the dancing had reached its climax, a deluge of rain descended, cooling the passions of the throng, everyone scattering and seeking shelter.

Finally, and with much relief, the Boers bade farewell to Mpande and set off for Pietermaritzburg. When but a few miles from home, they were met with the news that a messenger from Dingane had arrived at Pietermaritzburg and had addressed the assembled Boers on his master's behalf. He expressed for the Boers' benefit the king's cautionary opinion of Mpande: 'He is not a man; he has turned away his face; he is a woman. He was useless to Dingane his master, and he will be of no use to you. Do not trust him, for his face may turn again.'

Chapter 7

The Battle of Port Natal

Almost, it would seem, in an effort not to compromise the machinations of the Boers and Mpande, the British occupation force under the command of Captain Jarvis received orders to withdraw from Port Natal and return to the Cape. The redcoats were departing – for the moment at any rate. The alliance of Pretorius and Mpande, now free of any British restraint, prepared for war.

The redcoats, having lowered the Union Jack that had fluttered for months above the little fort they had named Victoria, departed on Christmas Eve 1839, aboard the schooner *Vectis*. Hardly was the vessel out of sight than the gleeful Boers took possession of the fort and ran up their own republican banner on the vacant flagstaff.

Within weeks a massive army had assembled, comprised of over a thousand mounted Boers and many thousands of Mpande's warriors, led by his acclaimed general, Nongalaza kaNondela. As the alliance advanced north to seek battle with Dingane, much of Dingane's army melted away as hundreds of his warriors decamped to join forces with Mpande.

Mpande, the king-in-waiting, did not accompany his army. The wily Boers had detained him and his eldest son, Cetshwayo, as insurance against any possible treachery. (Legend has it that to forestall any substitution of Cetshwayo with some other Zulu youth, the Boers, to make no mistake about his identity, took a nick out of his right ear.)

The white men played no part in the fighting that followed nor in the final defeat of Dingane. They stayed well away and the battle that ensued was fought between the two Zulu armies as of old: there were few or no firearms or horses to give either side an advantage. Finally,

although with over 2,000 dead on the battlefield, Nongalaza and his
warriors prevailed. Dingane, with a few loyal followers, fled north into
the Lebombo Mountains where, most likely, Dingane was tracked
down by the amaSwazi and killed.

Within six weeks of the British departure, the conflict was over. On
10 February 1840, Mpande, now recognised as the new king of the Zulus,
was subjected to a mock coronation and crowned by the Boers as though
by divine decree; understandably they also rejoiced and gloated at the
victory acquired at no cost to themselves. In addition they demanded
not only the coast and harbour already mentioned but, as a bonus and
compensation, 40,000 head of cattle, which they duly received.

The northern boundary of the new Natalia Republic, as agreed, was
the Tugela River. However, sixty miles from the coast, as the river veered
west towards its source, its main tributary, the Buffalo flowing down
from the north, assumed the boundary. But, thereafter, the demarcation
line became vague and would later be violently disputed by the Boers
and northern elements of the Zulu nation. To the south, towards the
Cape, where the amaPondo of Chief Faku held sway, there was no
acknowledged boundary at all. However, the furthest flung outpost of
the British Empire was not far away. One hundred and fifty miles south
of Port Natal, on the banks of the Mngazi River, there was a British fort
also named Mngazi.

The new Republic, not satisfied with the vast territory that its citizens
had, seemingly, with Heaven's help, miraculously acquired by right of
conquest, began armed excursions to the south. The ensuing uproar
would, however, soon awaken the dozing British Lion. Worse still for
the imprudent Boers, they naively invited both Dutch and American
vessels to use their harbour. In fact they believed that the supercargo
of a Dutch vessel, the *Brazillia*, was an official of the Netherlands
government. He assured the gullible Boers that both Holland and
France would uphold their cause in exchange for trade and harbour
facilities. The Boers, in turn, pledged to resist any British interference
with armed force if necessary. News of these happenings on its northern
border, with the possibility of a rival naval power occupying Port Natal,
was not long in reaching the ears of the Cape government, causing
Governor Napier to issue a proclamation, dated 2 December 1841,
advising the Boers that it was the government's intention to reoccupy

Port Natal with a military presence. The Proclamation concluded with the following caution:

> I hereby warn all British-born subjects, and particularly those who, after the 18th day of January 1806, have been born within the Colony [Cape Colony] of parents who at the time of their birth, by reason of their permanent residence in this Colony, or otherwise, owed allegiance to, and were subjects of, the Crown, that they cannot, by their removal from this Colony [Cape] to any place whatsoever, divest themselves of the allegiance which they owe by reason of their birth to the British Crown.

The Boer response, dated 21 February 1842, was emphatic that the emigrant farmers would, if necessary, defend their liberty by armed force. They began by pointing out that the Griquas, a people of mixed European and Khoikhoi blood, who had moved north/east out of the Cape Colony had, as an example, been recognised by the Cape government as an independent people. The Boers went on to mention that they had no hatred for the British and only wished to live in peace; that Chief Faku had no claim to the land that he occupied; that they had in their possession the contract made between Retief and Dingane; that they believed they had been unjustly labelled by the British as 'a rude people, who, tired of civilised laws and church discipline, sought to lead a libidinous' life. The response concluded: 'Should we, after such bloodshed and expense, be suppressed, the fire will merely have been extinguished to rage with more force on the day of vengeance.'

There could be no mistaking the Boer intent to fight and to complicate matters still further, there were a number of British settlers amongst the Boer community at Port Natal, the whole white population seemingly happy and prospering well. In fact, the *Voortrekker* government had offered 15,000 acres of the best land to the British settlers. So, being unable to find any further alternative, the Cape Government decided to bluff and intimidate the Boers by sending a military expedition to Port Natal in what was nothing but a forlorn hope that they would peacefully abandon their hard-won independence and return to the loathsome fold of the 'Great White Queen'.

The officer selected to command this expedition would, first and foremost, need to be a diplomat and a skilful negotiator; a man who, whilst expressing rapport and sympathy with the *Voortrekker*s and their

aspirations, would be able, with a kind but firm hand, to lead them back
to British authority. Unfortunately, the man chosen was largely devoid
of any such talents. Captain Thomas Charlton Smith was as tough
an old soldier as they came, and as events would reveal, completely
unsuited for this delicate task. He was the son of an army surgeon and
at the age of nine had entered the Royal Navy as a midshipman. By
his thirteenth birthday he had been wounded three times in battle and
had then transferred to the army, joining his father's regiment, the 27th
(Inniskilling) Regiment of Foot. He subsequently fought throughout
the Peninsular War and finally at Waterloo where the 27th suffered 68
per cent casualties, Smith himself being wounded yet again. Now at
the age of forty-four he commanded Fort Mngazi, the furthest-flung
of all the British garrisons on the Cape Frontier; and compounding
the tragedy of Smith's appointment was the vacillation of the Cape
government. Smith's orders from Napier were that he must act with
the greatest caution and that he must not express any recognition of the
Boers other than their being the Queen's subjects. Furthermore, Smith
and his redcoats should '. . . be civil and kind in their demeanor towards
the immigrant farmers because the great object of the government is to
consolidate these misguided men'. No easy task for Smith. Especially as
the *Voortrekkers* had steadfastly proclaimed:

> We are Dutch South Africans by birth; immediately after we quitted Her
> Majesty's territories in South Africa, we published our independence and
> from that time to this moment we have acted as an independent people,
> governed by ourselves according to our own laws, and consequently
> ceased to be British subjects; the country we inhabit we have legally
> acquired [by right of conquest?] and has never been a British province or
> colony to this moment.

The Boers also believed that Holland would support their bid for
independence, having being encouraged in this by Johan Smellekamp, the
supercargo of the visiting Dutch ship already mentioned who, it seems,
led the Boers to believe that he held some sort of diplomatic authority.
Yet, the Netherlands government had no intention of getting mixed up
in a confrontation with Great Britain, and as soon as the news of the
happenings at Port Natal reached Holland, the government announced
that it was in close alliance with Her Britannic Majesty and that the

King of Holland and his ministers would take every possible step to mark their entire disapproval of the unjustifiable use of their name.

Yet there was additional support for the *Voortrekkers* from a most unexpected quarter – although it could never be other than passive: Major Charters, who it will be remembered had led the earlier redcoat expedition to Port Natal, stated his unequivocal belief that the Boer migration from the Cape was legal and justifiable. Thus it was, in this turmoil of uncertain claims and conflicting opinions, that Captain Smith set out on a 200-mile march from Fort Mngazi to Port Natal. His force comprised 263 officers and men, a howitzer and two 6-pounder gun and included elements of the Royal Artillery, Royal Engineers, Sappers and Miners, Cape Mounted Rifles and two companies of his own regiment, the 27th Foot. In addition there were about sixty well-armed white wagoners to handle the 600 oxen and fifty-four wagons that completed the convoy. In the event of Smith's bluff being called, as indeed it would be, it was a detachment that, from the outset, was inadequate to take on its opponents and enforce British authority. Nine months later Smith would accuse Napier of sending him on an expedition with insufficient men and arms.

Fort Mngazi at that time was not the most comfortable spot; lonely and rife with disease. So much so that Mrs Lonsdale, the wife of Captain Lonsdale, insisted on accompanying the expedition with her two children despite every argument to dissuade her. Lonsdale had taken the place of Captain George Durnford who, struck down with rheumatism, would have to remain bedridden at the Fort but, would as we shall hear, catch up with the expedition later by sea.

The journey that lay ahead of Smith's convoy would be through some of the toughest but, in parts, most beautiful countryside in southern Africa: immense gorges that would force protracted detours, tropical forests, flooded rivers and sometimes, at low tide, beaches on which the giant skeletons of whales lay to amaze the awe-struck redcoats. It was recorded that in all, 122 streams or rivers had to be crossed – the approaches and exits to many seemingly too impossibly steep to negotiate. It was anticipated that the journey, at ten miles a day, would take three weeks but, as Durnford recorded, the contrary Mrs Lonsdale occasioned the convoy to delay for several days (he does not say exactly how she caused this to come about) and, consequently, by the time the great Mzimvubu ('Umyimvooboo') was reached, it was then in flood, causing a further ten days halt, much no doubt, to the fury of Smith and the embarrassment of Lonsdale. There were other officers who had brought their wives along, as had many of the wagon drivers, so that it came as no surprise to the convoy that one child was born *en route* whilst one soldier died of 'fatigue'. His lonely grave is still to be found some seventy miles short of Durban.

The Boers had no idea that a British invasion force was gradually drawing closer, the stealth of its approach being achieved by the deception of the local Natal Zulus for, of the two white 'tribes' that they had to contend with, the locals preferred the 'English'. Consequently, whenever a Zulu was questioned as to whether any British movement into republican territory had been seen, the answer was 'none'. Thus, much to the astonishment and rage of the Boers, Smith's convoy suddenly appeared on the hills at Robert Newton Dunn's farm, above the port, not more than half a dozen miles from the harbour itself. Had the Boers been aware of Smith's approach they could have mustered a commando of a thousand armed and mounted men that in a matter of hours would have had the British convoy, strung out for over two miles, at their mercy.

A short distance below Dunn's farm, named Seaview, there was the *Voortrekker* settlement of Congella, a spot much favoured for the fertility of its soil and the perennial stream that gushed from the rocks, tumbling sweet water in what seemed to be an appalling waste, into the sea. Over 150 years later the stream, now surrounded by a small tropical park, still flows forth as strong as ever.

But the Boers were not taken entirely unawares. It had been anticipated that the British would intrude upon their lives once again at some time or another and they had made a number of preparations, one of which had been the appointment, by the *Volksraad*, of Andreas Pretorius as Commandant-General, with the power to conscript commandos whose individual members would be required to swear an oath to defend their homeland.

Smith, having finally arrived and with the momentous struggle of the journey behind him, had important decisions to make. First he had to secure the harbour as reinforcements and supplies would come by sea. Major Charters' Fort Victoria was still there with the flag of the Republic of Natalia flying above it. Smith also required a good defensive position with a ready supply of drinking water – the fort met neither criteria so on the morning of the 4th May, accompanied by his officer of engineers, Lieutenant Gibb, Surgeon Fraser and several of the English settlers who had rode into camp that morning, Smith made his way down to the port. The settlers who accompanied him would now be seen as having aligned themselves with the invaders.

Smith also took with him a corporal and three men of the Cape Mounted Rifles as escort and, unmolested, Smith rode into Fort Victoria, pulled down the Republican flag, raised the Union Jack and spiked the Boer gun that commanded the harbour; not the best way to establish diplomatic relations. Then, after surveying the locality with the assistance of the English locals, Smith selected a defensive position on an area of open ground close to the harbour which offered a good field of fire for his guns, nearby grazing for the oxen and a supply of fresh water, albeit rather brackish.

11. A sketch of Port Natal circa 1842. To the left, what was once Fort Victoria, has now become the Boer Custom's Headquarters with the flag of the Republic of Natalia at the mast head. In the foreground small coasters are at anchor whilst a large ocean-going vessel looms on the horizon. (*Local History Museum, Durban*)

Meanwhile the news of the British occupation had spread like wildfire to the homesteads of the Republic and soon commandos of stern, determined, fully armed and self-sufficient men astride the best horseflesh in southern Africa, were riding towards Port Natal.

Pretorius, like Smith, had received orders not to fire the first shot and thought it best, so it seems, to keep a low profile least a meeting with the British commander might provoke a conflict from which neither could withdraw. Instead of an appearance in person, Pretorius sent a small deputation of three burgers, Meyer, Ferreira and Morewood, to see Smith and, on the strength of what they had been told by Smellekamp, inform him that the Republic of Natalia was in treaty with and under the protection of Holland. This must have come as news to Smith but he was unimpressed and sent the deputation on its way. Wasting no more time, the following morning the whole convoy descended the hills and with drawn swords and fixed bayonets marched through the little village of Congella and onto the open plain that had been selected the previous day as a campsite and which was known to the Zulus as *Ithafa labalindi* (The Plain of the Lookout). There the wagons were formed into a circular laager and entrenched while Fort Victoria, commanding

12. The British camp is turned into a makeshift fort with a moat before the laagered wagons. (*Africana Museum, Johannesburg*)

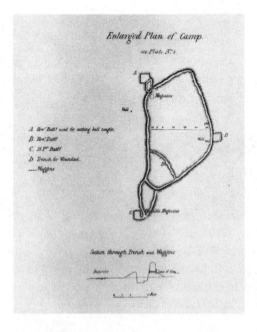

the harbour entrance, was staffed with some artillerymen, a cannon and a detachment of the 27th, all under the command of a Royal Artillery sergeant. 'Fort Victoria' sounds a grand name and is misleading for what it was, namely a stone-built storehouse, once belonging to a Port Natal trader, that had been reinforced during the previous British occupation under Major Charters.

Pretorius had kept out of the way but with the news of Smith's aggressive tactics, decided to make an appearance. He arrived at Congella several days later, having assembled a force of over sixty burghers to back him up. On receiving the news that Pretorius was in town Smith sent him an urgent notice to attend the British camp and state his intentions. The invitation was refused which infuriated Smith who, early the next day, at the head of a hundred men of the 27th, the Cape Mounted Rifles and a cannon loaded with grapeshot, marched on Congella causing panic and alarm along the route. On nearing the little town Smith and his army were confronted by a deputation of two burghers representing, they said, the *Volksraad* and the community of Port Natal. They requested Smith to halt but he brushed them aside and marched on. Finally Pretorius made an appearance: an imposing man, six feet tall, and like Smith a man with an impressive martial record – albeit that the force he had commanded at the moment of its greatest triumph had been a civilian one. Due to Pretorius' generalship, his men at Blood River had won one of the most remarkable battles in the history of warfare and he and Smith, men of such different cultures, were well matched. Of the two, Pretorius had a greater talent for diplomacy and was less intransigent.

Pretorius now stood astride the track, and as Smith approached doffed his hat like a European courtier and made a low bow. Perhaps Smith was taken aback by this show of gallantry; in any event he halted and, to further astonish him, Pretorius offered Smith and his redcoats the hospitality of Congella. As far as Smith was concerned such would amount to fraternising with the enemy; the offer was bluntly refused. Pretorius then protested that Smith's march and his take-over of Fort Victoria was extremely provocative and that the *Voortrekkers* would never consent to British rule or to becoming British subjects. In turn, Smith countered that he would not heed those presuming to question the right of British troops to march in British territory. Pretorius, no doubt to clear the air and ease the tension, requested time in which to consult with the *Volksraad*, the supreme *Voortrekker* authority, and a fifteen-day truce was agreed. Smith was happy with the stand-off which would provide time to put the finishing touches to his defences and to receive supplies via the harbour. Due to the delays that had been encountered during the expedition's epic journey, Smith's force was desperately short of provisions. Nevertheless, as would be expected from an officer with a record of active service such as Smith's, including the crowning accolade of a presence at Waterloo, Smith had no doubt of the invincibility of British arms as well as his own invincibility against a mob of armed farmers. He lacked the perception of Major Charters, who four years earlier had stated his belief that the Boers were 'most dexterous in the use of arms and with the support of native tribes were capable of besieging Cape Town Castle'.

Although Smith and Pretorius had agreed to a truce, during which there would be no provocative action, within days Smith perceived what he believed to be a threatening move towards his camp: Boer guards had been placed at intervals along the Congella track; an aggressive move in Smith's opinion. Pretorius apologised and removed them, but to ensure there was no misunderstanding, Smith informed Pretorius that should there be a similar incident, he would march on Congella and burn it to the ground along with the dwellings of any other hostile persons in the vicinity.

Ten days after the expedition had reached Port Natal a small supply ship, the *Pilot*, arrived bringing with it much needed provisions, the garrison having being almost on starvation rations for the last few days. The vessel also brought two large cannons, 18-pounders, to strengthen Smith's defences – one for Fort Victoria and one for the entrenched camp. But best of all, as far as the troops were concerned, was a plentiful supply of rum.

As the fifteen days sped by, *Voortrekker* reinforcements inconspicuously made their way to the port and the *Volksraad* moved the seat of government from Pietermaritzburg to Congella. On 16 May, Pretorius was instructed to deliver a letter to Smith accusing him of dishonouring *Voortrekker* sovereignty and demanding that he and his troops remove themselves from the Republic by noon. Smith took this inflammatory declaration with surprising calm and in reply requested that the

Voortrekkers abandon their hostile attitude and that he still regarded them as British subjects. Both Smith and Pretorius had been instructed not to fire the first shot but the *Volksraad*, no doubt feeling that they had Smith immobile behind his earthworks and wagons, decided on punitive action. The redcoats could be starved into submission: Pretorius resolved to drive off Smith's draught oxen. The redcoats had refused to leave; soon they would be unable to do so. In addition the Boer attitude that had been one of tolerance, changed: the local English settlers who, since the defeat of Dingane, had lived amongst the Boers as members of the community enjoying Boer protection, had been seen as owing allegiance to the Republic. Now the *Volksraad* issued a decree to the effect that collaboration with the British would be seen as treason and punishable by three years in prison.

Adulphe Delegorgue, the French hunter and artist whom we have encountered earlier in this book, was at Port Natal at the time having just returned from a hunting trip. He was immediately told that the British had come and in anticipation of being besieged the Boers had confiscated all the food: rice, flour, coffee and any other things that could be of use, causing an uproar amongst the traders. Hardly had Delegorgue considered the implications of this news than his cottage was suddenly invaded by a posse of Boer horsemen, 150 strong, who commandeered it for use as their centre of operations for the rustling of Smith's draught oxen. As the mounted men careered around driving the oxen before them, it became clear to Smith that his transport was being stolen and he ordered one of the cannon to immediately open fire, but no damage was done and the rustlers escaped unscathed. Infuriated, Smith ordered out a detachment of infantry in pursuit and it must have been at that moment – had it not occurred to him before – that he realised how vulnerable he was; how inadequate the force at his command and the folly of authority in placing an ineffectual military presence in hostile country hundreds of miles from reinforcements. The infantry could not, of course, pursue the mounted rustlers and were jeered and mocked as the caracoling horsemen disappeared with the oxen. Smith's expedition was now as immobile as a modern convoy that had run out of fuel. In addition, in Smith's view, the dignity of the British Crown had been affronted and treason committed. As Captain Lonsdale marched his dispirited detachment back to the camp, Smith decided to take immediate action to redeem British authority just as the Boers suspected he would. Smith later reported in a despatch to Cape Town that the Boer action '. . . rendered it absolutely necessary that some steps should be taken in order to prevent a repetition of such outrages'.

The night of 23 May was cloudless and lit by a brilliant moon. Smith's plan was to descend from his camp at 11 p.m. with a force consisting of Royal Artillery, Royal Engineers, a hundred rank and file of the 27th, five officers (one of whom was Captain Lonsdale who had commanded the abortive pursuit earlier in the day) and two mounted Cape Riflemen. Including Captain Smith, there were in all, 139 personnel. The force would make its way through some wooded country, already cleared of any spies, and onto the beach where, with the tide being low, it would continue unhindered along the hard sand until level with Congella. To support this manoeuvre Smith had acquired a flat-bottomed boat into which a howitzer had been secured under the command of an artillery sergeant. The boat was to row up a convenient channel and, on arrival of Smith's party, immediately open fire on Congella with shot and shell; at the same time Smith would likewise open fire with his two 6-pounders, mounted on carriages drawn by teams of the remaining oxen. Then, after a brief bombardment to demoralise the enemy (including women and children), the redcoats would charge with bayonets fixed. A good plan but, nevertheless, flawed. The Boers, alert to the likelihood of retaliation, had posted mounted pickets between Congella and the British camp and they detected the advancing column. A hurried ambush of 200 or more burghers, armed with hunting weapons far superior to the Brown Bess muskets of the infantry, had been rushed to a stand of mangrove trees just above the beach. Now, in the deep shade of their concealment, the Boers waited as the British drew nearer with Smith fuming at the absence of the boat-mounted howitzer which had got stuck on a sandbank and would take no part in the assault on Congella.

The Boer ambush party waited, until the British came level and then with the redcoats a mere 800 yards from Congella, they opened fire at point blank range, the soldiers silhouetted black against the moonlit beach. The redcoats sought to find a mark at which to aim while the artillery struggled to bring their guns to bear as the oxen, wounded and maddened by the commotion, went berserk plunging headlong into the despairing redcoats. Lieutenant Wyatt, of the Royal Artillery, mortally wounded, was one of the first to fall. Smith had but one option left: to form up and bayonet charge the mangrove trees but his men were too scattered to rally. There was no choice: retreat was the only option. Leaving the 6-pounders behind, trophies for the victors, Smith and his devastated men made a running retreat back to camp closely followed by the enemy who continued to harass the redcoats all the way whilst the incoming tide, seemingly in league with the Boers, swept away and drowned several soldiers who were endeavouring to take a shorter route along the beach.

Once inside the fortifications of the camp, the redcoats fought back and for the rest of the night a fire fight, with cannon and grapeshot on both sides, continued until dawn, but few casualties were sustained. With the coming of day the Boers withdrew to a safe distance, well out of range of the British guns, enabling Smith, on 25 May, to complete a long report to his commanding officer in the Cape. It was addressed to both Lieutenant-Colonel Hare and to the Lieutenant-Governor. It read in part:

> Sir, it is with feelings of deep regret that I have the honour to communicate to you the disastrous result of an attack made by the force under my command on the immigrant farmers congregated at the Congella Camp at this place.
>
> In my last dispatch, I detailed the various steps taken by the farmers to annoy the troops, and my determination to abstain, if possible, from hostilities, if it could be done without detriment to the honour of the Service ...

Smith went on to give a fair and accurate assessment of the battle and then continued:

> ... A severe loss resulted to the troops in consequence. Finding, therefore, that I was not likely to accomplish the purpose for which I had the attachment in motion, and that the men were falling fast, I thought it expedient to retire, effecting this object after some delay, the partial rising of the tide rendering the road difficult. The troops, however, reached camp about 2 o'clock in tolerable order, leaving behind them, I regret to say, the guns, which the death of the oxen, rendered it impossible to remove.

Thinking it probable that this partial success of the farmers might induce them to make an immediate attack on the camp, I made such preparations as I thought necessary; and found my suspicions realised shortly afterwards, a large body of them opening a heavy fire on three sides of it . . .

Smith then expressed his regret at the death of Lieutenant Wyatt and applauded the gallant conduct of Captain Lonsdale and Lieutenant Lennard, both of whom had been severely wounded. He continued:

The loss on the part of the Boers is difficult to estimate but I'm told it has been severe. The whole of this day they have made no movements; but I have to give them the credit of treating such of the wounded as fell into their hands with great humanity. These, with the bodies of those who fell, they sent to the camp this afternoon and tomorrow the sad duty of interring our departed comrades will take place.

What steps the farmers may subsequently take I cannot at this moment surmise with any degree of certainty; but I think it probable they will again demand that I should quit the territory they call their own within a specific time. I shall, of course, do what I can to maintain myself in my present position but considering the number of the disaffected, and the means they possess of molesting the troops, I beg to urge the necessity of a speedy reinforcement, as I scarcely consider the troops at present stationed here sufficient for the performance of the duty to which they had been assigned.

I have the honour and etc.
Signed: T C Smith, Captain
27th Regiment, Commandant.

Smith had realised that he and his men could not possibly survive, nor British esteem and authority prevail, without reinforcements, and he desperately pondered how to get his dispatch to the Cape 600 miles away. He turned for help to George Cato, a British resident of Port Natal and a settler of long standing. Cato in turn recommended Dick King as the best possible courier. King was also a British local, his presence at the port going back to the time of Allen Gardiner, who could converse fluently in both Zulu and the Dutch language spoken by the Boers. Being an acknowledged horseman and an intrepid hunter, King was the man made for the moment. It was proposed that two of the Cape Mounted Rifles' horses should convey King and his young native servant, Ndongeni. Later that day, under the cover of darkness, George Cato, his brother Joseph and the two riders led the horses to the Point, close by Fort Victoria, where a boat was tied. The Cato brothers rowed whilst King and his Zulu companion held the reins of the horses swimming along behind. Finally, the boat and horses touched bottom on the Bluff and the riders prepared to head south on what was to become, perhaps, the most legendary ride in the history of southern Africa. As the horsemen stealthily made their way up the beach into the bush, the Cato brothers, with equal caution, commenced to row, as silently as possible, back across the bay.

At some point during the course of the day – exactly when is uncertain – a schooner, the *Pilot*, commanded by Captain Ian McDonald, had arrived at the port, as had another vessel, the *Mazeppa*, bringing Smith's supplies from the Cape. Amongst the consumable treasures there was a sorely needed supply of rum and to add to Smith's defences, equally sorely needed, a long-barrelled 18-pounder gun. However, the Boers, elated with their unexpected success of the previous day in which they perceived the help of the Almighty, now saw another opportunity. Pretorius, having organised a commando of a hundred burgers, despatched them by a long circuitous route, around the British positions, until they eventually burst from the bush almost under the noses of the redcoat detachment supervising the unloading of the vessels. Greatly outnumbered, the soldiers hurriedly retreated into the ramshackle fort where they kept the enemy at bay having sustained two men killed and two wounded. It was a situation that could only worsen: with no water supply and the prospect of the 'fort' being pounded to bits by the cannons now being brought to bear, Sergeant Barry, the NCO in charge, surrendered. The soldiers were taken prisoner and the gleeful Boers, stocked up with British provisions, marched them off to Congella where they were treated with consideration – not so the ten British settlers who were arrested the following morning, George Cato and Henry Ogle amongst them. They were put into the stocks and chained night and day. After a week, having been convicted of treason, they were marched to Pietermaritzburg and imprisoned in conditions of incredible vileness while the soldiers were given parole to walk around the town.

Smith and his besieged troops now had to apply all their knowledge and every endeavour to improving the defences of the 'camp'. The area occupied inside the perimeter of stockaded wagons was approximately two acres and in shape a lop-sided square. Inside the laager the earlier trenches were deepened, with parapets on either side, which in turn were strengthened with sods. A 'shelter' trench for the wounded, with lay-byes, was cut internally across the width of the camp and magazines were constructed at the southern and northern ends of the perimeter. The remaining 18-pounder gun was situated facing south with two other smaller gun batteries facing north and east. The well that lay outside the western perimeter was deepened and the brackish marsh that supplied much of the water was carefully nurtured. Into this confined and vulnerable space were crammed close on 500 people, including women and children. Added to the burden were the sick and wounded, some of whom were seriously maimed with limbs requiring amputation; Dr Fraser, the 27th's medical officer would need all his skill and endurance if a number of his patients were not to die. The following day a deputation approached the camp with the proposition that Captain Smith and his men surrender, board the vessels in the harbour and sail away to the Cape. However, there were conditions attached that Smith found outrageously unacceptable and after a few days negotiations came to an end.

  The siege now began in earnest and on the morning of 31 May the Boers, having copied the sod-made batteries and embrasures of Smith's camp, opened a bombardment with the cannons so recently captured from the enemy, sending 122 roundshot crashing into the British defences. Captain Lonsdale, who, it will be remembered had been severely wounded in the abortive attack on Congella, had, for the last six days, been confined to the tent which he was lucky enough to share with his wife and two small children. In a letter written later to his mother, he remembered the time as a period during which, due to the nature of his wound, he had hardly been able to move, but:

On the morning of the 31st May, just before sunrise, we were saluted by a 6-pound shot, which passed through the officers' mess tent, knocking their kettles and cooking apparatus in all directions. Everyone, of course, went to his station in the ditch: the Boers then kept up an incessant fire from four pieces of artillery and small arms, never ceasing for a moment during the whole day till sunset. During the whole day Margaret and Jane [his wife and daughter] were lying on the ground in the tent close by me. Many shot, both large and small, passed through the tent close to us. James [his son] was lying in my other tent on the ground, with his legs on the legs of a table, and his dog with him, when a 6-pound shot struck the legs of the table just above him, and cut them in two, and struck him in the face with some of the splinters. . . . When the attack of the day was over, all the officers came to our tents expecting to find us all dead.

The following morning the Lonsdale family moved to the protection of a shelter trench and once again the bombardment commenced and continued until noon when a Boer deputation appeared carrying a flag of truce. They proposed, very gallantly, that the women and children should leave the camp whereupon the Boers would place them, for their own protection, aboard the *Mazeppa*, it becoming a sort of temporary prison ship. There they would be safe from the fighting. This considerate offer was sensibly accepted by Smith and the women and children, including Mrs Lonsdale, were escorted out of harm's way down to the harbour. Once gone, the truce ended and not only was the bombardment renewed with vigour, but also each night hundreds of Boers emerged from hiding in order to extend their trenches and embrasures closer and closer to the camp so that within a few days, they were in a position to fire with impunity on anything that moved. It was a situation that could not be tolerated and on the night of 18 June, the twenty-fourth day of the siege, Smith ordered a night attack. Unfortunately for the redcoats, at close quarters the Boers heard and saw the British coming and opened fire, killing Ensign Prior and two men of the 27th. The redcoats fired in return and then, without any hesitation, charged with the bayonet catching and killing many of the enemy before they could get away. Then with additional help from the camp the redcoats set about destroying, as best they could, the enemy embrasures and filling in the closer trenches. The Boers never attempted to recover their lost ground, nor carry the camp by direct assault but the unrelenting bombardment continued while the redcoats, reduced to living on dead crows, scraps of horse flesh and anything edible, were, as Lonsdale described to his mother, close to starvation:

All this time nearly all our provisions were gone; we were living on our horses and biscuit dust – six ounces of the former and four of the latter per day; sometimes we had a little corn. We dug a well in our camp, but the water was bad. Sometimes it was difficult to cook our little provisions for the want of wood. The wounded suffered very much, as the doctor had nothing in the way of medical comforts. I was lying in the trench twenty-seven days, hardly able to move and not so much as a jacket on.

While Smith and his redcoats continued to grit their teeth, unbeknown to them things had been happening. It will be remembered that the Cato brothers had rowed Dick King across the bay with George Cato ending up in the stocks. However, Joseph Cato had evaded capture, having hidden aboard the *Mazeppa*, and was still there when the women and children were marched aboard. The Boers, not being a seafaring nation, knew little about boats or sailing, so as a precaution against the *Mazeppa* being stolen and put to sea, had removed the anchors, believing that no one would take the boat if it were incapable of being brought to a halt; they should, of course, have taken the rudder. The *Mazeppa* not only had her rudder intact, she was, in addition, merely tied up to the wharf by a couple of cables and had on board Joseph Cato, a capable ship's captain.

Joseph determined, with the first favourable weather conditions, to hijack the *Mazeppa* and sail off in the hope of finding a British warship; the women and children would be his crew. However, the ship, once underway, would come under the Boer cannon guarding the harbour and would be a short-range target for anyone with a gun: some protection was required. The lady prisoners, making the excuse of spring-cleaning their quarters, took out all the blankets for airing, hanging them along the sides of the vessel nearest to the wharf where they would give a degree of protection.

On 10 June, just as the tide was right, a lively breeze caused a fluttering of waves across the harbour and Joseph waited no longer. The women, having being instructed in the tasks they were to perform, were seen, under Joseph's instructions, cutting the cables and hoisting the sails: slowly the vessel gained momentum. For several moments the Boers failed to comprehend what was happening right under their very noses and then it was too late: too much water lay between them and the ship.

The Boers resorted to the only course left at their disposal: they opened fire but the cannon shot was hopelessly misdirected and the small arms fire ineffectual: the *Mazeppa*, with her wildly-cheering crew of women and children, sailed away down the harbour and out to the open sea. Now it seemed that Smith and his men had a chance – albeit a fairly remote one – of their plight being revealed but, unbeknown to them, a rescue mission was already on its way from the Cape. The intrepid Dick King, accompanied by his companion Ndongeni for the first half of the journey, riding though country teeming with wild animals, crisscrossed by deep gorges and rivers infested by crocodiles – and in spite of coming close to being killed by amaBongeni warriors who had mistaken him for a Boer – had arrived at Grahamstown, having covered 600 miles in ten days. A fine equestrian statue commemorating Dick King's magnificent ride is still a prominent feature of Durban's Marine Esplanade.

Soon the drums were beating and the redcoats marching: the first to hear King's news was the 27th Regiment in Grahamstown, a hundred of whom, the grenadier company under the command of Captain Durnford, were soon on the road to Port Elizabeth eighty miles away. Meanwhile another rider had carried the news 480 miles on to Cape Town causing the redcoats of the 25th Regiment to be hurried aboard HMS *Southampton*, a fifty-gun frigate that, fortuitously, had been at anchor in the harbour. The whole relieving force was placed under the command of none other than Colonel Abraham Cloete, the sinister figure of fifteen years earlier, who it will be remembered, would not permit King Shaka's emissaries to proceed to Cape Town.

Although the grenadier company of the 27th had a head start on the rest of the relieving force, they had no ship awaiting them at Port Elizabeth but their luck was in as Captain William Bell of the *Conch*, a trading schooner, was not only an adventurer but also a patriot who was prepared to put his vessel at risk for Queen and Country – but not so, it would seem, his crew; when the news of the impending voyage reached the ship they were suddenly taken ill. Bell later wrote that he took a doctor with him to the vessel but he knew the symptoms of the illness and the cure better than the medical man, and straight away prescribed three dozen lashes for any man who deserted or went ashore. Bell continued:

13. HMS *Southampton* arrives off Port Natal bringing troops and giving their landing covering fire. (*Africana Museum, Johannesburg*)

I found the grenadiers of the 27th Regiment drawn up in line, stowing away a half-aum of Cape Smoke [cheap brandy] that the commandant had given them, at the same time entertaining the town's people with songs. After they embarked in the boats, my gallant volunteers were ordered to the front for embarkation. Many efforts were made to discourage me from going, and I was repeatedly told that I was going to serve a government that would not thank me. . . . About midnight a wind came from the north-west, and before daylight we were underway, the soldiers cheering the ships in the harbour as we passed them. . . . We had to contend against adverse winds and currents, and only reached Natal after a passage of thirteen days. Nevertheless the time passed merrily, as the old 27th produced a fine lot of officers and soldiers. On sighting the bluff I told Captain Durnford, commander of the troops, that we could not enter the harbour with the wind then blowing, and that we should be obliged to enter in the outer roads, and wait for a fair wind. He asked me if I could devise a plan to get some of the Boers on board. I proposed that the soldiers should go below, when a few miles to the westward of the bluff, in which the captain concurred. The men were then ordered below, which was cheerfully obeyed, leaving the hatches off to give them as much air as possible; the officers in

plain clothes remained on deck. On coming around the bluff we were
soon convinced that the rebels were in full possession of the harbour
entrance, and could distinctly hear firing between the Boers and the
troops in the camp. There was also a vessel in the harbour, which proved
to be the brig 'Pilot', of Cape Town, which had been taken possession
of by the Boers. We came to anchor in the usual way, making it appear
that we were unconscious of what was going on. We waited some time,
but finding that no boat came out, we lowered ours, and prepared to
go in with the 'flag of truce'. They had just pushed off, when a boat
was observed coming; we therefore called our boat back. All this time
the soldiers were below almost suffocated. As the boat approached I
observed two persons sitting, and as I expected them to be of some
importance, I went to the gangway to receive them. As the boat neared
the ship, I observed one of them to be the port captain; the other
although previously acquainted with, I did not know at first sight, on
account of his rich uniform; he proved to be the 'military secretary'.

14. Capt. William Bell of the
Conch in later life after he
had become Harbour Master
of Durban. (*KZN Archives,
Pietermaritzburg*)

The visiting dignitaries came aboard and Bell continued:

I shall never forget their surprise and change of countenance. The first thing that met their view was the grenadiers sitting in the main hatchway as thick as bees. . . . The port captain appeared to have some doubts whether he had made a satisfactory impression on our minds with regard to his kind feelings towards the English, and repeated his former assurance of fidelity. He gave us a very truthful statement of what had occurred subsequent to King's leaving with dispatches for the old colony [the Cape Colony].

As we have heard Lieutenant Prior and some men had been killed while making an attack on the enemy's entrenchment, and that the camp was in a deplorable state. Horse flesh with a little biscuit dust, and a few oats, occasionally shooting a stray crow hovering over the camp after the offal, were all they had for subsistence. The two Boer officials wondered whether or not Captain Durnford was going to hang them from the yardarm there and then. They were greatly relieved when instead he requested them to take a letter to Commandant Pretorius which would request permission for the assistant surgeon of the 27th to go ashore with medical supplies for Smith's wounded – such would also be the means of informing the camp that relief was at hand. It was agreed that the following morning Durnford would send a boat for an answer. As the day progressed the firing ashore intensified but as darkness fell Durnford sent up a rocket in the direction of the camp which was immediately acknowledged by a rocket in return. Smith and his men were still holding out.

The following day the mate of the *Conch*, accompanied by a sergeant of the 27th, rode ashore to seek a reply to Durnford's letter. They were met by Boer officials who informed them that neither the surgeon nor anyone else would be permitted to go to the camp or go ashore.

Durnford, with the grenadier company at his back, was tempted to get ashore by some means or another and storm the Point, but commonsense prevailed and the redcoats, crammed aboard the *Conch* like cattle in a truck, settled down to await whatever fate would provide – their patience was awarded almost immediately: far away to the south, only discernable with Captain Bell's powerful telescope, the tops of three masts, barely visible, were peeping above the horizon; after due scrutiny Bell pronounced them to be the rigging of a man-of-war; HMS *Southampton* would shortly arrive. Durnford rather recklessly decided he would go and meet her. He later described the occasion:

> I ordered the ship's boat for I was Admiral and everything else, and putting a compass into her started with the captain to board, determined to bring her to her anchorage that night, and after pulling at least fifteen miles, we did get on board in the pitch dark. I could not distinguish one person from another but found it was the frigate with Colonel Cloete, Major D'Urban and three hundred of the 25th on board. So down into the cabin we went with all the bigwigs, and pulling out our plans we settled what was to be done the next morning. I left them again about 10 o'clock and got to my own vessel about 1, having left directions that a shell and a rocket should be fired every quarter of an hour till I returned. . . . And about 2 the frigate came to anchor close alongside of us. We then went to supper and to bed.

But the best-laid plans can go awry and the breeze that had been expected with the coming of dawn did not materialise and the situation remained static: a battle waiting to commence; the Boers lining the shore with riflemen on both sides of the harbour and with cannon loaded at the narrow entrance whilst, just out of range, the British vessels also waited, the time being spent in rigging planks of yellowwood along the sides of the *Conch* to give protection to the exposed helmsmen and troops – it was well known that one of the Boer tactics in the defense of their harbour would be to aim for the helmsmen thus sending any invading vessel out of control. But, as far as the British were concerned, not all the morning was wasted: the captain of HMS *Southampton* desired to get as close to the shore as safety would allow, both from the point of view of enemy cannon fire and the danger of going aground. Captain Bell was summoned aboard the warship and with his knowledge of the harbour, agreed to supervise the warping of the vessel – that is moving it only by means of hauling on ropes with one end secured to the ship and the other attached to anchors ashore. This manoeuvre was successfully completed and by noon the *Southampton*, with her gun ports open, lay broadside-on to the Boer defences. The *Conch*, although a schooner, was nevertheless armed, and with Captain Turner of the Royal Artillery on board, egging on Captain Bell, the vessel was also warped to a position that brought her guns within range of the Boer harbour defenses. The gunners of both ships then tried the range, cheered on by the crews and redcoats, as shot and shell rained down on the enemy entrenchments. By noon the tide had risen and with the sudden coming of an easterly breeze from off the sea, it was decided that the *Conch* should go in towing behind her six naval longboats laden with redcoats of the 25th and, having run the gauntlet of the Boer battery and the marksmen lining the shore, make a landing close by Fort Victoria whilst two boats under the command of Captain Wells of the 25th, would cast off earlier and storm the bluff on the opposite side of the harbour. At about 3 p.m. the little armada, carrying approximately 220 redcoats plus a number of sailors, who had strict orders that on landing they were to stand by and guard the boats, headed for the harbour entrance and the onslaught of shot and shell that would greet them. Captain Bell, at the helm of the *Conch*, remembered:

> The firing was now at its height, and bullets whistling in all directions. One struck the main boom about six inches above my head . . . We were now completely enveloped in smoke, so much so that I found it difficult to see the channel. Here one of the men who had just been shot was brought to the main hatchway for the purpose of being passed in to the cockpit, but the surgeon seeing the wound was mortal, did not see the necessity of passing him below. At the same time I observed another man, making his way to Captain Durnford, with the stock of his musket in one hand and the barrel in the other, with the iron ramrod very much bent.
>
> We were now rounding the Point and fast approaching the anchorage, our shells [from both the *Conch* and the *Southampton*] plowing up the sand hills, and causing a great stir. When off the engineer's house at the Point, the launch and the remainder of the boats were cast loose and pushed on shore. . . . During all this time the *Southampton* was not idle, the shot and shell dropping too close to us and the boat to be pleasant. Orders had been given for the sailors not to leave the boats but no sooner had they touched ground then Jack [a nickname for sailors] was out and over the sand hills cutlass in hand towards the flagstaff, at the risk of being knocked over by the shot from their own ship.

Captain Bell also grounded the *Conch* and on jumping ashore found the vessel to have been riddled by so many bullets that it was close to sinking, the water being 'up to the thwarts'. However, plugging with strips of blanket and energetic baling made her seaworthy for the moment. Temporarily indifferent to the condition of the vessel, Durnford and his men went ashore 'like greyhounds', while some of the sailors, espying the Republican flag flying from the staff close by Fort Victoria, immediately set about bringing it down by scaling the staff like monkeys. Unfortunately, it could not take their weight and slowly collapsed. Undeterred, the 'rebel' flag was torn away and, lacking a Union Jack, the sailors hoisted an ensign from one of the longboats but in their haste raised it upside down which, in nautical communication, indicates distress. The *Southampton's* lookout quickly recognised the signal and, believing the shore party to be in danger, opened fire which, in turn, caused the flag to be hurriedly reversed whereupon the firing ceased.

Taking command of the situation, Colonel Cloete ordered his bugler to sound assembly recalling the rampaging redcoats, then, having had his force formed up into three sections, advanced on the port. But the Boers were gone; gone without hardly firing a shot once the troops were ashore. British casualties had been light – two killed and a few wounded. Delighted with the success of the assault, Cloete and his men advanced on Smith's camp, the stench of which could be discerned a quarter of a mile away. Yet the spirits of those but recently besieged were high and with fife and drum they marched out to the regimental air, 'The Sprig of Shillelagh'. But what the relieving force found appalled them. Captain Bell later wrote:

> The main entrenchment across the camp appeared to have been converted into a hospital. I found men with their legs and arms off, and some having suffered from dysentery; the only shelter they had from the hot sun by day and the cold by night was the hides of the horses they had just killed for food; the stench from these hides and the putrid offal lying about was most offensive. Great credit is due to Dr. Fraser; although in want of almost everything that was requisite, every amputation he undertook succeeded.

However, a joyful event soon followed. On 27 May a ship that was assumed to be *The Maid of Mona*, a schooner bringing reinforcements from the Cape, was seen sailing off the Point. As the vessel drew

closer it was recognised as none other than the *Mazeppa* that, after
her triumphant escape, had sailed north in what had turned out to be
a futile attempt to find a British warship. Now the *Mazeppa* cautiously
peeped into the harbour and, on seeing the *Southampton*, sailed straight
in and over the bar, deliberately grounding on a sandbar enabling her
delighted female crew to find their husbands.

But in truth the battle was neither won nor lost: the Boers, who
well outnumbered the British troops, were still in the vicinity having
throughout the siege and the redcoats' seaborne assault, suffered but a
handful of casualties. Major William D'Urban, the son of Sir Benjamin
D'Urban, wrote to his father on 29 June describing the tense situation
at the time:

> Two days after we arrived here we marched for Congella, but the
> Boers did not wait for our approach, and after posting a proclamation
> we returned. . . . The farmers' [the Boers] have carried all the military
> prisoners they took, and also a great many individuals who would not
> join them, to Pietermaritzburg, and report says that the latter are not
> well treated. I do not myself see the end of this business. We cannot be
> satisfied with leaving these prisoners in their present hands . . .

Cloete, seemingly not a popular or charismatic person, was,
nevertheless, the man for the occasion; perhaps he and the Boers found
an affinity due to Cloete being of Dutch birth. Eventually, and against
the angry protests of many who would have had the Boer leaders hanged
as traitors, Cloete pardoned all and, without a further shot being fired,
Port Natal settled down to an uneasy calm until, a few years later, it was
proclaimed part of the Crown Colony of Natal.

Many of the Boers who had resisted the redcoat invasion stayed
and, retaining their farms, prospered under British rule, but others,
seeking the independence they craved, loaded their wagons and once
again trekked off into the vast interior: one such person was Pretorius
and another a seventeen-year-old lad by the name of Paul Kruger who
would continue the fight for more than half a century.

But what was it that had taken the fight out of the Boers when the
British landed? They had shown themselves to be the most skilled
mounted infantry in southern Africa; and in taking on the Zulu army
at Blood River, the most audacious and courageous of men. There is

little doubt that had they serious opposed the landing the redcoats' rescue mission would have ended up in a similar position to that of Captain Smith.

D'Urban in writing to his father commented:

> You will observe that our loss is very small, and most surprising it is that it was so. I can only account for it by supposing that they fired principally at the schooner and as our advance was very rapid, the shots intended for it flew over our heads. They were, I imagine, a good deal shaken by finding that the ship [HMS *Southampton*] could throw shot and shell to reach them [2,000 yards]. At the place we landed the bush and sand hills composed ground of such a description that a few resolute men might have destroyed the whole of us.
>
> When I went over the ground a few days after the landing I felt that my life had been given me. There are two store houses too, stockaded [Fort Victoria] from behind which they might have fired with deadly affect, and we could only muster about fifty men in the first landing from the boats, which had to return to the schooner for more men.

The answer would seem to be that the Boers, faced with the might of HMS *Southampton*, saw it as some sort of marine juggernaut against whose power they had no answer: it would be impossible for them to defend their harbour or any nautical enterprise, when they had no more marine capability than a few rowing boats. It was clear they could not compete: the veldt was their habitat. But what did the Zulu kingdom think of it all? White man fighting white man. One may be sure that King Mpande's spies kept him fully aware of every move – furthermore, what did he think of the mighty *Southampton*? Mpande was not so naïve as to still think of it as a sea monster, if he ever had. Unfortunately, we have no record of Mpande's thoughts and although he and the Boers had a pact that if either were attacked the other would, as an ally come to the other's defence, the Zulu king had made no move to aid the Boers. Now his neighbours across the river were the British and the redcoats were drawing closer to the heart of the Zulu kingdom.

Chapter 8

The Colony and the Kingdom

The British having taken from the Boers the land the Boers had taken from the Zulus, the region settled down to a period of relative calm. The Tugela River was acknowledged as the boundary between the colony and the kingdom but the coastal strip, and additional territory surrounding St. Lucia Bay, was returned to Zululand. Reckoning the commencement of Mpande's reign from the time of Dingane's death, his kingship would last thirty-two relatively peaceful years, a period without any serious confrontation with his white colonial neighbours. Less than two decades had passed since the first white men had waded ashore to pay their respects to King Shaka and, as little better than castaways, had been received with generosity while they in turn had had little to offer except a few firearms and macassa hair oil. Nevertheless, the white man had acquired half the territory over which Shaka had once held sway. Apart from the battle the Boers had fought on the banks of what they called 'Blood River', the territory had, strangely enough, been acquired by either the white men fighting between themselves or having the Zulus fight against each other. By the white man's own reckoning, 3,000 Zulus had perished at Blood River and a further 2,000 in the more recent battles. On the other hand, white casualties inflicted by the Zulus, including those of Piet Retief and his men, were little more then 100 whilst casualties inflicted, white upon white, between the Boers and redcoats, numbered more or less the same.

At the time Mpande became king, the borders of Zululand were contained by the Indian Ocean to the east, the new colony of Natal to the south, the Swazi kingdom in the north while to the west the border drifted into the lands of vassal clans and tribes beyond which there were other African kingdoms yet to be explored and exploited by the white man. Nevertheless, by the time of Mpande's death, the Zulu kingdom would be all but surrounded by white dominated territory, and with its army of 40,000 warriors with no-one to fight, would be reckoned as an archaic but dangerous hindrance to the white man marching north. However, that was for the future; for the present Mpande and the Zulu people would be left to get on with their ancient way of life without too much interference from their bossy colonial neighbours. There would still be desertions from the kingdom with runaways seeking protection and employment, but these defectors were absorbed by the colony and were no longer marched back to Zululand for punishment. Generally, the Zulus shunned working as labourers for the white man but there were those willing to do so, adding to the mounting number of Natal Zulus who would soon vastly outnumber the colonial whites.

Encounters with the Zulu people who were still living their traditional way of life, were now confined to those who would, for whatever reason, journey north beyond the Tugela River: traders, hunters and the odd missionary who happened to be fortunate enough to obtain Mpande's permission to preach within his kingdom. However, most missionaries had to be content to evangelise amongst the ever-growing number of defectors from the kingdom who were known, in colloquial terminology, as 'Natal kaffirs'. Just such a missionary was Wilhelm Posselt, a German of the Berlin Missionary Society.

When Posselt arrived in Natal, Mpande had been king for four relatively peaceful years but Posselt, like other missionaries, would exaggerate the savagery and barbarism of the Zulu people in order to excite and awe his sponsors and to exaggerate the dangers of his mission. He told his German kin:

The amaZulu, on the north-eastern border of the Colony, are the most powerful and warlike nation . . . Its constitution represents the most complete despotism of the lowest and rudest kind. There the king sits like a demi-god in his large kraal. His people approach him on their knees only to within a given distance, which may not be transgressed, adoring him and with loud voices exalting him to the highest heavens. The only purpose for which this monster the king, lives and to which he devotes his wild life is to satisfy the lust of his unclean heart to the fullest degree and to secure his life and his reign through the elimination of whole sections of his people, his relatives, parents, wives and children.

Posselt, having described Mpande and his people, neither of whom he had ever seen as yet, went on to describe his congregation:

The Zulu kaffirs [those Zulus who had defected to Natal] are also robust, broad-chested, well-built people of average height. However, there are many who, like Saul, are one head taller than the rest. Among the men one often finds really good looking fellows and one such a fellow stands before me, straight as a dart, with well-formed limbs and a broad chest, I always wish that our own king might have a few regiments of guardsmen of this quality.

Once they reach adolescence, young men will dress their hair according to the dictates of their latest fashion, much as the Parisian ladies do in regards to their clothes. Now they will rub their hair with smelly lard and red ochre and turn it into little balls; then they will let it hang down in shaggy strands like sheep's wool; or they will shape it into a series of crests, or they will comb it forward to form a horn on their forehead etc. Men will shape their hair into a high, round nest on their crown and harden the outer rim with gum, which is polished.

Then, describing the girls, one can almost hear Posselt's voice, hushed with disapproval: 'Girls just wear a string around their waist from which a few short frills are suspended, and walk about in this shameless state till they get married. Only then will they cover at least the lower part of their body, while the top part continues to remain uncovered.'

If Posselt disapproved of those Zulus as yet untouched by civilisation, he was equally critical of those who had become urbanised, especially those seemingly converted to Christianity, who came to church to swank and be admired:

Once a Zulu takes to wearing of European clothing, as is the custom among converts, there is, especially among the young no limit to their desire for ostentation and dressing up.... Not only must their boots be highly polished, but must also 'cry', as they say, that is, they must squeak. A white handkerchief is put into the pocket not only a corner is visible but at least half of it hangs out. One does not walk with the gait of a normal human being, but one struts, or 'staps', as they say here, that is walking haughtily. The girls insist on wearing the confounded crinoline, an apron around the waist, and a sash over the shoulders. When they come to church they arrange to arrive when the service has already begun in order to draw attention and admiration.

He and Allen Gardiner would have got on well.

While white missionaries were almost queuing up for a share in saving Zulu souls, trader/settlers began to flood Natal. Between 1849 and 1852, 5,000 arrived, the vast majority from England. Most came through entrepreneurial immigration schemes and many with barely the minimum resource needed for survival.

Perhaps typical of would-be trader/settlers, was William Clayton Humphreys, a cocky young Englishman of good education, aged twenty-two. With the little capital he had on arrival at Port Natal in 1851, he joined up with a Mr Holden bound on a trading expedition into 'the interior'. It is interesting to note that at the time, twenty-eight years after Farewell had first seen Port Natal, the forests of magnificent timber that Farewell had so admired were still in evidence, as was much of the game.

Port Natal for fifteen miles from the coast, has the appearance of a dense forest full of fine timber either for ship or wagon building. The pasturage is extremely rich. The whole face of the country is covered with grass from one to eight feet high. The country a short distance inland abounds in elephants, lions, tigers, panthers [leopards], hyenas, buffaloes, elands, buck, hippopotami, wild boars, wolves [wild dogs], porcupines, monkeys, ant-eaters, etc. In the rivers there are seacows, crocodiles, otters, etc. Of reptiles there are a fine variety of serpents.

Having got his kit ashore and being unemployed, Humphries had nothing better to do than spend the next month attempting to shoot birds (with little success) along the Umgeni River, a little way out of town. But within that short period of time he seems to have become an authority on local affairs including King Mpande: 'The Zulu country belongs to His Highness King Panda [sic], one of the most cruel, bloodthirsty and despotic monarchs I ever heard of. He can muster fifty thousand warriors and is continually quarrelling and fighting with the neighbouring nations.' Such were the nightmare tales told by the locals that Humphries almost abandoned the idea of venturing into Zululand: 'Mr. Holden told me such awful accounts of the cruelty of the brutes that he almost frightened me from going.' But once the little expedition consisting of Holden, the wagon (which Humphreys called a cart), six oxen, a small white boy to lead the beasts and three 'kaffir' servants-cum-trade negotiators was under way, Humphreys assumed the mantle of swaggering white supremacy, the colour of his skin automatically putting him above the Zulu people, no matter what their rank or standing or on which side of the Tugela he encountered them. Their kindness and hospitality towards him and to whites in general, he assumed as a right and unashamedly cadged and stole almost as though bestowing a favour on those he abused. Seldom did the expedition offer to pay for food or for the overnight accommodation that they scrounged.

> There are hundreds of kraals on the Umvoti. It is a missionary station and as usual the kaffirs who call themselves Christians are more inhospitable and saucy than any other. They would not give us any milk or beef though they had been killing an ox that afternoon, however, as I was exceedingly hungry I determined to have a piece of their meat either by fair means or foul.

Thus the traders trundled on into Zululand, Humphreys incessantly thinking of food. Near the Umvoti River, ten miles from Port Natal, they came upon an eland – 'The handsomest beast I ever saw' – with a calf. Humphreys immediately perceived possibilities for his dinner and, with three assegais in hand, set off in pursuit of the calf but, alas for him, it easily made its escape.

Along the way there was no lack of missionaries. One Sunday morning the traders encountered an impressive gathering:

> At about 10 o'clock a Zulu boy went on all the surrounding hills with a Chinese gong and struck it for about five minutes on each; in a short time the Zulus began to assemble until they numbered 163, principally females, many had come a long way. It was one of the most interesting sights I had ever witnessed. They squatted altogether on the grass in

front of the hut and a service commenced by the missionary praying, he afterwards read a chapter from the bible (in the Zulu language of course) and they afterwards sung a hymn very nicely. The missionary then put up a placard with the Zulu alphabet on and they pronounced each letter after him. Altogether it was a most pleasing sight. Most of the congregation was composed of young females, many of them positively pretty, I never saw any before to equal many of them.

Just outside present-day Eshowe, which was once deep in Zulu country, there is a prominence known as 'Martyrs Rock'. Legend has it that the one and only Christian convert was visited by a deputation from the King – which King, whether it was Dingane, Mpande or Cetshwayo, remains uncertain. However, the *induna* of the deputation posed the question: 'did the convert believe there was a King residing in the sky who was greater than his own Zulu King?' The convert replied: 'Yes', that was his belief. The *induna* responded that he was sure the convert would understand that the King of the Zulus could not condone such a belief and the convert was invited to retract his statement, failing which the *induna* would have no option but to execute him forthwith as an example to others. Undeterred the convert held firm and was led away to where his execution – made more impressive by its location on the rocky prominence – was duly carried out.

Back to Humphreys again who, having heard that a 'great chief' resided near his camp, decided to visit, indicating the confidence Humphreys and his like had in the supremacy of a white skin; Humphreys, in reality, being little better than a white vagrant. In comparison the man who would receive him with courtesy and hospitality was a kingmaker, none other than Nongalaza kaNondela, Mpande's renowned general, once commander of an army 20,000 strong, who it will be remembered had defeated Dingane in open battle eleven years previously and in doing so had procured the throne for his king. Indeed one of the greatest chiefs.

I arrived there about 4 p.m. and was surprised to see a larger kraal than I ever saw before. He had certainly not less than 2,000 head of beautiful cattle besides sheep and goats. He had about two hundred wives and three to four hundred children. He was exceedingly kind to me and treated me to a pot of thin amas with boiled mabele in which I made a first rate meal of and afterwards drunk more than a quart of tchualla or beer . . .

Journeying on, a day or two later Humphreys discovered that he was only twenty miles from King Mpande's royal home and nonchalantly commented in his journal: 'I would have gone to see him if I had been well.' As it was he and Holden had arrived at one of the king's military kraals occupied by a regiment of soldiers:

> I had no idea that the Zulus ever had such a kraal as the one I was now at. It was built up as the rest but the outer fence was fully a mile and greater in circumference and enclosed about a thousand huts. About a score of soldiers came out to the cart but they were a saucy lot of devils and were most of them drunk with tchualla. We met the queen of the kraal (one of Panda's wives), she was very kind and agreeable but [much to Humphreys' indignation] did not give us anything.

And so the expedition made its way deeper into the Zulu kingdom, the two traders abusing Zulu hospitality and shooting game as the whim took them. There is little mention as to their trading activities, the enterprise seemingly being left in the hands of their native employees who, needless to say, were suspected of skulduggery.

Having been on their trading venture for two months with nothing to show for it, and with their staff having gone to barter their goods but having failed to return, Humphreys and Holden began to fear the worst. So it was with great relief that he saw his men reappear driving before them fifty head of cattle. According to Humphreys' calculations the number should have been fifty-five: the men were five short and despite loud protests were immediately accused of having sold them. They pleaded that the missing beasts had died on the road.

So the trading expedition, of indifferent success, made its way back to Port Natal, stopping briefly at Verulam in order to bring the men before the magistrate, Mr Cleghorn, on a charge of stealing the 'missing' cattle. One would think Mr Cleghorn had little in the way of evidence to consider but, given by the white men, it was enough, and all the herders were found guilty and fined two cows each (their homesteads were nearby from which the fines could be secured). One of the men protested; protested too loudly, it seems, for Mr Cleghorn, considering him to be 'saucy', ordered him to be flogged. No doubt they all wondered whether it would not be preferable to be back in Zululand again, under the rule of King Mpande.

Humphreys must have admired Cleghorn's power and authority
as immediately on return he apprenticed himself to a local law firm,
qualifying as an attorney five years later. Eventually he became the town
treasurer of Durban and in 1866 'apparently absconded with the town
treasury funds' and fled. History does not record whether or not he was
caught and brought before Mr Cleghorn for justice.

White female visitors to the Zulu kingdom were rare whilst those
who, in addition, could speak the Zulu language were unique. Such
a woman was Catherine Barter who had followed her trader brother
Charles out from England in order to keep house for him. Of a good
county family the siblings, in social standing, were several cuts above
that of the average Natal settler. Nevertheless, either for amusement, or
out of necessity, Charles was happy to engage in trade: beads, baubles
and cloth in exchange for cattle. In addition he led hunting expeditions
for wealthy clients into Zululand.

Catherine wrote a short account of an expedition that she and her
brother made into Zululand and published her tale under the dramatic
title of *Alone Amongst the Zulus*. She made this particular journey for the
most part, unaccompanied by Charles or any other white person and
her story reflects the tranquil and easygoing state of affairs that existed
between the colony and the kingdom. The colonists, either as traders
or hunters, required little, if any, formal permission from the Zulu
monarch in order to carry out their enterprises within his kingdom.

Proceeding deep into Zulu country Catherine recalled a visit paid on
a previous occasion to a rather rough old Zulu worthy whose prickly
manner could well have been brought about by too many scrounging
whites (such as Humphreys) taking advantage of traditional Zulu
hospitality:

From the plain of the Matikulu, we soon came to the kraal of a great
prince called Nongalazi, he was the king's uncle [also, as we have heard,
the King's renowned General], and reported to be rich, so we hoped he
might sell us a cow or two. We outspanned not far from his gate, but he
did not appear. We sent to let him know that we were there and after some
delay he came out with a few followers, but was very short in his answers.
'He had a white man of his own, whose blankets were now heaped up in
one of his huts; he could take some of those if he needed them.'

Perhaps Catherine, who was more skilful with the Zulu language than her brother, had taken it upon herself to personally bargain with the prince. She, the prince no doubt thought, needed to be put in her place and turning to Charles enquired why, if he wanted cattle, did he not sell his sister? Catherine with wry humour observed: 'He did not, however, go as far as to offer to purchase me.'

Yet, within two years of Catherine's tranquil journey into Zululand the country erupted in civil war culminating in one of the most bloody battles in the history of southern Africa. However, apart from a few white men, the traders were not involved; it was Zulu against Zulu in a war of succession fought between the forces of the ageing King Mpande's two sons, the half-brothers Cetshwayo and Mbuyazi.

Cetshwayo was not only Mpande's first son by his chief wife, it was he whom Mpande had presented to the Boers as his heir back in 1839. Despite this, Mbuyazi was Mpande's favourite, as the king had made clear on several occasions; also, he had implied that Mbuyazi was to be his successor. By 1856 Cetshwayo, highly intelligent and courageous, found the situation intolerable and decided to establish his succession by conquest.

Throughout the kingdom, both princes had their supporters, each group bearing a name that would become its battle cry. Cetshwayo's warriors were known as the 'uSuthu' while Mbuyazi's were called the 'iziGqoza'. Of the two factions, Cetshwayo's was by far the most numerous.

King Mpande, aware of the rivalry between his sons, had attempted to put distance between them and their respective armies but the young princes, strutting with pride and ambition, were determined to meet in battle. Mbuyazi, having examined the advancing uSuthu army, suddenly realised how numerically superior it was and decided to retire south with all his people towards the Tugela River where he hoped not only to enlist further Zulu support but, with offers of land and cattle, to entice white men with their guns to join his cause.

Hurrying south, Mbuyazi first called upon a trader, Ephraim Rathbone, who at that time, had an abode ten miles from the Tugela on the Zulu side of the river. Mbuyazi found him with several other traders who were making their way back to Natal with a large herd of cattle. But the white men wisely refused to get involved. Instead,

Rathbone sent word to the Natal Border Agent, Captain Joshua Walmesley, advising that there was a bloody conflict in the making. Walmesley had as his administrative assistant a young white man by the name of John Dunn, a man destined to greatly influence the future of Cetshwayo and the fate of the Zulu nation. Dunn was a man of pure colonial lineage being the offspring of a hunter/trader, Robert Dunn, who had settled in Natal during Shaka's era and had married Ann, a daughter of Alexander Biggar. From an early age the Dunns' had allowed their son – 'Janteni', as the Zulus called him – to run wild in the untamed country above Durban Bay that still teemed with game including lion and elephant. With a gun, a pony, and accompanied by Zulu companions, young John Dunn roamed free, his education in the ways of the wild being as thorough as his formal education was sparse. When he was thirteen years of age, his father was killed while hunting elephant, whereupon his mother decided to return to the eastern Cape and to take with her John and her three daughters. But the boy had other ideas and evading all efforts to have him embark with the rest of the family, he remained in Natal and for several years lived with the Zulus, becoming as fluent in their language as his own and completely at ease with their customs and way of life.

After a couple of years, young Dunn, now in every respect a Zulu except for the colour of his skin, was approached by – or even apprehended by – Joshua Walmesley; no doubt Walmesley thought that it was 'not on' that a white youth should 'go native'. In any event, Walmesley restrained Dunn from continuing with his carefree existence and, in a fatherly way, gave him the formal education that he lacked. In addition Walmesley tutored Dunn in the intricacies of white social behaviour and etiquette, so much so that within a few years Dunn was equally at ease as a Zulu, and a confidant of the Zulu monarch, as he was as a colonial gentleman hobnobbing with the nabobs of the British Empire. By the time he was twenty-two Dunn, by virtue of his hunting skills and by acting as a guide to wealthy visitors had, in addition to his post as assistant border-agent, made enough money to acquire the beginnings of a transport business, all the time improving the quality of his oxen and wagons. It was at this stage of his career that a panicking Mbuyazi arrived across the Tugela begging for armed assistance for which he promised to pay in cattle and land. Walmesley prevented Dunn from getting involved but, the story goes, gave him permission to cross the river with a 130 armed men, some from the Border Police and the remainder being Dunn's black hunters, many of them mounted. Ostensibly Dunn's involvement in the affair was that of a negotiator endeavouring to broker a peace between the warring princes, but his subsequent actions make it clear that he was in it for the loot that would fall to the victors. Writing thirty years later, Dunn maintained that Walmesley was aware that he intended to fight for Mbuyazi but, as an official of the colonial government, it is extremely unlikely that Walmesley would have condoned Dunn's participation.

The following day Dunn crossed into Zululand:

It was a raw, cold, drizzling morning when the call to arms was sounded. On our army being assembled, I asked Umbulazi if our scouts knew anything of the movements of the enemy. The answer was that he did not know. This I took to be a bad omen, and so did the warriors, for there was a murmur amongst them. I now had a strong suspicion that an attempt would be made by the enemy to cut us off from the Tugela. I therefore immediately called upon my men to follow me, and rode off towards the river. This was the last I saw of Umbulazi. What I suspected turned out to be true; and as luck would have it, I rode straight for the head of the right wing of the uSuthu that was trying to cut us off. I rode to within about 400 yards, and called out to them to wait for us [so that we could fight them] if they were not cowards, and then galloped back and hastened my small force of about 250, with shields and assegais, and about 40 more men with muskets of every queer variety. Seeing a man on horseback caused a feeling of uneasiness amongst the uSuthu, a horse being at that time an object of terror to many of them, and for a time the uSuthu remained rooted to the spot on which they stood and where I had left them. As soon as I got my men up – although there must have been ten to one opposed to us – I went straight at them, seeing that that was the only chance of getting out of the now fast-closing circle. Seeing such a small force daring to attack such odds caused a panic amongst the uSuthu, as they felt sure that I must be backed up by a very much larger force, and after very little fighting we drove them before us for about half a mile, killing many. I then re-called my men, and although my intentions had been to have only cut my way through, and make for Natal, I now felt confident from the success we had, and being excited, I made up my mind to see the end of it.

It was a rash decision as, having underestimated the enemy, it was not long before Dunn and his little band were fighting to keep at bay the whole of the uSuthu right horn, it being only Dunn's dubious firepower that was keeping the enemy in check. Nevertheless, Dunn's audacious act allowed many of Mbulazi's women, children and stragglers to reach the Tugela and a remote chance of survival, rather than being overrun *en route* and slaughtered. Yet, when the fleeing host had its back to the river a panic set in, not only amongst Mbulazi's followers, but likewise amongst Dunn's men: 'A panic had seized all, and the scene was a sight never to be forgotten.'

Dunn goes on to describe the beginnings of the massacre that followed and to mention that the white traders, who had been at Rathbone's homestead a few days earlier, were at that moment camped on the banks of the river. On seeing the carnage that was about to descend on them, the traders abandoned their wagons and cattle and plunged into the river, fortunately being saved by the ferryman who brought his boat to the rescue. Dunn continues:

> As soon as I got to the river I was at once rushed at by men, women and children begging me to save them. Several poor mothers held out their babes to me offering them to me as my property if I would only save them. And now the uSuthu were fairly amongst us, stabbing right and left without mercy, and regardless of sex, and as I saw that my only chance was try and swim for it, I urged my horse into the water, but was no sooner in than I was besieged from all sides by men clinging to me, so that my horse was, so to say, completely rooted to the spot. I now jumped off, stripped myself, all but hat and shirt, and taking nothing but my gun which I held aloft, swam with one hand. Yes, I handed over my horse to a Hottentot and swam for dear life.

Dunn goes on to relate how he got out into deep water, losing his gun in the process, to be rescued by the ferry boat, whilst in the shallows the slaughter continued without mercy, men, women and children alike being the victims of the victorious warriors: 'The uSuthu were, with terrible earnestness, hard at work with the deadly assegai.'

1   Utimuni, a nephew of King Shaka, painted by Angas. His uniform, as an officer of an elite Zulu regiment, contains items of finery such as the globulus tufts in his headdress from the feathers of the green roller, a bird found only in the interior of Africa. (*Campbell Collection, Durban*)

2   (Above) Two rival regiments, one is distinguished by black shields and the other by white, parade before King Mpande. (*Amafa, Durban*)

3   (Below, left) Adolphe Delegorgue, a young French naturalist and hunter, travelled widely within Zululand during the reign of King Mpande. (*Amafa, Durban*)

4   (Below, right) The Boer women were equally adept at defending a laager. Note the nonchalance of the lady on the left as, with a ramrod between her teeth, she pours black powder down the muzzle of a gun.

5 Piet Retief anxiously discusses whether or not to enter Dingane's palace without firearms while, at the gate, a Zulu induna entices another Boer to step inside. (*Don Collection, Durban Municipal Library*)

6 King Dingane's capital of Mgungundlovu, with Retief and his party surrounded in the middle of the parade ground. (*Don Collection, Durban Municipal Library*)

7 Following the murder of Piet Retief, Dingane sent his impis to destroy all the Boer encampments along the Drakensberg foothills.

8 Dingane's vast palace of Mgungundlovu before it was torched by his own hand.

9   (Above, left) King Shaka kaSenzangakhona, as drawn by Captain Allen Gardiner. The shield appears to be extraordinarily large and unwieldy and the spear bears no resemblance to a Zulu assegai.

10   (Above, right) King Mpande kaSenzangakhona Zulu, seated on his elaborately carved throne, is protected against the sun by his shield bearer. (*Amafa, Durban*)

11   (Below) The coasting vessel *Mazeppa* escapes to the open sea seeking a British warship. Boer riflemen ineffectually pursue. (*Local History Museum, Durban*)

12 (Above, left) Joseph Cato, in later life, who captained the *Mazeppa* in 1842. (*KZN Archives, Pietermaritzburg*)

13 (Above, right) Ndongeni in later life. As a youth he accompanied Dick King for much of the way to Grahamstown. (*Campbell Collection, Durban*)

14 (Below) The Boers, having captured several British canons, continuously bombarded the besieged camp. Note the canon shot holes through the tents and wagons. To the right, some of the wives take shelter. (*Africana Museum, Johannesburg*)

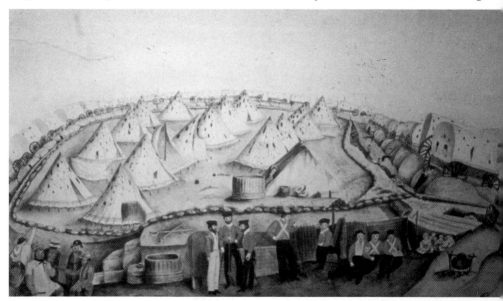

15 The *Conch*, towing naval long-boats, crammed with troops, into Port Natal harbour. Note the white smoke from Boer guns situated on the Bluff. (*Local History Museum, Durban*)

16 Lieutenant-Colonel Abraham Cloete, who commanded the assault on Port Natal. (*Africana Museum, Johannesburg*)

17 (Above) The type of warrior who would have attended Cetshwayo's coronation in their thousands. (*KZN Archives, Pietermaritzburg*)

18 (Top, right) Chief Langalibalele at the time of the Hlubi rebellion. His hat and old military coat give him a piratical appearance. (*KZN Archives, Pietermaritzburg*)

19 (Right) Prince Dabulamanzi kaMpande, Cetshwayo's half-brother, who challenged the colonials to a shooting competition.

20   The gunners of the Natal Volunteer Artillery who fired a 17-gun salute as King Cetshwayo was crowned. (*Local History Museum, Durban*)

21   The Durnford brothers: Anthony, right, with his young brother Arthur. This photograph was taken before Anthony grew his distinctive moustache that reached to his shoulders. (*Campbell Collection, Durban*)

22 The summit of Bushman's Pass today. Nothing has changed except for the cross erected above the grave of Troopers Erskine, Potterill and Bond. It is a place seldom visited. (*Campbell Collection, Durban*)

23 Lord Chelmsford, Officer-Commanding British forces in southern Africa. (*Local History Museum, Durban*)

24 The British made every effort to enlist native allies. Warriors of the amaNgwane tribe, who had a score to settle with the Zulus, were recruited by Durnford for the Natal Native Horse. (*KZN Archives, Pietermaritzburg*)

25 The splendid physique of the Zulu warriors was much admired by the British. (*Ron Lock Collection*)

26 Native allies were recruited as far away as Swaziland. One British officer made the comment '… I saw some Swazis, splendid looking fellows indeed in their wonderful clothing of skins and feathers.' (Ron Lock Collection)

27 The feathers of a Sakabuli bird headdress and a lion claw necklace indicate a regimental commander of high rank.

28   A warrior, fully fledged but most likely about to participate in a wedding ceremony or other peaceful pursuit. (*Local History Museum, Durban*)

29 The Battle of Isandlwana raged for about an hour. One Zulu coming in sight of the camp remembers that the whole place was a twisting mass of soldiers and Zulus.

30 For the benefit of the young soldiers, an old warrior describes how the Zulus won the Battle of Isandlwana. (*KZN Archives, Pietermaritzburg*)

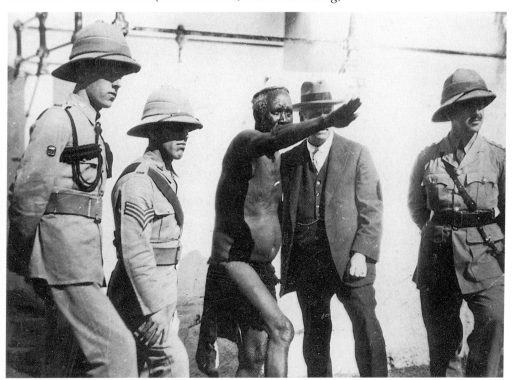

31 The defenders of Rorke's Drift, outnumbered twenty to one, fought for twelve hours without a break in the fighting. Eleven Victoria Crosses were awarded for this action, drawing attention away from the disaster of Isandlwana. (*Ron Lock Collection*)

32 Cetshwayo's portrait by Carl Sohn, commissioned by Queen Victoria, presents a very different countenance, one of intelligence and humour. (*By gracious permission of Her Majesty the Queen; Local History Museum, Durban*)

Dunn endeavoured to beg or buy another gun from the traders but for fear of retribution should the uSuthu cross the river, the traders were playing it as safely as possible and were not parting with any of their firearms.

Originally Dunn rode into the river but had abandoned his horse in mid-stream in an attempt to save it from the many grasping hands who desperately hoped the beast would tow them from the prospect of a watery grave. This thoughtful action saved the horse while most of Dunn's little army of 310 men perished.

Having survived, Dunn realised news of the slaughter would spread like wildfire to Port Natal where it would cause an unprecedented panic, provoking more mischief and bloodshed. So, borrowing a pair of trousers, he having discarded his own in the river, he mounted his horse and, at a gallop, rode for the port.

As for Mbuyazi, his body was never identified, giving rise in later years to the rumour that he still lived; but there is no doubt that he was numbered amongst the slain.

There was understandably alarm amongst the Natal settlers, many believing that the Zulu army would, with dire consequences, invade the colony. But Cetshwayo, having eliminated his rival, withdrew immediately the slaughter was over, leaving behind thousands of corpses whose bones would litter the banks of the Tugela for decades to come. In their excitement some of Cetshwayo's triumphant warriors had made off with all the cattle that the traders, in panic, had abandoned during their flight across the Tugela. Dunn, having clearly backed the wrong man, was undeterred and smartly set about turning the looted cattle to his advantage. With his intimate knowledge of Zulu character and custom, he was confident that, the battle over, Cetshwayo would harbour neither resentment nor a desire for revenge.

The traders had appealed to the colonial authorities to assist in the recovery of the livestock, which numbered close on one thousand, and an attempt had been made to negotiate their return by sending no other than Henry Francis Fynn, now a man in his mid-fifties, to parley with Cetshwayo. But Fynn, having returned empty-handed, Dunn volunteered to go. It would seem to have been a perilous step to take bearing in mind that Dunn and his gunmen had caused significant slaughter in the uSuthu ranks during the recent battle. Nevertheless, with Walmesley's reluctant permission, Dunn set off, supposedly to hunt buffalo and, unmolested, finally met up with Cetshwayo. The meeting was cordial and after waiting for several days for the scattered cattle to be collected, Dunn and his hunters herded them back across the Tugela with Dunn eventually being rewarded with £250 for his trouble.

It seems that there had been an immediate rapport between Cetshwayo and the white man with Cetshwayo seeing in Dunn not only a means of better communication with the colonial government but also a go-between and personal advisor in all his dealings with his white neighbours. In fact, it was not long before Dunn was acting as a conduit for the procurement of firearms.

In time Cetshwayo's regard for Dunn would blossom into affection and he would regard him as a brother – indeed, Dunn, having taken several Zulu wives including one of Cetshwayo's royal sisters, became the future king's brother-in-law. Yet, Cetshwayo's recollection of their first meeting, which he recorded many years later, markedly differs to Dunn's account:

> One very cold and stormy night in winter I was seated before a large fire in my hut when there was a noise without as if someone was arriving. I asked the cause from my attendants and they told me that a white man in a miserable state of destitution had just arrived and claimed my hospitality. I ordered the servants to bring him in, a tall, splendidly made man appeared. He was dressed in rags, for his clothes had been torn to pieces in fighting through the bush, and he was shivering from fever and ague. I drew my cloak and asked him to sit by the fire, and told the servants to bring food and clothing. I loved this white man as a brother, and made him one of my indunas, giving him land and wives, daughters of my chiefs.

It is likely then that Dunn, during the time that he roamed with his Zulu companions prior to his association with Walmesley, had made the acquaintance of Cetshwayo which would explain Dunn's lack of concern at re-entering Zululand to seek the traders' cattle. It was lucky for Dunn that at the time Cetshwayo did not hold the opinion he formed of him twenty-three years later, for then he said of Dunn, speaking metaphorically: 'Who would stay with a rat in his hut that ate his food?'

Chapter 9

Coronation of a Zulu King

Although Mbuyazi and his supporters had been destroyed, except for a few who had escaped into Natal, Cetshwayo soon found that his succession as king of the Zulu nation was by no means assured for there were other royal princes, the offspring of King Mpande and his many brides, ready to assert themselves. There was for instance his half-brother, Prince Hamu kaNzibe, who fretted that although senior in age to Cetshwayo he stood far behind him in the succession because his mother had not been selected by Mpande as his 'Great Wife', a situation that, as Cetshwayo would later discover, would not deter Hamu's ambition to become king. Hamu and his supporters had, in fact, fought staunchly for Cetshwayo at Ndondakusuka. The real reason for such apparent loyalty could well have been Hamu's plan to rid himself of Mbuyazi before setting about the elimination of Cetshwayo. Unlike other princes, Hamu lacked Mpande's favour, but not so Mthongu, Mpande's fourteen-year-old son by Nomantshali, a junior wife greatly loved by the ageing king. Nomantshali was ambitious for her son and, as Cetshwayo came to realise, it was her desire, as was Mpande's, that Mthongu become king in preference to all others.

On realisation of this new and perilous threat to his ambitions, Cetshwayo determined to act with the ruthlessness and expedience that the situation demanded. He summoned Bhejana, the head of his household and a captain of the nGobamakhosi Regiment, and ordered him to proceed at once to Nomanthali's village and to, forthwith, kill her and all her children. But on Bhejana's arrival at Nomanthali's homestead only her younger son Mpoyiyana was present, Nomanthali and Mthongu having gone to stay with other royal relatives. Fearful

15. Sigcwelegewele kaMhlekeleke, commander of the elite Nkobamakosi/nGobamakhosi Regiment. (*KZN Archives, Pietermaritzburg*)

that his mission on behalf of Cetshwayo was in jeopardy, Bhejana took Mpoyiyana prisoner and hastened to kwaNodwengu, the royal capital, where he mistakenly believed Mthongu and his mother to be. On arrival, and with great bravado, Bhejana was blatantly disrespectful to Mpande and demanded that Nomanthali and her son present themselves. The old king, furious but impotent, repeatedly denied – as was quite true – the presence of his wife and son putting Bhejana into an almost uncontrollable rage, as he dared not go into the royal *isigodlo* ('harem') to seek them out knowing full well that to do so as a commoner, the penalty would be death, irrespective of under whose orders he might be acting. But the young Mpoyiyana was still his prisoner, and were he to slay him it would not be seen as so serious an offence as that of a commoner entering the *isigodlo*. So Bhejana and his men dragged Mpoyiyana from Mpande's grasp and with the boy wailing with terror, took him off and killed him.

When this bungled operation was reported to Cetshwayo, he was abashed and infuriated that his father had been subjected to such indignity and grief. Nevertheless, the pursuit of Nomanthali and Mthongu continued and eventually the mother was tracked down and killed. Mthongu, however, evaded his pursuers, escaping into Boer-held territory where he would become a pawn in future negotiations: his life for more land.

It was against this background in 1861, only months after Mthongu's escape, that the Natal government, in the form of Theophilus Shepstone, decided to send a deputation to Mpande. Shepstone was aware that (after Mthongu's escape) the Boers of the Vryheid Republic, which was little more than a bankrupt white banana republic, had concluded a deal with Cetshwayo, whereby they would hand over Mthongu – on condition that he was not harmed – in exchange for land, land that would include a corridor to the sea for the use of both the Vryheid and Transvaal Boers. The British – and especially Shepstone – believed this was not in the best interests of the Empire and Shepstone took it upon himself to assess the situation and scuttle Boer ambitions by a personal visit to the Zulu kingdom.

16. Theophilus Shepstone at about the time of Cetshwayo's coronation. (*Campbell Collection, Durban*)

Shepstone, like Dunn, was also a man of impressive colonial lineage, having arrived in Africa in 1820 at the age of three with his settler parents. Growing up amongst the Xhosa, whose language is similar to that of the Zulus, he was acting as an interpreter to the military by the time he was fourteen years of age and it was in that capacity that he had accompanied Major Charters to Natal in 1838. It will be remembered that Charters' expedition remained for but a while and then departed. When the colony of Natal was proclaimed some five years later, Shepstone returned and acquired the position of Diplomatic Agent to all the black people that had settled themselves within the colony. Thereafter, he spread his net further afield, making contacts with chiefs and monarchs of the many clans and tribes beyond the borders of Natal, so much so that any dealings that black people might contemplate with the whites – and vice versa – were in the first instance made by, or through, Shepstone. As one native potentate put it: 'My entry into the white man's domain was ever through Shepstone's door.'

Although Shepstone would have regarded his expedition into Zululand at that particular time of recent upheaval, as a dangerous one, he had no intention of showing the least concern, making his way unarmed to Mpande's capital by a meandering route in order that as many people as possible would know of his coming. Mpande, aware of the prestige with which his approaching guest was held, summoned Cetshwayo to be present at the forthcoming *indaba* (conference) that was to take place at kwaNodwengu. Cetshwayo, torn between resentment that he should be ordered to listen to what would undoubtedly be a lecture by the white man and curiosity as to the real purpose of Shepstone's visit, found himself in a quandary. However, believing that his father might well persuade Shepstone – and through him the Natal government – to support the nomination of Mthongu as the future king, Cetshwayo truculently decided to attend, making it clear, however, by taking with him a fully armed contingent of the crack uThulwana Regiment, that he was the power in Zululand.

When Cetshwayo arrived at Nodwengu at the head of his belligerent warriors, he was in a pugnacious mood, made immediately more dangerous by the news that Shepstone's head man, Ngoza, who in Cetshwayo's eyes was nothing more than a commoner and Natal kaffir, had had the effrontery to enter the royal *isigodlo*. His purpose,

Cetshwayo had pondered, might well have been to convey a message from Mthongu. But whatever Ngoza's purpose, it mattered little, he had defiled a royal place and the penalty, for a common dog such as he, was immediate execution. This boil of contention that was bound to erupt, was at first not mentioned, instead Cetshwayo, demanded of Shepstone that Mthongu be delivered back to Zululand. When it became apparent that Shepstone would never agree, Cetshwayo became distraught and ordered his warriors to perform. They, as distraught as their commander, began to stamp and shout in frenzied rhythm, the climax of which could well have been the slaughter of Shepstone and all his followers. Mpande did his best to halt the maddened dance but, despite his ministers belabouring the prancing warriors with clubs and sticks, it continued towards its frightening climax. Then Shepstone rose. He slowly raised his arm and pointed over and beyond the wall of warriors. Such was his presence that his gesture had the power to pause the dancers where belabouring clubs had failed. In the moment of silence that followed, Shepstone, with the demeanour of a Zulu nobleman spoke:

> I know your purpose is to kill me. That is an easy thing to do as I come among you unarmed. But I tell you Zulus that for every drop of blood that falls to the ground, ten thousand red coated soldiers will come out of the sea yonder, from the country of which Natal is but one of its cattle kraals, and will bitterly avenge me.

The spell was broken. It would not be a repeat of the killing of Retief after all. The spear points were lowered as the warriors gazed, seemingly compelled, towards the east as though expecting a redcoat army to crest the horizon at any moment. In the calm that followed, the meeting eventually proceeded with decorum and purpose. (It must be mentioned that Shepstone's splendid act of bravado was recorded by Henry Rider Haggard, the future author of *King Solomon's Mines* and was, most probably, recounted to him by Shepstone himself some seventeen years later after the event, at the time when Haggard, twenty-two years of age and impressionable, was employed by Shepstone as a secretary.) To Cetshwayo's delight, Shepstone supported his claim to which Mpande formerly concurred. Cetshwayo would indeed be the next king of the Zulu nation – and he would not have long to wait. Thus a veil of tranquillity again obscured the violent passions of disappointed contenders for the throne. The unhurried life of the nation meandered along while traders and hunters from the colony travelled the kingdom unafraid.

In due course, on 18 October 1872, Mpande, unlike the two previous Zulu monarchs, Shaka and Dingane, who had suffered violent deaths, died peacefully bringing to a close a relatively undramatic reign of almost thirty years. His passing was not immediately made known. In keeping with Zulu custom at the time, the death of a monarch was kept secret in order that his successor could rally sufficient support to daunt any opposition.

The old king was buried with many personal items accompanying him to the grave. It was customary for household staff, and perhaps a wife, to be slain in order that they could accompany the king to the next world. Mpande, when close to death, and well aware of the fate in store for his personal body servant and friend of many years, advised him to flee and escape the fate of 'a mat' upon which the dead king would lie during his passage to the spirit world.

If Mpande's funeral at kwaNodwengu was not a moment of great pageantry, the next public event, Cetshwayo's coronation, would be the most spectacular ceremony ever to take place in Zululand. Yet, amongst his brothers and powerful chiefs, there were still those who, given the opportunity – or those who were brave enough to manipulate one – would contest Cetshwayo's succession. Well aware of his would-be rivals, Cetshwayo prudently sought the support of his colonial neighbours who would also be anxious that the power in Zululand be transferred as peacefully as possible. Thus high-ranking messengers, including John Dunn, carrying a formal request for colonial participation in the forthcoming coronation ceremony were despatched to Pietermaritzburg:

> The nation asks that Somtseu [Shepstone] may prepare himself to go to Zululand when the winter is near and establish what is wanting among the Zulu people, for he knows all about it, and occupies the position of Father to the King's children. Another embassy will be sent to fetch him when the time comes; we ask only that he may prepare.

The Zulu nation wishes to be more at one with the government of Natal; it desires to be covered with the same mantle: it wishes Somtseu to go and establish this unity by the charge which he will deliver when he arranges the family of the King, and that he shall breathe the spirit by which the nation is to be governed.

We are also commissioned to urge what has already been urged so frequently, that the government of Natal be extended so as to intervene between the Zulus and the territory of the Transvaal Republic.

Shepstone, well aware of the prestige he would acquire in the role of kingmaker set about his preparations and determined that on this occasion, unlike his visit to Mpande of 1861, he would proceed with all the pomp and circumstance that his status and the occasion demanded. He would be accompanied by an armed escort, including two pieces of artillery, drawn from Natal's mini-army of week-end soldiers. These were not red soldiers; these were colonial cousins who wore blue coats, a colour that, five years later, would save many of them from death during the rout that followed the Battle of Isandlwana: warriors would bypass fleeing colonials in preference to overtaking and killing redcoated Imperial infantry. But all that was in the future. For the present, a total of 123 men, including bandsmen, had been assembled from almost a dozen different units. The cavalcade set off for the Zulu capital on 1 August 1873:

> The different contingents mustered at Baynes Drift, and were joined the same evening by the Secretary for Native Affairs [Shepstone]. The march yesterday was intentionally a short one to guard against any contingency which might arise from the unaccustomed moving of such a large number of men and material. Most perfect good humour and discipline prevailed, and the conduct has been all that could be desired. The band of the Maritzburg Rifles performed each night to an appreciative audience. Along the road we have been met with great hospitality and civility . . .
>
> Leaving the Umhloti early, we breakfast near a coffee plantation, a stream nearby being resorted to by every one to remove traces of the dusty ride . . . We camped at Rev. Grout's mission station having so far experienced good weather . . .
>
> Tugela, 6th August,
> . . . Great difficulty experienced in crossing Sinquasi Drift. The column leaves here tomorrow and crosses into Zululand . . .

8th August,

Crossed the Tugela today and camped a mile from the drift. The men were now informed that they were under the Mutiny Act. Spare time is occupied in cooking, looking after horses and playing cricket and quoits. . . .

9th August,

On the banks of the Tugela, from which it would take us eight days to reach the royal kraal. Zulus prove very friendly, bringing eggs etc. to sell. Health of all excellent. . . .

Amatikulu, 10th August,

Reached here yesterday after a long trek of sixteen and a half miles. The principal wagon stuck in a drift until 9pm; thirty-six oxen being inspanned to pull it out. A present of fat oxen was received from Cetshwayo. The camp was pitched with military precision. . . . Church parade was held this morning, the men formed a square and a short service was read by Major Giles. The band played after the service. Our start was delayed this morning by horses straying, four or five still being missing.

St. Pauls, 12th August,

A further instalment of fat oxen in good condition was received from Cetshwayo. Natives prove very friendly, with women, girls, and children collecting to see the column go past. . . . The band played to the delight of the crowd of our visitors. . . .

White Umfolozi, 17th August,

The column encamped here on the edge of the bush country and fifteen miles from Nodwengu, the royal kraal. Owing to the death of Masiphula, the Zulu Prime Minister, it was necessary to stay here for four days. The country around is very broken and stony. Athletic sports, etc. were held, also a cricket match between the coast and up-country volunteers, which resulted in a win for the latter. . . .

25th August,

The camp was moved back to day about 400 yards for sanitary reasons. A party was formed to inspect the scene of the murder of Piet Retief and his followers. Traces of many huts were found. [The old capital of Mgungundlovu.] The judgement seat was seen, beads etc. being taken as relics. On returning to camp the welcome order was given to push on to Nodwengu tomorrow. . . . The final halting place was reached this morning and camp was pitched close to a Norwegian mission station [that of the Rev. Schroeder], in sight of three of the royal kraals. . . . On the line of march the troops were disposed as follows: An advance guard of twenty men followed by a troop, then Mr. Shepstone's wagon, followed by another troop, succeeded by two guns of the Durban Artillery. . . . The band played in the evening, exciting great curiosity. . . . After the camp had been formed, several of the leading men of the country came to offer their hearty welcome. The band, which was hidden from view by a small bush, struck up during the interview. They had never heard or seen such a thing before and, until brought nearer at their request, it was amusing to watch the struggle between their dignity and their curiosity, and to note that, what seldom occurs with a Zulu, the latter triumphed. . . .

28th August,
Cetshwayo paid his long put-off visit to Mr. Shepstone. He approached the camp at 3 pm., accompanied by about fifteen hundred followers. Major Giles had prepared the escort to receive him, the mounted volunteers with the artillery being drawn up on the right. The shaking of hands by Mr. Shepstone was the signal for firing of a salute by the Durban Artillery. Cetshwayo expressed his pleasure and thankfulness at the coming of the expedition, walked towards the camp, listened to the band, and watched the movements of the mounted volunteers, which were most creditably performed, considering the nature of the ground.

On Monday, 1st September, preparations were early commenced to carry out the coronation. A large marquee, brought for the purpose, was erected in the centre space of the military kraal, being decorated inside with shawls, blankets and other showy articles which had been brought as presents. At noon the whole of the party proceeded to the Umbambongwenga kraal, where the ceremony was to be performed . . . The brilliant uniforms of the officers formed a contrast with the costumes of the clergy and the miscellaneous dresses of the party. The mounted volunteers, artillery, and band of the Maritzburg Rifles formed up on the right of the marquee; Cetshwayo and his councillors with Mr. Shepstone and his party being on the left . . .

Thus did the diarist of the Natal Carbineers contingent record the benign progress of Shepstone's column, giving the impression of peaceful accord with their Zulu hosts. Yet, unbeknown to his escort and the many other colonial hangers-on that had mostly joined the column out of curiosity, Shepstone fumed: it was he who was to have been the kingmaker but, it was suddenly disclosed, Cetshwayo had in fact already been crowned king.

John Dunn, who by this time had resided in Zululand for close on seventeen years, will explain, but first it must be mentioned that Dunn had become a friend and confidant to Cetshwayo and in his own right a power in the land; he was also accepted in the highest social circles on both sides of the Tugela. Through his friendship with Cetshwayo he had acquired considerable wealth; so much so that he had, as a coronation gift for Cetshwayo, procured the finest carriage, drawn by four matched grey horses, that money could buy.

Although Cetshwayo wanted the visible backing of Britain in the form of Shepstone's anointing of him, most of the old chiefs and ministers of the kingdom regarded the participation of whites on such a sacred occasion as unacceptable interference. And, as Cetshwayo's succession – even on the threshold of his coronation – was far from guaranteed, as will be seen, he decided to go along with the dictates of his councillors

17. The smart carriage, drawn by white horses, that John Dunn gave to Cetshwayo to mark his coronation.

and first be crowned traditionally; then, having kept the colonials waiting, participate in Shepstone's ceremony. But let Dunn describe the events, as thousands of warriors began to gather, that transpired whilst Shepstone, affronted and infuriated, was made to wait.

The ground round about where the photographer was stationed was selected for the assembly, and as soon as we – i.e., Cetshwayo, myself, and the staff of the former – arrived on the spot, the north-eastern party [Chief Sibebu's warriors] moved in sight, and, on getting about half-a-mile from us, they commenced to form in order. From what I could make out from the remarks made to me, I gathered that our people were beginning to feel uneasy, and now believed in the rumour that Cetshwayo was to be taken by force. [It was also rumoured that Mbuyazi had not died in battle with his brother so many years before and that he was now, accompanied by Shepstone, on his way to contest Cetshwayo's succession.] I now thought it time to speak to Cetshwayo, which I did, and while I was talking, Sibebu's party made an advance. Uhamu, Umnyamana, and their party were sitting on a mound to the west, so that if mischief was meant, we were between two fires, which showed very bad generalship on the part of Cetshwayo. Usibepu's party first advanced slowly, and then came on with a rush, and some of Cetshwayo's staff began to prepare for flight. I alone told Cetshwayo that unless the advancing party was stopped, there would be a fight. I had nothing in my hand, by the way, but my hunting-crop. From the expression on Cetshwayo's face when he answered me, I could see that he had never considered the danger. Looking round to the hill on the west of us, I could see that the party with Uhamu had also taken alarm. I could now see that Cetshwayo began to take a more serious view of the situation. He gave me quiet orders for our party to arm themselves, as we had come on to the ground unarmed – at least Cetshwayo's followers had, but I had 200 of my hunters with me. These were always in the habit of carrying their guns and ammunition with them, so that I, with them, would make a stand. Fortunately, on the arrival of Cetshwayo's messengers, the leaders of Usibepu's party had influence enough to stop the advance, or else there certainly would have been great slaughter. This fact I found out long afterwards. As soon as I saw the check in Usibepu's party, I left Cetshwayo, who I could see did not know exactly how to act, and passing through my men to give them confidence – telling them, however, to prepare for the worst – and after telling one of my men who I knew to be a bad shot, that, in the event of a scrimmage, I would take

his gun, I walked quietly up to where Umnyamana was sitting. [Dunn
then assured Mnyamana kaNgqengelele that the arming of his men
was only a precaution and that neither he nor the king had anything
to fear. Dunn remained with Mnyamana and Hamu until Cetshwayo
came along.] He came up to where I was, and the whole of the parties
came up and formed a great circle. As each lot came up it fired blank
charges, but they fired so close to one another in some instances that
there was a serious danger of being knocked over by the powder. In fact,
Sedcweledcwele, one of the principal men on our side and Colonel of
the Ngobamakosi Regiment, had a charge so closely fired behind him
that the paper and wadding from the gun cut a hole in his cows tails
which comprised a principal part of his dress, and also burnt a hole in his
shoulder. If the man who had fired the shot had had his gun loaded with
a heavy charge of powder the affair might have proved fatal. Everything,
however, passed off quietly, and I firmly believe that it was owing to my
advising Cetshwayo to send messengers to check Usibepu's party in their
advance that a general massacre was avoided.

Writing thirteen years later Dunn makes light of Cetshwayo keeping
Shepstone waiting. Dunn records that Cetshwayo, having been
crowned by Masipula, organised a massive hunt in which the whole
army participated, the spoils of the chase providing the nation – most
of whom, men, women and children, were present – with sustenance
for many days to come. Whether Shepstone arrived or not seemed to
be of little importance. Not at all flattering to the would-be colonial
King Maker. Dunn who kept Cetshwayo company recorded: 'All this
time we were awaiting the arrival of Mr. Shepstone, and after the lapse
of three days without any news of him, it was decided to move on
to the vicinity of Nodwengo Kraal [a military barracks close to the
royal residence at Ondini] . . . At last it was announced that Somseu
[Shepstone] had crossed the Tugela . . .'
Dunn's narrative is entirely at odds with the colonial version of
events that makes clear Cetshwayo would have undoubtedly known
of Shepstone's whereabouts and progress from the moment he set out
from Durban. One of Shepstone's week-end soldiers, Trooper Blamey,
exaggerating the dangers to give even more spice to a unique adventure,
takes up the tale. But, before starting on Blamey's account, we must
attend to Dunn once again as he records the opening scene of the

probable murder of none other than Masipula, the Prime Minister, who, but days earlier had crowned Cetshwayo king. Masipula likely suffered a similar fate to that of previous Zulu dignitaries whose deaths, as we have seen, tended to follow fast on the ascension of a new king. In Masipula's case there was added cause why Cetshwayo's should seek his death: whilst Prime Minister to Mpande, he had frequently snubbed Cetshwayo in public and, even more to his peril, had made it known that he favoured both Mbulazi and Mthongu in preference to Cetshwayo. However, Masipula's death would not be a hideous public affair as had been the death of Mpande's minister that Delegorgue had witnessed thirty-five years earlier. Dunn was most discreet in recording what transpired, leaving the reader to draw his own conclusions:

> . . . On breaking up of the meeting Masipula called on me as he was passing to his kraal where he resided. After sitting with me for some time in my tent, he got up to leave, and turning to me, said, 'Good-bye, child of Mr. Dunn, I have finished my part and am now going to lie down – I am now going to sleep – look after your own affairs – I have no more a voice in matters' – meaning that he wished to retire from public life, as Umpande [*sic*], to whom he had been chief Induna, was dead, and; so he now wished to end his days in peace. The poor old fellow little thought, when he thus spoke, that his end was so near – that the words he then said to me were among his last and that the sleep he wished for was to be everlasting, for that same evening, as soon as he got to the Umlambongwenya kraal, where he was staying, on entering his hut, he was suddenly taken ill, and died before morning. There was, of course, much consternation amongst the people, and, as usual, many rumours afloat, one of which was, that having displeased the King, something had been put into his beer.

It seems likely that it had. The girls who had prepared his beer when he had drunk in the presence of his new king, called out 'Farewell Father' and had laughed as he bid the assembly 'Good night'.

Trooper Blamey continues:

> . . . Day after day we marched on in the Zulu country to where Cetshwayo was to be crowned. Cetshwayo had his suspicions that we were bringing Umblas [Mbuyazi] to crown him in his stead, almost every day Zulu spies would come to the camp and follow along to see if Umblas were

with us. When we got to Umtonganeni [Mtonjaneni], Cetshwayo sent word to say that we were not to cross any further for a few days as his people were mourning the death of their Prime Minister, and also sent word to say he wished to be crowned at the Upata where Dingane slaughtered the Dutch in former years. Mr. Shepstone was very much annoyed at this message, and, knowing what treachery this savage nation was capable of, had his suspicions aroused that a death trap was being planned for our destruction. Well, here we had to stay for about two weeks, messages going backwards and forwards from Cetshwayo and Mr. Shepstone every day, and at night the Zulu spies were continually around our camp. Our kaffir servants got so nervous at what was going on that they used to clear out of our camp after dark and sleep a few miles away in the grass fearing we should be attacked. One evening Mr. Shepstone gave orders to us all to be on the alert and prepare for an attack, each man to have his gun and revolver loaded by his side all night. Not many of us closed our eyes and we were thankful to see the next sunrise, escaped so far from the cold assegai going though our bodies. It was about the next night that I was sent out on horse guard with another trooper, all the horses were feeding loose a few hundred yards away from camp, it was a bright moonlit night and after walking round the horses for some time my chum and I sat down and began talking about our dear home we had left far away behind. At once our conversation was disturbed by a low whistle and a little further away another whistle, at last a third whistle we could hear in the distance. My chum thought it was reed bucks. 'You stupid!' I said. 'They are Zulu spies.' A few minutes later the different whistles were repeated, my chum was now convinced danger was close to us. I said, 'Look here, if the camp is attacked, I shall catch two of the fastest horses in the troop and make for Natal for all I am worth, it won't be any use our going to the camp; they will all be butchered by the time we get there.' We were both trembling and whispering in low tones to each other for fear of being heard by these savages. He said, 'I will follow your example if the attack comes.' Then he whispered, 'Oh my father said it was not safe for Mr. Shepstone to take only a few men like ourselves into the heart of a savage nation.' This tickled my feelings and I laid back in fits of laughter. Fortunately no attack came and after a few days of long waiting it was arranged that we should march on towards Cetshwayo's kraal at Mathlahatini. We went until about two miles off the Uniyambogweni Kraal (where Cetshwayo and his army lived). We camped for about three or four days whilst the coronation was being arranged.

18. Men of Shepstone's escort, carbineers and gunners, relax in camp close to the Umbambongwenga kraal where the coronation ceremony was performed. (*Local History Museum, Durban*)

At last, a month after leaving Natal, Shepstone was about to take centre stage. He and his retinue of colonial dignitaries were duly received by Cetshwayo who was escorted by his royal brothers, ministers, regimental commanders and hundreds of warriors. The *indaba* that was about to commence, which would be conducted in the Zulu tongue and much illustrated with metaphors, would be an interminable colloquy to those who did not speak the language. Therefore, Shepstone, in order to avoid a fidgeting and distracting colonial audience, wisely dismissed most of his followers. Later he officially described the proceeding in the *Government Blue Books*:

Cetshwayo received us cordially as before: those who, from not understanding the language or other reason did not wish to stay through the long interview before us, were, by Cetshwayo's orders, shown whatever there was to be seen of the Royal Family and apartments and returned to camp. Major Durnford and my son, with the Natal native indunas, sat down with me to an interview with Cetshwayo and the counsellors, that

lasted for five hours without intermission. It was of the most interesting
and earnest kind, and was conducted with great ability and frankness by
Cetshwayo . . . Had it not been for the straightforward manner in which
Cetshwayo insisted upon their getting direct to the point, it would have
been impossible to have got through the serious subjects we were bound
to decide in the time we did. For instance, they had been evading an
important point, and fencing for some time, when Cetshwayo said,
'Silence, all of you! Do you hear the wind?' – 'Yes', they replied. 'What
does it say?' – 'We cannot discover that it says anything!' 'That is exactly
what you have been doing. Don't you see what my father [Shepstone]
means? Why do you not say so-and so?', hitting the point exactly. He
treated me with the most marked respect, and always addressed and
spoke of me as his father.

The five-hour session was occupied by Shepstone pushing the
conditions – that he would later would refer to as 'laws' – that
Cetshwayo would be obliged to accept if he were to have British
backing. Subsequently, five years later when Britain's representatives
were searching to find the excuses to justify the invasion of Zululand,
Cetshwayo's disregard of these 'laws' together with a couple of other
seized-upon incidents, would be enough to send thousands of red
soldiers marching across the Tugela River and into Zululand.

Shepstone goes on to describe the conclusion of the marathon
indaba:

> It was late before our conference ended, and on taking leave of Cetshwayo
> I impressed upon him the absolute necessity for his avoiding bloodshed
> the next day, which was to be devoted to the old but dangerous custom of
> general recrimination. I cautioned him that it afforded an opportunity for
> every man who hated his neighbour to injure him, and probably cause the
> loss of life by reckless and false accusations. He promised that he would
> do all he could. He said it was difficult to restrain Zulus on such occasions.
> The next morning I sent a message to him to the same effect. I informed
> him that my orders from my government were imperative: that I could not
> consent to become a witness to the shedding of blood, and if I found that
> my caution was being unheeded, we should at once all leave the country.

If Shepstone was doing his best to prevent bloodshed and avoid any
confrontation that could lead to a repetition of Piet Retief's fate – of

which his men were constantly reminding one another – it was his very escort who mischievously egged on the possibility of a set-to. Trooper Blamey takes up the tale:

> The afternoon before the coronation Cetshwayo and all his headmen came over to the camp to us. Dabula Manzie [Dabulamanzi kaMpande, a royal half-brother and in the war to come a famous and fiery general], one of the best rifle-shots in the Zulu army, challenged any of us to hit a bottle 100 yards off. We said – pointing to one of our little drummer boys who was one of our best shots – 'If you can beat this child in shooting, then talk to us men.' A bottle was placed on an ant heap, Dabula Manzie had first shot and missed, our little boy, out with the rifle, and put the bullet just under the bottle. We said, 'Don't talk to us men after this about your shooting'. After staying for about two hours, Cetshwayo and all his followers went back to their kraal. That night we had a grand display of fire works, rockets going sky-high and breaking up into star-shaped things. – This was all done to show the Zulu people what wonders we had with us.

19. Prince Dabulamanzi kaMpande, Zulu General with escort. It was he who led the attack on Rorke's Drift.

But for all their bluster, the colonial soldiers were apprehensive and full of the jitters. Blamey again:

Next morning we had an early breakfast, all excitement, getting to fall in to march over to the kraal for the coronation. 9 am. the bugle sounded, each one saddled up and fell into line. A long speech was made to us by Major Giles, sitting on his horse in front of us. 'My men', he said, 'load your rifles and revolvers now.' After this was done, he said, 'Every man of you must be on the alert whilst we are over at the coronation, and if we are attacked, fire at the Zulus for all you are worth, and die like true Britons, shoulder to shoulder.' Then the word to march came and we followed in the rear of Mr. Shepstone: we had two cannon with us, belonging to the Durban Artillery, under the command of Mr. Escombe, one of the finest and bravest of men in the whole column. We soon got over to the kraal and found ourselves surrounded by thousands of Zulus. Mr. Shepstone kept close to Cetshwayo's side all the time we were there (Cetshwayo was sitting in an armchair which Mr. Shepstone had brought with us), and after a long speech to the Zulu nation he put a scarlet velvet cap on Cetshwayo, and said: 'I now crown you King with this cap and I am sent here to crown you King by our great mother, the Queen of England.'

That is Trooper Blamey's account of the event – Shepstone's is rather different:

On Monday, 1st September, preparations were early commenced to carry out the installation. Mr. Consul Cato, assisted by Messrs. C. and G. Shepstone, went over and pitched a large marquee, brought for the occasion, in the centre space of the military kraal. They decorated it inside with the shawls, blankets, and other showy articles which had been brought as presents. In the middle of one side stood a table covered with drapery, with a mirror, in front of which had been placed the headdress; the design was taken from the Zulu war headdress, suggested by Mr. Dunn, after consultation, I believe, with the Zulus, improved upon by the master tailor of the 75th Regiment, and dignified with Zulu trappings of war subdued to a peaceful purpose. There also stood his Chair of State, with the scarlet and gold mantle upon it so that the marquee presented a very tasteful appearance.

Cetshwayo co-operated with enthusiasm and was keen to pursue Shepstone's idea that at some time during the ceremony, Shepstone would 'take possession' of Cetshwayo and in a twinkling transform him from an immature prince to a mighty monarch: 'I must take him from their sight a minor and present him to them a man; I must take him as a prince and restore him to them a king.' It would have to be a sort of 'top of the bill' conjuring trick performed in front of their very eyes. But, as a precaution, just in case of a mishap, Shepstone deemed it wise not to include the appearance of all the Zulu regiments at the climax of the royal revelation. Shepstone continues:

> Major Giles organised the order of procession, in which we entered the lower gate with the band playing. I was accompanied by the officers and gentlemen already named, and others who were desirous of seeing what took place. The brilliant uniforms of the officers formed a contrast with the costume of the clergy and the miscellaneous dresses of some of my companions, and added much to the appearance of the procession. The artillery, the mounted volunteers, and the band of the Maritzburg Rifles formed on the right of the marquee, my natives on the left, Cetshwayo with his counsellors and my party formed a group in front. The Zulu people described three quarters of a circle about fifty yards off, and may be estimated at from 8,000 to 10,000, mostly young men. These latter were forced into their position not by words of command so much as by the free use of sticks by their officers; it seemed to be many blows first and then a word; and some of them appeared to be severely hurt. . . . When the order desired was established, Cetshwayo wished to examine the guns. Captain Escombe explained the loading to him and he was surprised at the facility with which an open cylinder could be closed for firing, but seemed disappointed that the guns were not larger. On returning to our seats I stood and explained in the native language the nature and importance of the ceremony I had come to perform, the condescension and good will of the Government of Natal, shown by allowing me to come, and by sending such a complimentary escort to accompany me; and after adding such introductory remarks as appeared necessary, I proceeded to the business in hand. I thought it would be best that all the points I wished to establish and impress should be presented in the shape of questions and that I should require audible assent to each to be given by all the brothers of Cetshwayo, and the rulers and counsellors of the country who formed my audience, for the common people were too far off to hear me speak.

Shepstone had decided that he would read from a paper that he had prepared, all the points to which he would require the 'audible and hearty assent' of his audience. That having been done, the paper from which he had read would be kept as written evidence of the 'laws' to which Cetshwayo and the Zulu people had agreed. Shepstone, in theatrical mode and dressed to suit the occasion in a gold-braided uniform with cocked hat, then delivered his proclamation:

> Have not I entered Zululand at the request of the Zulu Nation to install their king? Have not I been requested to come because I was chief witness to his nomination by his father at Nodwengu?
>
> Is not Cetshwayo the son that was then nominated, and is not he who the Zulus now wish me to install?
>
> So say you all?

Shepstone received the hearty response that he had hoped for and in a most profound and imperial manner continued to describe the rest of the conditions with which he and his government expected the Zulu nation to comply: that the life of any man or woman, high or low, be vested in the king on behalf of the nation; that for any man to take the life of another, without the king's consent, would be as to take that which belonged to the nation; that any man be allowed to answer before the king any charge that may be brought against him and that he be not condemned before having the opportunity to do so; that the Zulu people agree that the punishment of death for every crime destroys a nation. Having got a rousing response, Shepstone demanded of the gathering whether or not he stood in the place of the king's father and, having got his answer he required, Shepstone proclaimed that the indiscriminate shedding of blood must cease; that no Zulu be condemned without trial; that no Zulu life be taken until a trial had been conducted and right of appeal exercised; and lastly that the death penalty for minor crimes be substituted for the compensation of property.

Heralds then proclaimed the 'laws' to the assembled throng while Shepstone led Cetshwayo into the marquee where the transformation was to take place, the doorway being guarded by two armed gunners of the Durban Volunteer Artillery. Shepstone immediately set about fulfilling the masquerade:

Cetshwayo was robed in the scarlet mantle, the headdress/crown was placed upon his head and, the transformation to King complete, Shepstone took him forth to be presented to his people.

Shepstone continued: 'In the meanwhile, a carpet, presented to him by Captain Macleod and Mr. Fairlie, had been spread, the chair of State we had brought him placed upon it facing the people, and another of less pretentious character, but so disguised as to look suited to the occasion, was put alongside for me.' Some of warriors in the front row, entering into the spirit of the charade, pretended amazement at the sight of their new king, uttering exclamations of wonder, pretending to doubt his identity. Shepstone recalled with satisfaction: 'Thus he, who a few moments before had been but a minor and a prince, had now become a man and king.' A signal was given and the Durban Volunteer Artillery fired a seventeen-gun salute with great precision; the colonial soldiers presented arms and the band of the Maritzburg Rifles struck up a rousing tune. But there was still drama to come.

The vast throng of warriors, not to be outdone by the colonials, now presented their own traditional salute: raising their shields high, they struck at them with sticks and clubs, as though they were beating a thousand drums, setting forth a shattering explosion of noise.

20. Ten thousand warriors were present at Cetshwayo's coronation but only sticks were permitted to be carried, assegais being strictly forbidden. (*KZN Archives, Pietermaritzburg*)

It caught the troopers by surprise. Having earlier dismounted, they had left their horses unattended except for one man who was quite unable to control the stampede that followed the bedlam of the beaten shields. In their terror the flying horses, falling over one another in their haste, galloped off in all directions, some heading directly at the royal party. As Shepstone later remarked: 'This belonged to a class of accident that sometimes produces disasters, and for the moment one seemed likely to happen.' However, the horses were soon brought under control and the new king, quick to appreciate the reasons for the stampede, remarked: 'They had left their horses and they stampeded at the noise of the shields.' Shepstone later wrote: 'The quickness with which the accident was remedied soon changed the aspects of affairs, and turned adverse criticism into admiration at the smartness with which the mischief had been stopped.' (Well done, Trooper Blamey.)

The ceremony now complete, the colonials prepared to move off but not before a photograph of the assembly was taken. Yet, the fear of causing an upset still ran high and when the famous artist and explorer, Thomas Baines, was requested by the photographer, J. W. Buchanan of Durban, to duck his head under the black cloth to check the camera angle, Baines refused fearing that such action might be taken as a form of wizardry aimed against the king. However, with or without Baines' assistance, a picture was taken but, unfortunately during the moments of exposure, the king moved his head creating the illusion that he possessed two faces; a sort-of unintentional affirmation of his metamorphosis from prince to monarch.

The following day, Shepstone and his column, taking with them a present of elephant ivory and the good wishes of the king, headed back towards the Tugela, most of the contingent confident that peace and goodwill had been established between the kingdom and colony. Yet, within little more than five years, many who had attended the coronation, both Zulu and colonial, would perish on the bloody battlefields of the Anglo-Zulu War, a war that would destroy forever the old order of the Zulu kingdom.

However, allow Trooper Blamey, as rascally as ever, to have the last word on the coronation as he describes how he and his comrades, unabashedly, pillaged both black and white during their journey home:

The first night we slept at a Norwegian mission station, these white Norwegian women couldn't talk English, so I had to interpret for Mr. Escombe in Zulu to them and put in a few words on my own account. I told them we were very hungry and that this great man, (Mr. Escombe), was one of our Queen's representatives, and that it would go well with them if not only ourselves, but our horses, were fed. This put the fear of death into them, and they hustled about and gave us all they had. Next morning we saddled up, and after thanking them for their hospitality, we rode on . . . Towards midday both ourselves and our horses felt very hungry, and in the distance in front we spied a large Zulu kraal. Mr. Escombe asked if it would be possible to buy some food for ourselves and horses. My reply was, 'No money will buy us food, but if you will only do what I may suggest, we may get well fed. Do this when we get near the kraal. I will be your herald and ride on to the kraal, shouting your praises, each man to fall in single file behind you.' This plan being arranged, I rode off to the kraal, full gallop, shouting like a lunatic. Out all the women and men came, looking terrified, asking me who are these people that are coming? I replied, 'Its our great chief, make ready at once for him and his followers, his animals are hungry also.' Not another word. Off into their huts they went, kaffir beer and baskets of mealies were soon brought out. Presently our great man arrived, looking very dignified, all of his followers paying great respect. I crouched down at his approach, and took his horse and presented him with all this food; after we and our animals had had a good fill, we saddled up and off we went after thanking them for their food.

But retribution was on its way for Blamey. That evening the weather changed and, without any shelter, Blamey and his companions spent a wretched night huddled in the pouring rain.

Chapter 10

Defeat and Disgrace

The amaHlubi were one of the many clans and tribes that Shaka had scattered in the formation of the Zulu kingdom. They were an ancient people speaking their own dialect and with a hairstyle quite unlike that of the Zulu but similar to that of the Masai of East Africa. Their original home had been the cattle country surrounding the headwaters of the White and Black Mfolozi Rivers but, under their young chief, Langalibalele, they had been gradually driven south-west into the foothills of the Drakensberg Mountains where, tucked away amongst the cliffs and valleys, they hoped to find sanctuary. This location of the tribe also suited the Natal government: the white settlers closest to the mountains were subject to frequent Bushmen cattle raids made in retaliation of the white man's hunting of the eland, the provider of all the Bushman's needs from food to an object of worship. The government therefore saw the amaHlubi as a convenient barrier between the settlers and the raiders.

The Hlubi slowly prospered despite growing demands made by the government for taxes: first an annual tax for every standing hut; then a tax of so much per head of cattle, but due to the fear of an armed confrontation the proposal was dropped. Next the government, in the person of Sir Theophilus Shepstone, announced a tax on every new marriage which not only caused a wave of resentment but also a stampede to the altar before the law came into effect. Inevitably, the young men, angry at the continual demands on their tribe, and their own pockets, caused them to seek employment that would give them the highest remuneration, which usually meant the Kimberley diamond mines where a firearm would also form part of their wages.

Despite several other confrontations over the years such as the occasion when Langalibalele refused permission for members of the tribe to take up employment with a Ladysmith farmer, and numerous incidents of late payment of taxes, the Hlubi and the government had not come to blows. Nevertheless, there had always been a hint of violence close to the surface in all the tribe's dealings with authority. By the early 1870s the Hlubi numbered 10,000 and, by encroaching on state-owned land, they had extended their area of occupation by many square miles. There was, therefore, a growing feeling of apprehension amongst the whites that with Langalibalele and his associated clans to the south, and the Zulu kingdom to the north, they were in a precarious position.

There was a particular animosity between Langalibalele and the Estcourt magistrate, John MacFarlane, who, in 1873, having been instructed to evoke an existing law that required all natives to licence their firearms, decided to apply the regulation only to the Hlubi tribe. The ensuing instruction, which was delivered to Langalibalele, was a difficult one to implement: not only was it most unlikely that Langalibalele would have known who amongst his followers did or did not possess a gun, it was even more unlikely that those who did would ever consent to their weapons being handed over to a white magistrate – the belief being that if they were, they would never get them back.

Langalibalele journeyed to Estcourt to discuss the problem with MacFarlane but found him absent; instead his assistant interviewed Langalibalele and ended up by abusing him. Eventually the chief returned home to await the outcome of his unfortunate visit; and a summons to Pietermaritzburg, the seat of Shepstone's authority, was not long in coming: a far more serious matter for the Hlubi who believed it meant death. On two occasions over the last decades, chiefs of other clans, who had been summoned to Pietermaritzburg in person – the ultimate indignity – had then suffered the dispersal of their clan by government armed forces. Likewise, it was remembered when, years earlier, Langalibalele's elder brother had been summoned to Dingane's presence and he, like so many others, had ended up on the Hill of Execution. Consequently, any summons to appear before an overlord, black or white, was regarded with distrust and fear. Thus the issue of appearing in person before Shepstone, and

Langalibalele's refusal to do so, became more a bone of contention than the registration of the Hlubi firearms.

In July, to further aggravate the situation, it was reported that red soldiers had arrived at Estcourt. The Hlubi immediately assumed their purpose was to arrest Langalibalele and attack the tribe. But their fears were unfounded; the men were the colonial blue-coated cousins of the red soldiers, most likely training for the part they were about to play as Shepstone's escort to Cetshwayo's coronation which, as we have seen earlier, was imminent.

By now Langalibalele, at close on sixty, could be considered very much an elder – certainly not 'fine-looking' as he had been described thirty years previously. No longer attired in the barbaric splendour of tribal regalia but in cast-off European clothing, he appeared as a rather ugly and scruffy old man with little to recommend his physical appearance.

Due to an old knee injury, a handicap that both MacFarlane and Shepstone were aware of, he most likely tottered along with the aid of a stick. The upshot was his elders advised against the journey to Pietermaritzburg and, to placate the government, Langalibalele began

21. Fort Durnford, near Estcourt, was designed by Major Durnford and constructed prior to the Langalibalele incident. Subsequently, it became the headquarters of the Natal Mounted Police. It is now a museum. (*KZN Archives, Pietermaritzburg*)

to impose his own taxes in preparation for the stiff fine that would undoubtedly be imposed. But Shepstone, having returned at last from the Zulu king's enthronement, would not have it: Langalibalele must appear before him as ordered. Once again a summons was sent to the Hlubi chief and it was also made clear that it was not a matter that could be settled by the payment of a fine no matter how impressive and solicitous. To ensure Langalibalele understood the seriousness of his position should he resist further, an ultimatum was dispatched. The messenger selected to deliver the communication, one Mahoija, was on Sir Benjamin Pine's staff and as such was seen by Shepstone not only as a direct representative of the Lieutenant-Governor but also of Queen Victoria herself. However, Mahoija's status was ignored and he was ridiculed, threatened and finally, so he maintained, stripped naked and sent packing.

There were other black marks to add to Langalibalele's insubordinate score board: that he and his tribe were poised to quit Natal, taking all their cattle with them into Basutoland, thus escaping the government's retribution, was one. Much more seriously, rumours held him to be in collusion with King Cetshwayo in evoking all the clans and tribes in a general uprising. The white settlers, outnumbered eighteen to one, were understandably highly nervous. There was little in the way of military strength to back up Sir Benjamin's threats. The only imperial troops were a company of the 75th (Stirlingshire) Regiment, a section of artillery with two 6-pounder guns which, in view of the terrain in which they would have to operate, would have been best left back at the barracks. For the rest they were all settler volunteer units: the Richmond Rifles, the Weenen Yeomanry, two troops of the Carbineers – those of Karkloof and Pietermaritzburg (referred hereafter as the Natal Carbineers) under the command of Captain Charles Barter – and hastily raised levies of – it was hoped – loyal natives. Whatever the odds, Langalibalele must be brought back and pay the consequences for – as Shepstone and Governor Pine saw it – rebellion.

So the drums began to roll and a plan contrived to catch the fleeing tribe in a pincer movement that would close, blocking its escape, at the top of the Bushmen's River Pass at a height of 9,500 feet. But the colonial authorities had no idea whatsoever of the character of the country, its extent or the terrain. The width of the pincer, within which

22. The Karkloof Troop of the Natal Carbineers. Capt. Barter, with the white beard, is seated centre middle row. (*KZN Archives, Pietermaritzburg*)

the troops would be expected to deploy, was fifty miles as the crow flies. It would also be found that terrain advised as being a flat plateau would be little short of alpine, and the pass to the summit, up which the right arm of the pincer had been order to advance, did not exist at all.

While the outlying farmers and their families hastened to either the semi-safety of Estcourt or Pietermaritzburg, the military forces made for Fort Nottingham, where there was a genial atmosphere of military camaraderie, with both Sir Benjamin Pine and Sir Theophilus Shepstone in campaign attire, ready to assume overall command from Lieutenant Colonel Thomas Milles, of the 75th Regiment, the senior imperial officer present.

Spies had brought intelligence that the amaHlubi were already on the move up Bushman's River Pass into Basutoland where, technically, Sir Benjamin Pine's pursuit could not be followed without the approval of the British governor-general in Cape Town. Speed then was of the essence.

The Carbineers, with the rest of the troops, had marched out of Pietermaritzburg with bands playing but by the time the cavalry men had ridden the thirty miles to Fort Nottingham in inclement weather, had drawn rations and forty rounds of ammunition, they were ready for bed. Yet, just as the troopers (several of whom had recently formed part of Shepstone's escort to Cetshwayo's coronation) were pulling off their boots, the bugle sounded the order 'Saddle up' and the men all fell in and were marched off to their horses.

By leaving Fort Nottingham at 8.30 p.m. it was anticipated that by 8.30 a.m. the following morning, and with the assistance of the right pincer, they would be in a position at the top of Bushman's River Pass to hold the amaHlubi at bay and force them back down the pass into the arms of the Natal authorities.

However, to consider such a feat possible was optimistic ignorance: a night march in complete darkness over wholly unknown country, treacherous terrain, with intermittent rain, to find a pass of which none knew the location, was a recipe for the disaster that would surely come about.

Hardly had the Carbineers, seventy-eight in number, got settled in their saddles then command of their column was taken over by an aloof imperial redcoat officer by the name of Major Anthony Durnford of the Royal Engineers, newly arrived in the colony. Why Milles should have taken the command away from Barter at the last moment is a mystery. Perhaps Durnford persuaded him to do so for although Durnford had been in the army for twenty-five years, he was yet to have seen action, and perhaps he saw this as an opportunity to hear shots fired in anger. Not understandably Barter, who was a man of importance in the Colony, he having at various times been a newspaper editor, a member of the legislative assembly, author, magistrate and, of course, commanding officer of the Natal Carbineers, would have been indignant, to say the least. Both men, Durnford and Barter, in appearance, could only be described as distinguished for even in that age of grossly long and luxuriant facial hair being fashionable, they would have drawn attention: Durnford by a moustache that reached his shoulders and Barter by a snow-white Santa Claus beard.

Durnford was accompanied by one of Shepstone's interpreters, Elijah Kambule and about fifteen Basutu guides of the baTlokwa tribe led by Chief Hlubi who, despite his name, was not of the amaHlubi; all were mounted and armed and, so it would seem, first and foremost gave their loyalty to Durnford. Orders had been given that each man was to carry his own personal rations of boiled beef, biscuits, rum and extra ammunition but these instructions had either been misunderstood or ignored by the Carbineers. Instead the provisions had been loaded onto pack horses led escorted by four troopers.

The dispirited command set off on time as planned, disappearing into the drizzle and darkness, their departure having a mysterious and secretive air about it for none, except Barter, knew the name of their new commander nor their intended destination.

After marching for about three hours it was discovered that the pack horses and escort were missing. A halt was called and the men allowed to lie down for a while whilst the Basutos tracked back only to return some time later unsuccessful: the rations and ammunition were lost and would not be seen again until the column returned to Fort Nottingham. Shortly after midnight the men were ordered to 'mount up' and then 'Ball cartridge load; aim and fire slow', arousing some excitement. Thus presuming the enemy to be near at hand they once again moved off into the darkness.

Captain Barter recorded his impressions of the ride that followed:

Travelling through the night, we emerged upon the said plateau and for some time rode over a fine grass country. Suddenly, however, turning to the right we found ourselves facing a stupendous mountain, its sides scarred and scoured with water furrows, and discovered that this obstacle lay between us and our destination. All this time our Commanding Officer pressed on, eager to fulfil his instructions . . . After one or two minor inequalities of ground, we came to the edge of an abrupt descent of slippery grass, very steep and long, so trying to the necessarily dismounted men that a considerable number were thoroughly knocked up before they reached the bottom . . . We commenced the ascent of a precipitous hill, which, in any other spot, would be a mountain. Here several of the Natal Carbineers succumbed, of whom three made their way back.

All the following day they rode without interruption, except for brief halts, until the column was into its second night in the saddle, with the moon, despite intermittent cloud cover, bright enough to show the way. With no sign of the pack horses, the Carbineers had not eaten for almost forty-eight hours until Durnford ordered his baTlokwas to share their rations which they had kept tied to their saddles as ordered.

Nevertheless, morale was high even when it was realised the 4,000-foot wall that towered above them would somehow have to be scaled.

Durnford's orders had been to reach the summit by way of the Giant's Castle Pass, but the Batlokwas had mistakenly veered off six miles to the south. They were now leading the column into the entrance of the Hlatimba Pass that soared, impossibly steep, into the sky. Barter described the climb:

> The scene before us was savage in the extreme. Down the bare side of the mountain hung ribbons of water, showing the spot to be the very birth place and nursery of the rivers; above, huge krantzes [gorges] crowned, while the masses of unburnt dry grass, hanging like a vast curtain, made a sombre and malignant aspect to the scene. How we slipped and struggled, fell feet up, and struggled again, or lay panting on the ground, despairing of accomplishing the task.

Trooper Henry Bucknall also remembered the climb:

> . . . Everyone was too tired to give more than a passing glance at the stupendous masses of projecting rock above us, like a rugged wall, half a mile high; we would scramble up twenty or thirty yards, then sit down, scramble another twenty, and sit down again, leading our horses, which made it much more tiring than it would have been without them . . .

The night would not be without accident: Major Durnford, perhaps leading the way with too much enthusiasm on his little grey horse, Chieftain, took a tumble, man and horse bouncing down the side of the mountain, where a rocky projection stopped their fall into the abyss below. Trooper Robert Erskine was, at a considerable risk to himself, the first to reach Durnford who was badly injured: a dislocated shoulder, broken ribs and head injuries. Chieftain, however, had miraculously escaped unharmed.

It would not be unfair to say that at this point the column had become a shambles: it was almost a day late for its rendezvous with the right pincer, its commander was seriously injured and miles from any medical assistance, its second-in-command, Captain Barter, being considerably older than anyone else, was far behind; it was spread out for over a mile or more and it was more or less lost.

During the course of the night Trooper Erskine climbed down to Durnford on several occasions, taking him rum and blankets and with the assistance of other troopers managed to reset Durnford's shoulder.

Trooper Bucknall again describes the proceedings:

> ... Our gallant Major fainted at the bottom of the steep part, and Trooper Erskine stayed behind with him. I will give you my own feelings because I knew what they were, and all were very much alike. I was crawling on about ten yards at a time, with heart palpitating and every nerve in my body, arms and legs aching like rheumatism, bathed in perspiration, and a cutting cold wind blowing ...

By about 2.30 a.m. on Tuesday, and in bright moonlight, in ones and twos, the Carbineers began to arrive at the top of the Hlatimba Pass. Durnford, who proved himself to be a man of grit and iron will, had himself placed in a blanket and hauled to the top where he fainted from the pain. Barter, with the assistance and encouragement of younger men, also made the summit. All were ravenously hungry but, in the greater need for sleep, hunger was forgotten. As each man reached the summit he threw himself down and, without thought for a sentry to stand guard, tried to sleep; but the bitter cold only permitted the briefest slumber.

The Carbineers had started from Fort Nottingham, numbering fifty-seven all ranks. They now totalled only thirty-five excluding Lieutenant Parkinson and a couple of troopers who had been detailed off to await stragglers and form a rear guard; the mounted Batlokwas had all kept up with the column. After reaching the summit, Durnford had lain unconscious for half an hour then, at about 3 a.m., he raised himself and calling for Elijah Kambule, the interpreter, to bring Chieftain, announced he was ready to proceed. With assistance, and with his arm in a sling, he was lifted into the saddle. Finally the column moved off, riding over boggy ground strewn with stones but good enough for a canter in places, lifting morale.

At 5 a.m. the sun neared the eastern horizon, turning the landscape, 4,000 feet below, into strangely shaped silhouettes resembling a raging sea and, despite their hardships, all were in awe of the magnificence of the scenery it was their privilege to witness.

As the sun rose higher, and having ridden some ten miles south from the Hlatimba Pass, it was possible to see considerable activity in the distance: men and cattle emerging from another pass while mounted men watched nearby. Urging their horses forward over the rugged terrain, the column finally arrived at the head of the pass frightening the herdsmen and the cattle alike. Although a day late – through no fault of their own – the first impression was Langalibalele would soon be their prisoner. Perhaps it was this thought that led to an upsurge in confidence that would have disastrous consequences. Durnford ordered the men to dismount, release the horses to graze, to form a cordon across the pass and to drive both warriors and cattle back down into Natal.

All in the column were still ravenously hungry and here before them was beef on the hoof: it was suggested they should slaughter one of the cattle. It was then that Durnford revealed he had strict orders from the Lieutenant-Governor that on no account must the column fire the first shot and for that reason the beast he proposed to be the victim could not be shot. Furthermore, he said, he would also pay for it so that its killing would not appear to the amaHlubi as an act of aggression, but with no other option, its slaying would have to be done by a spear thrust delivered by one of the baTlokwas. A beast was selected but the killing of it proved to be more difficult than anticipated: it got away bellowing and wounded. So the baTlokwas selected another which proved to be as difficult to kill as the first; and it was not until four or five of the Hlubi cattle had been wounded did they succeed in killing one. It is not difficult to imagine the fury with which the Hlubi warriors watched this fiasco. Worse still, Durnford, who had wanted to pay compensation was, with tragic consequences, dissuaded by Barter from doing so.

While the Carbineers tried to stomach raw meat, the highly-incensed and aggressive young warriors began to push their way through the cordon, jeering, jostling, waving weaponry in the faces of the Carbineers and asking when the real soldiers would arrive.

With orders not to fire, and the Hlubi warriors increasing in number with every moment that passed, the Carbineers were in an impossible position. The baTlokwa were also strictly instructed not to fire in what was becoming an extremely volatile situation; Elijah Kambule cautioned Hlubi, the baTlokwa chief, that should one of his men fire first, he, Kambule, would blow the man's brains out.

Suddenly it seemed that the tables had been turned: a body of horsemen were observed coming up from the rear and the immediate assumption was they were Captain Allison's men of the right pincer. But Allison and his levy, after a futile search for the pass that did not exist, had long since returned to camp many miles away. Durnford and Kambule rode forward, supported by the baTlokwas, only to discover the hard truth of their predicament. They were, in fact, mounted amaHlubi, most probably the rearguard of Langalibalele's escort, and now reinforcements for the warriors still coming up the pass. There ensued a long wrangle between Durnford and the amaHlubi chief, translated by Kambule, that went on for almost an hour during which time Durnford, acknowledging the danger he was in, sent a note back to headquarters at Fort Nottingham, stating he was surrounded and asking for help. This note was subsequently found in the possession of an amaHlubi warrior; presumably the baTlokwa courier had been intercepted and killed.

Meanwhile at the pass the situation had worsened: the high ground on either side had been occupied by Hlubi marksmen who called upon those coming up the pass to join them where they would be able to fire down with impunity upon the Carbineers. In addition the young warriors, under the noses of the Carbineers, were sharpening their spears on the rocks and pantomiming what they intended to do with them. Durnford, still attempting to accomplish the orders he had been given, handed his diary, detailing events so far, to Kambule for safekeeping, then rode alone to the lip of the pass where he by gesture, or being lucky enough to find a headman who could speak English, tried to persuade the exodus back into Natal. The reply was only on condition that Durnford and his column went first – which was, of course, completely unacceptable. Furthermore, the headman indicated that Durnford's presence was inciting the young warriors and feared that he would no longer be able to restrain them.

During Durnford's absence the Carbineers had become surrounded by two or three hundred amaHlubi, all anxious to fight. Barter later admitted he had been of the opinion that once the Carbineers withdrew, the amaHlubi's urge for battle would vanish, but he was proven wrong. Elijah Kambule, better able to gauge the temperament and intent of the amaHlubi than anyone, went to Sergeant John Jackson begging him to: 'Tell our Commander that the rebels would soon attack', to which Jackson replied that he could not advise Durnford in such a manner whereas Kambule, himself, could. Barter then ordered Jackson to go to Durnford and tell him, from Barter, that: 'These men want to fight'. Jackson delivered the message and was told by Durnford to go back to his place whilst Durnford, to no avail, pointed his revolver at the warriors and ordered them back down the pass.

By now, presumably on Barter's orders, the Carbineers had remounted and several had asked Barter to go to Durnford and advise him to retire but, as Barter later wrote: 'Our Commanding Officer, as gallant and determined a man as ever breathed, would have cheerfully sacrificed not only us, but himself, in the execution of his orders.' Inevitably there would be an inquiry into the tragedy that was about to follow with much of the blame being attributed to Sergeant William Clark, an imperial army pensioner who as the drill instructor, and due to his age, had not been compelled to accompany the column yet had done so nevertheless. Not been a colonist, he would find himself a scapegoat, it being maintained by Durnford that Clarke largely caused, if not instigated, the panic that ensued. Barter also implicated Clarke in the rout stating that after the Carbineers had stood passive to the mockery of their foes for an hour, some of the older Carbineers had gone to Barter pointing out the column was surrounded and it ought to retire before the excitement of the young warriors reached a climax. And, to quote Barter: 'These feelings were not calmed by Sergeant Clarke who had loudly shouted we were going to be murdered, etc.' He continued: 'I decidedly thought, and think so still, that to match thirty-two men, jaded and sick with hunger, even with the very efficient aid of the Batlokwas, would have been madness.' Barter again observed that Durnford seemed prepared to sacrifice the lives of the whole column when he shouted, in a last attempt to hold the pass: 'Will no one stand with me?'

The response was gallant but inadequate: Erskine, who had attended Durnford's injuries, was first, followed by Troopers Bond and Potterill, but no others. Durnford, sick with pain, frustration and disappointment, later maintained that at about this juncture, Barter reported that many of the Carbineers had said they would all be massacred if they did not move. To which Durnford said he replied: 'Do you mean to report to me officially that you can no longer depend upon your men?' Barter makes no mention of this, merely recalling that Durnford eventually yielded to his advice and addressed the column saying: 'Gentlemen, I am sorry to inform you, your Captain informs me that he cannot place confidence in you.'

In the hubbub that followed, Durnford at last gave the order to retire but the way was now blocked by a mass of warriors who clustered around the Carbineers close enough to give any man or horse a spear thrust. Barter ordered: 'Fours right', and the column, well under control and with pistols drawn, moved off four abreast, Sergeant Varty at the front. The column was making its way back to the Hlatimba Pass and, apart from killing one of the Hlubi cattle, no actual harm had been done. But the young warriors were now completely out of hand and had been presented with the backs of the retreating Carbineers who, having encountered a narrowing of the little ridge along which they were riding, were ordered to halt while they formed into half sections, two abreast.

Meanwhile, Durnford, Kambule and the Batlokwas had veered off taking high ground to the right. Inevitably, one warrior could constrain himself no longer. A shot was fired followed by a volley at close quarters, so close the Hlubi could not miss. Down went three troopers, Erskine, Bond and Potterill, to be pounced upon by the gleeful warriors who immediately set about stripping the bodies. Elijah Kambule shortly suffered the same fate as did several of the baTlokwa, leaving Durnford isolated with warriors on both sides grasping at Chieftain's reins. Durnford has it that he drew his revolver, and shooting left and right killed two men, with Chieftain carrying him from the fray.

In the blame-game that followed, Durnford becomes little less than frantic in accusing others while indulging in self-vindication. He related to his brother, Lieutenant-Colonel Edward Durnford, how Chieftain had carried him through a barrage of shots and grabbing hands: 'And then my gallant beast followed the line of retreating heroes, [sarcasm], reins loose on neck, over a fearful country, myself shooting right and left, all the time perfectly regardless of everything except a burning desire to shoot my own cowards [the Carbineers].'

Whatever the conduct of the Carbineers might have been, it could not possibly have justified Durnford's 'burning desire' to shoot them.

23. The artist/explorer Thomas Baines was commissioned, by a person unknown, to paint an impression of the skirmish — obviously based on a description by someone who was present. This preliminary sketch depicts (1) in the middle foreground Elijah Kambule stabbing a Hlubi warrior while another Hlubi takes aim at Kambule. (2) To Kambule's right warriors point their guns and run '… to capture the Major.' (3) Middle left of the picture, warriors shoot the carbineers at point blank range. (4) In the background, warriors have taken possession of the high ground on both sides of the pass and open fire while other warriors attempt to spear the fleeing carbineers. (*Natal Museum, Pietermaritzburg*)

Rather his concern should have been to see his command safely off the mountain; he also has the whole column galloping away in headlong flight. Not so. Barter recalled:

> Just as we rounded the corner nearest the hill, I saw poor Erskine struck, and am certain that he was dead before he reached the ground. He had supported the Major in his wish to continue the occupation of the pass, and had behaved with gallantry which distinguishes all his family.

Sergeant Varty's horse falling dead, he seized the grey which had carried poor Erskine, to be again unhorsed by a chance shot. This time he must have been lost but for the assistance of Troopers Fannin and Speirs, one of whom caught a lead horse, and the other helped to shift the saddle from the dead steed to the living one.

This was not the action of cowards but rather of Victoria Cross material. Trooper Jackson recalled:

Major Durnford's spare horse running loose, I went after him, the fire of the rebels still going on, and after catching him I rode towards a group of our men, finding that Varty was again unhorsed. The horse I handed to Trooper Fannin, and he, Trooper Speirs, and Trooper Bucknall, assisted Varty, at great risk to themselves. We were all in the range of rebel fire at the time, and Varty was once more mounted. I rode to the rest of the troop who was standing still, and then saw Major Durnford cantering past us alone, shouting: 'Carbineers, Carbineers!' but he did not draw rein at the time. He gave no order. We found later that Elijah Kambule and some Batlokwa were killed. We obeyed his last order to retire by the way we came. He took another way. We did fire a few shots but the men hid behind stones, Speirs dropping one who came out in the open. Sergeant Clark, our Drill Instructor, called on us to ride to a ledge of rock, as we were under the rebels' fire. We did so and dismounted, but seeing our Commander, with some Batlokwas and four or five men, going towards Giant's Castle, we mounted and followed at a walk. The horse of Trooper Church was knocked up, and Bucknall put Church on his horse and walked. The horse of Jaffray was also knocked up, and Jaffray abandoned him and walked with us. About noon we reached Giant's Castle Pass [Hlatimba Pass] and there we found our Commander, also Lieutenant Parkinson, with some twelve others and our pack horses, carrying ammunition and biscuits.

Sergeant Varty, possibly the most experienced frontiersman/soldier amongst those present, having accompanied many expeditions into the High Berg in pursuit of Bushmen raiders, modestly recounted the retirement which starts on page 3 of his manuscript, the first two pages being missing. He was rightly indignant that Durnford should accuse the Carbineers of 'bolting':

. . . to my assistance, and these men were, according to the military authority [Durnford] bolting. Trooper Speirs caught me poor Erskine's horse that was rushing past with saddle turned almost under its belly, and he not only brought me the horse but, dismounted and got me my rifle and its bucket, a work of some little difficulty as the dead horse lay on it. I tried also to get my saddle off, as it was a very good one, but could not. I then ungirthed Erskine's horse and put on the saddle and rode off to join my comrades. Several stood around me, amongst them Mr. Bucknall, who dismounted and fired. . . . I also saw our Commander close to me with his face to the hill and heard him say something about 'If we were Englishmen'. Someone replied that it would be madness to stay here, in fact we had lost confidence in our leader. On the fresh horse I rode perhaps a hundred yards when he, previously wounded, received another shot in the flank and pulled up suddenly. Three or four of my companions tried to catch another horse for me. . . . Sergeant Jackson caught me Major Durnford's spare charger and rode back with it. . . . Mr. Fannin being a better mounted man than Jackson, received the horse and brought it to me. The horse was a fine spirited animal, half wild with the shooting. The grey of Erskine's was an animal of small girth, the fresh horse was large. Fannin sat on his horse holding mine and I did my best to put the saddle on, but for some time could not do so, as the girths would not meet.

All this time the kaffirs were firing at us, and as we were about 150 yards in the rear, we formed rather a large mark and drew their principal fire. But strange to say, though so close they failed to hit either us or our horses, though one or two shots threw up soil in my face, and one or two whistled unpleasantly close. Trooper Speirs dismounted close to us, but moved off a little to the side as he thought we were too large a target. Yet, [as Durnford would have it] these men were bolting! Fannin, myself and others fired a few shots and we retired to join the bulk of our men, whom I caught up, perhaps a half mile in advance, riding slowly, Major Durnford being with them. I apologised to him for taking his horse and his reply was that I was perfectly welcome and the only condition required was that if the horse that he was riding failed, he must ride behind me. One of our men, Walter Jaffray, had his horse shot through the kneecap and at a distance of about four miles from the Bushman's River Pass the horse gave up. He therefore shouldered his rifle, walked on, and got to the Giant's Castle Pass at least five minutes before anybody else so that if he bolted, he did it very deliberately and in rather slow time.

Trooper Bucknall also has a say:

Coming into the line the others had gone round, some heavy ground turned my horse out of it, for he was labouring hard. Others had gone through, and one horse was floundering, its rider, a Batlokwa pitched over his head, jumped up, and trying to get him out, kaffirs rushed in, stabling and floundering together; bullets whistling and fizzing around, as our bad bullets do, but the shooting was horrible, that is, they did not hit as they ought to have done at the distances, which was from forty to a hundred yards. Most of them went over our heads.

Later Bucknall recalls that he was close to Varty and the others at the time they attempting to catch Varty a new horse when, just at that moment, Durnford 'passed me with his revolver in his hand, shouting, "Halt! Whatever are they running for?"' Bucknall replied that he had heard that someone behind had been brought down to which Durnford replied: 'What a shame to leave a companion.'

24. Whoever commissioned the painting must have disapproved of the preliminary sketch as it bears little resemblance to the final product in which Barter, on the white horse, Durnford in the centre, and Kambule, wearing a sort of sombrero, sit resolute at the head of the pass facing the oncoming amaHlubi, while in the background, the carbineers, in line, stand firm. Unfortunately the final painting has disappeared without trace.

Finally the retreating column, still followed by a few aggressive amaHlubi, reached the Hlatimba Pass where they found Lieutenant Parkinson and the stragglers with ammunition and biscuits. But Durnford would have no pause, ordering the men to proceed immediately down the pass. He fainted part of the way down and was revived with sips of watered gin administered by Trooper Button. Parkinson and several others had got ahead and were well down the pass where Parkinson had given orders to halt and 'off-saddle'. When Durnford caught up it seems he flew into a rage and although they were all now at the bottom of the pass he would not hear of giving the horses a break as he perceived the column to be in danger still.

Now let us hear how Durnford, as related by his brother, Lieutenant-Colonel Edward Durnford, attempted not only to blame the Carbineers for the fiasco but to make himself an African legend at the same time.

He [Durnford] was afterwards told that his cheeks had been required by the natives for the composition of some important medicine, and that a great fighting man has that pleasing notoriety thrust upon him. His conduct on this occasion certainly made a great impression upon the natives for the story was reported amongst them thirty miles away, on the afternoon of the same day, that the troops had run away, leaving their chief behind, and that he was the only man there, and had but one arm. In the excitement of the moment, he was quite unconscious of the severe wound which he had received in the left arm, and was only made aware of the fact by finding his hand full of warm blood, which had run down inside the sleeve of his patrol jacket. That patrol jacket was found afterwards to be pierced by assegais in so many places, that it seemed as though he must have borne a charmed life to have escaped as he did.

Edward Durnford continued his brother's story as his brother reached the top of Hlatimba Pass:

Lieutenant Parkinson, with the pack horses and about a dozen stragglers, was met at the head of the pass, and here again, had it been possible, Major Durnford would have made a stand until he could be reinforced. But the demoralisation of the force was so complete that this could not be done. The men went helter-skelter down the pass, their rear still being covered by the Batlokwas. When at last he gave up in vain his attempt to rally his white command, for his strength, severely tried by all he had gone through, was failing fast, and his voice was gone through shouting, he turned his horse, and rode back alone through the Batlokwas towards the pass, resolved at all events to sell his own life dearly amongst the foe. The Batlokwas at first, as one of them afterwards said:

'We thought he might have dropped something, and wanted to find it' – their own natural hardihood making his return in that case seem nothing surprising to them. But, when they saw that he was riding back straight to the pass alone, they became alarmed and some of them who followed galloped up beside him and although he made no reply to their questions, they knew by the expression of his face that he was going back to die.

Faithful and obedient followers as they had hitherto prove themselves, they now took the law into their own hands and, seizing his horse's bridle, they brought him back.

Durnford then admitted to being led to the bottom of the pass where the column was met by a messenger bringing news that a contingent of redcoat infantry was on its way, but as Edward Durnford related:

Thinking it probable that, encouraged by the flight of the white man, the whole tribe would pursue, and being familiar with the ground, they would endeavour to cut his party off in some of the deep valleys, Major Durnford altered the line of retreat from that of the advance of the previous night, and would permit no halt until dusk. They upsaddled in an hour's time and reached the camp utterly exhausted, men and horses, at 1am.

As one can imagine, there was uproar in Natal: three young Carbineers had been killed and their bodies cut open; Potterill's body (he being the youngest at twenty-two) had had the left hand cut off from which to make medicine; the rebel, Langalibalele, had got clear away with all his tribe and cattle; and rumours were rife that in collusion with King Cetshwayo, Natal was to be invaded at any moment.

The colony turned not only on the government, blaming it for the fiasco, but on Durnford also, blaming him for the death of its sons; and because Durnford's hands had been tied by the order not to fire first, his reputation was tarnished with the nickname 'Don't fire Durnford'. Yet in the weeks that followed, Durnford despite his injuries, neither

25. George Shepstone, a son of Theophilus Shepstone, was a corporal during the encounter at Bushman's Pass. Five years later, as Durnford's staff officer, he held the rank of lieutenant in the Natal Native Horse. It was he who, at Isandlwana, brought news of the Zulu army's advance on the British camp. (*KZN Archives, Pietermaritzburg*)

reported sick or gave up the chase, leading an expedition to the top of Bushman's Pass only two weeks after the skirmish.

Although Langalibalele had retreated deep into the barren heights of Basutoland, the pincers at last began to close. Captain Allison, with 1,500 native levies and a large force of mounted Basutos were hot on his trail while redcoat soldiers of the 75th Regiment, also supported by local levies, waited at the bottom of the Natal passes.

On 17 November Langalibalele, leaving behind a trail made by 7,000 cattle that could not be missed, was overhauled by Allison. He and his sons were brought into Pietermaritzburg a month later, Allison having paid the levies and Basutos with most of the cattle and horses for services rendered. The colonists were clamouring for retribution and the savage sentence on the amaHlubi went some way to placating the white population. Langalibalele was sentenced to exile on Robben Island while Lieutenant-Governor Pine set in action a program to disperse not only the amaHlubi but also their neighbours, the amaPutini, who had not been involved other than looking after some of the Hlubi cattle.

Now it was the turn of the Natal levies to plunder. Villages were burnt to the ground, cattle stolen, unarmed men, women and children were hunted down and killed in cold blood. *The Natal Colonist* commented that Pine, who had issued the order not to fire, the first shot, was now indifferent to '. . . the horrid butchery that was going on'. Durnford at the time was engaged in dynamiting the passes and saw little of the actual ravaging of the amaHlubi but would shortly write to Bishop Colenso, a champion of the native people, a pathetic letter: 'There have been sad sights – women and children butchered by <u>our</u> black allies (too often, unhappily, by the permission and encouragement of the white leaders . . .), old men too . . . The burnt villages – dead women – it was all horrible. And the destitution of the women and children left is fearful. The women are all made slaves! What will England say?'

England's reply was not long in coming: Lieutenant-Governor Pine was recalled in disgrace to be replaced by Major-General Sir Garnet Wolseley. But, perhaps of more importance, what would Cetshwayo, the next-door neighbour, think? It had only been a few weeks since Shepstone, much to blame for the whole bloody affair, had lectured the Zulu King on the theme 'Thou shalt not kill'.

Cetshwayo, through his spy system, would be aware of all the shameful details and would have much to ponder on: could, in fact, his neighbours be contemplating the conquest of his own kingdom? It would not be long before he knew.

Chapter 11

Looking for a Good Excuse

Shepstone, on his return from Cetshwayo's coronation, had hoped that, as colonial kingmaker, and by persuading Cetshwayo to accept the 'new laws' he had foisted on him, he had achieved the pacification of colony and kingdom for the foreseeable future or, that is, for so long as it suited him. However, that essential element 'trust' that may well have existed between black and white as Shepstone, with his escort of Carbineers and gunners, had marched back to Natal, would have largely been dispelled by the treatment since meted out to the amaHlubi. What had been done to them, could with a great army of redcoats, be inflicted on the Zulu. Cetshwayo therefore concluded the Zulu army must be emboldened and the regiments increased to parallel those of King Shaka's day. However, the Colony did not see this as a Zulu precaution against attack but rather as an indication of their own plans to do so.

Cetshwayo was not far wrong in gauging his neighbour's intent: Natal, in the form of various interested parties, had long contemplated the conquest of Zululand in one way or another. For instance, John William Colenso, the Bishop of Natal, who had fiercely defended Langalibalele, had for many years been hoping for a Christian conquest of Zululand by deposing the reigning monarch and installing in his stead the Christianised pretender Mthungu, Cetshwayo's half-brother, who was Colenso's pupil and who resided under his roof. Now that Cetshwayo, who was plainly anti-missionary, reigned it was a high priority amongst all the churchmen that Cetshwayo be removed – or, better still, that Zululand be annexed by Britain.

By 1873 there were numerous missionaries from a variety of nations within the kingdom, all having been permitted to set up shop by King

Mpande. However, their frustration must have been great – and, no doubt, regarded as a bad investment by the various philanthropic institutions who financed them – for they had hardly a convert to boast of; and now that Cetshwayo was on the throne their task would be doubly difficult. In fact, it was Cetshwayo's immediate intention to expel all the missionaries but was persuaded by Shepstone to allow those currently resident to remain. Mpande had regarded the missionaries as the source of all the white man's knowledge and the conduit through which white man's possessions could be obtained. Cetshwayo on the other hand, preferred to shun the missionaries and obtain his wants through the white traders. In 1877, F. B. Finney, the border agent, and a man as knowledgeable of the Zulu kingdom as any, appraised the Governor of Natal of the new king's attitude:

> During the reign of the late king umPande [*sic*], the missionaries were considered almost as a necessity in Zululand . . . Bishop Schreuder especially enjoyed the friendship of umPande, and for many years had great influence over him. That state of things now has entirely altered. Cetshwayo's disposition differs greatly from that of his father, he is more self-reliant, arrogant, and conservative. If he wants anything, he can find many traders ready and willing to supply his wants, and he, together with his chiefs, can see no good in either the missionaries or their work. He does not believe in their doctrines, and looks on any Zulu who professes so to do as a Zulu spoiled. He feels that each mission station is a separate power, set up in his land, which to a great extent is calculated to rob him of his influence over the people he governs and forms a place of refuge for all the *abatakati* [witches] and those who wish to throw off their allegiance to him. This is no new idea on his part, as from the first, he wished to get rid of the missionaries. I have good reason for believing that some of the missionaries have very unwisely interfered in Zulu politics.

How right Finney was. The Reverend Robertson, a prominent old hand amongst the British missionary contingent, was deeply involved in political intrigue. He not only kept up a stream of alarmist correspondence to the outside world, he was also the anonymous authority on Zululand for the *Natal Mercury*. Robertson, in common with his fellow missionaries, irrespective of nationality or denomination, was hoping and angling for the British annexation of Zululand. The missionaries would have Cetshwayo seen as a bloodthirsty and ruthless monarch whose subjects would delight in his demise, yet Robertson, the most virulent of Cetshwayo's accusers, secretly held an entirely different and benign opinion of the king. In 1877 he wrote to his bishop:

Regarding the king, you have nothing to fear if you do not interfere with him . . . Lately the king said to me, 'I love the English. I am not umPande's son. I am the child of Queen Victoria. But I am also a King in my own country and must be treated as such. Somseu [Shepstone] must speak gently to me. I shall not hear dictation. I shall perish first.'

Just as the missionaries were determined to have full rein inside Zululand, so Shepstone was equally anxious to have unrestricted right-of-way through the kingdom for the passage of migrant labour who were fast becoming an essential factor in the booming agriculture and mining activities in Natal and the Cape. In both areas labour was scarce but plentiful beyond Zululand. Shepstone had once credited Shaka and his military state for saving south-east Africa from the ravages of slavery, thus, within Natal, there was no pool of recently freed slaves to draw upon for labour, nor was there a people with a tradition of manual work, the Zulu warriors scorning the very thought of exchanging the spear for a spade. The Kimberley diamond diggings alone were gobbling up any potential workers as fast as they appeared and had even managed to attract a few young bucks of the warrior class when it became known that the mines would pay for their labour with firearms. Shepstone wanted right of passage for amaTsonga labour through the Zulu kingdom, by way of a coastal route. This he managed to achieve with John Dunn securing the lucrative appointment of government agent. Yet Tsonga labour would not fill Natal's needs and another route to the west was essential, a route that would give access to the limitless supply of manpower in Central Africa that had been created by the recent cessation of the slave trade in Zanzibar.

Such a route was possible, not through Zululand proper, but via an adjacent stretch of land known, for good reason, as the Disputed Territory. In the early days of the Boer alliance with Mpande, and after the British occupation of Natal in 1842, many Boers trekked north to create what became the Transvaal Republic whilst others put down roots in a triangle of land that had its southern tip situated at present-day Rorke's Drift, and its northern boundary parallel with the Pongolo River, an area of some 3,000 square miles. The Boer settlers held that, in one way or another, they had acquired ownership which the Zulus, who had been the previous occupants, heartily contested. Hence the name the Disputed Territory. Later, the Natal government would offer to act as referee in the dispute but, in the meantime, shortly after Cetshwayo's coronation, Shepstone was contemplating the acquisition of the Disputed Territory for Natal, as was the current governor, Sir Garnet Wolseley, who confided to his diary in May 1875:

> I hear from Mr. Shepstone that Cetshwayo the King of the Zulus is now ready for war and means to begin by fighting the native tribes on his frontier. I wish his attention could be directed to the Transvaal; he hates the Dutch [the Boer settlers] who have always cheated and dealt unfairly with him; a war between these two parties would be very useful to us. It would reduce the King's power immensely, perhaps break it up altogether, and it would prevent the Transvaal from obtaining money to make the Delagoa Bay Railroad and make it more keenly anxious to gave us the strip of disputed territory lying between them and the Zulu Kingdom, a piece of land that we want very badly . . . I have only to give the King the slightest hint, and he would pitch into the Transvaal there and then. I wish I could do so without compromising the Government at home. When his messengers arrive I will see what can be done. It is a glorious opportunity for England, for we ought to try and force the Transvaal into our arms.

The war that Wolseley believed Cetshwayo to be contemplating was undoubtedly the one against the amaSwazi that he had already decided to abandon, but it served the purpose of the colonial schemers to have the Zulu nation seen as permanently poised for war. Shortly after his coronation, Cetshwayo believed it necessary, by established tradition, to embark upon a war. Let John Dunn, who acted as go-between for Cetshwayo and the then Governor of Natal, Sir Benjamin Pine, explain:

> All now remained quiet until he [Cetshwayo] took it into his head that he ought to establish his supremacy by following out an ancient custom of washing the spears of the nation in the blood of some neighbouring tribe. When he conceived this idea, he sent for me to write a letter to

the Natal Government, stating his wish to go against the amaSwazi. To this he received the following reply, on the margin of the despatch (now in my possession) containing the reply, the autograph of Sir Benjamin Chilley Campbell Pine, is affixed:

'Reply of His Excellency Sir Benjamin Chilley Campbell Pine, K.C.M.G., Lieut.-Governor of Natal, to Cetywayo, Chief of the Zulu Nation.

Office of Secretary for Native Affairs,
October 22, 1874.

'The Lieutenant-Governor has received the letter sent by Cetywayo, and the reasons given for making war upon the amaSwazi.

'The Lieutenant-Governor sees no cause whatever for making war, and informs Cetywayo that such an intention on the part of the Zulus meets with his entire disapproval.

'Cetywayo must also remember that the amaSwazi are almost entirely surrounded by white people who have settled in the country, and it will be impossible for the Zulus, if war is made, to avoid getting into difficulties with them.

'Many years ago the Lieutenant-Governor sent a letter to the late King M'Pande, requesting him to allow the amaSwazi to live in peace from any further attacks from the Zulus, he promised to do so, and kept his word. [Pine had served as Lieutenant Governor on a previous occasion.]

'The Lieutenant-Governor trusts that what he has said will be sufficient to deter Cetywayo and the Zulu Nation from entertaining such a project.

'By command of His Excellency,
'(Signed) J. W. SHEPSTONE,
'Acting Secretary for Native Affairs.'

Dunn comments further: 'The above letter made the King change his plans, although it enraged him, as I could plainly see.' (Especially, no doubt, in view of Pine's recent decimation of the amaHlubi.) It is also ironic that the colonial government should prevent the king making war against the Swazis when, only three years later the same government would strive to get the amaSwazi to attack the Zulus: '. . . Offer the Swazi king fifty horses with saddles and bridles and 200 cows if his men moved to Pongola and keep the Zulus out of the Transvaal. Try to get this done for half the price.'

There can be no doubt that the British intent, either that of the home government, the colonial government, or both, was the conquest of a great deal more of southern Africa than that over which the Union Jack flew at the time of Cetshwayo's coronation; and in order to accomplish that ambition the Zulu kingdom must come under British control. Only six weeks prior to Shepstone putting the tailor-made crown on Cetshwayo's head, the *Natal Mercury* thundered: 'Natal must consequently carry out a Monroe doctrine of its own, and insist that the Anglo-Saxon race shall hold undisputed sway from Cape Town to the Zambezi . . .' The greatest fear of the thinly-scattered population of white settlers was that of a general uprising, a fear that was fed by the realisation that a network of intelligence and collaboration existed amongst the tribes of southern Africa and, of even greater dread, the Zulu Army of 40,000 warriors.

It seems then, that all Britain needed in order to invade Zululand was a good excuse. By late 1878 Cetshwayo was aware that it was Britain's intention to take his Kingdom, for he remarked to John Dunn: 'I am not a child; I see the English wish to have my country; but if they come in I will fight.'

There were great expectations amongst the British military that there might be a campaign in the offing. As far back as 1877 it had been regarded as a certainty by Sir Garnet Wolseley who, when at Aldershot, was asked whether or not he thought there might be an immediate war, replied: 'No, Shepstone will keep him [Cetshwayo] quiet until we are ready', to which a colleague, Colonel Butler replied: 'When we fight the Zulus, we shall want 10,000 men . . .'. A serious under-estimate as it turned out but none would have thought so at the time.

Lieutenant-General Frederic Augustus Thesiger, 2nd Baron Chelmsford, the new general-officer-commanding Her Majesty's Forces in southern Africa, who, by mid-1878 had successfully brought to an end the Ninth Frontier War in the Eastern Cape, and was looking for further military laurels, got more to the point when writing to, recently knighted, Sir Theophilus Shepstone, in July of the same year:

The Zulus have been very kind to us in abstaining from any hostile movements during the time we were so bitterly engaged [with the Ninth Frontier War] in this colony [the Cape]. If they will only wait until next month, I hope to have the troops better prepared than they are at present ... If we are to have a fight with the Zulus, I am anxious that our arrangements should be as complete as it is possible to make them – half measures do not answer with natives – they must be thoroughly crushed to make them believe in our superiority.

And, during the same month, despite contending that 'my reports from Natal breathe nothing but peace', Chelmsford wrote to the War Office in London saying: 'It is more than probable that steps will have to be taken to check the arrogance of Ketywayo [Cetshwayo], Chief of the Zulus.'

So, looking around for an excuse, the best on offer seemed to be Cetshwayo's disregard of the 'laws' that Shepstone had proclaimed. Executions were still a not uncommon occurrence in Zululand, as indeed they were elsewhere in the world. John Dunn tells of the first after Cetshwayo had been crowned: 'One of the Royal household servants had stolen several tins of "Chlorodyne" from the King and taken them off to his house with the idea of giving his brew-potted beer more punch. The unfortunate man was tracked down and arrested.'

Dunn witnessed him being brought in:

One morning, about eight o'clock, I was sitting in front of one of my wagons talking to some of my men when I saw a gathering of the Indunas at the gate of the King's kraal. I remarked that there was some mischief brewing. After they had been talking for some little while, I saw all at once a scrimmage, and a man knocked down and pounced on. Seeing me in view, the Indunas sent to tell me that they had been trying the thief, and that he was to be killed. The poor fellow lay on the ground for a short time, for he had only been stunned: His arms had been twisted right round behind his head and tied together straight over his head. As soon as he recovered his senses he prepared to march. Having often witnessed a similar scene he knew, from terrible experience, the routine. So he got up of his own accord, and without being told, took the path to the place of execution, and was followed by about half-a-dozen men, who had been told off to go and finish him.

This was the first man killed after the coronation of Cetywayo, almost before Sir Theo. Shepstone could have reached Maritzburg. But it served the fellow right, as he was guilty of a great breach of trust. The Zulu is only to be ruled by fear of death, or the confiscation of his entire property.'

Cetshwayo, of course, denied that he had agreed to abide by Shepstone's 'laws', maintaining that they were merely part of Shepstone's ritual, and that he would not forsake his kingly prerogative of executing of his subjects as he saw fit. '"Did I ever tell Mr. Shepstone I would not kill?" he enquired. "Did he tell the white people I made such an agreement because if he did, he has deceived them . . . Why does the Governor of Natal speak to me about my laws? Do I come to Natal and dictate to him about his laws?"'

So, the Colonial authorities waited; Cetshwayo's breaking of the 'laws' could hardly justify war – and then two incidents occurred that, had they been stage-managed, could not have served the colonial government better.

One of Cetshwayo's favourite subjects, Sihayo kaXongo, occupied a chiefdom on the north bank of the Buffalo River opposite the Rorke's Drift Mission Station. Sihayo possessed a number of wives, two of whom decided to quit their husband and, with their respective lovers, flee across the river and take up residence in Natal where they would be safe from Sihayo's wrath – or so they thought. But they had reckoned without Sihayo's sons who were resentful of the shame brought upon their father and, led by the eldest boy, Mehlokazulu kaSihayo, an officer of the iNgobamakhosi Regiment, a group of thirty mounted warriors in war attire crossed into Natal. There they found one of the adulteresses, and took her back to Zulu soil where, in plain sight of the Natal natives across the river – who were suitably terrified by this time – they killed her. The following day, Mehlokazulu sallied forth again, with a much larger war party, and apprehended the other wife, dragged her back across the river, and, as with the first adulteress, put her to death.

The Colony of Natal was outraged and clamoured for retribution. The Lieutenant-Governor, Sir Henry Bulwer, demanded that Sihayo's sons and the rest of the war party be handed over for trial under British law. Cetshwayo protested, saying in reply, that adultery was punishable by death in Zululand and that the young men were merely protecting their father's name and honour. With this incident being far from resolved, in September there was a further 'outrage'. Two officials of the Colonial Engineer's Department, Messrs. W. H. Deighton and D. Smith, were supervising work on the ford across the Tugela at Middle Drift (a chosen invasion route into Zululand), when they were apprehended by a party of warriors after they had crossed the river to survey the Zulu bank. Not only were the two white men apprehended, they were partly stripped and manhandled although they were then released otherwise unharmed. This affair caused a fury of colonial indignation for which recompense would also be demanded. (A few months later, after a British army had crossed into Zululand to avenge these affronts, a Natal newspaper gloating thundered: 'I have seen . . . the red and blue uniforms of men who have gathered . . . to vindicate the just cause of an offended civilisation, and to assert the outraged authority of the British Crown; I have seen the climax of a policy which must end in the undisputed supremacy of British rule over all the native tribes that live south of the Limpopo.') Similarly there were incidents in the Disputed Territories seen as Zulu harassment, mainly directed at native Christian converts. Thus, in the latter months of 1878 there had been sufficient incidents to thoroughly alarm the settlers, sending them to bed with the thought that a vast Zulu army might descend upon the colony at any moment.

There were, however, some good tidings for King Cetshwayo that the Governor-General of the Cape Colony and Her Majesty's High Commissioner for Southern Africa, Sir Henry Bartle Edward Frere, was keeping up his sleeve for the moment: the Boundary Commission had reached a conclusion and had awarded more than half the disputed territory to Zululand. Frere had decided to disclose the award coupled with an ultimatum the terms of which he believed King Cetshwayo would find it impossible to comply. However, in the invitation sent to Cetshwayo to meet with the colonial government, there was no hint of the bombshell that was about to be delivered. Consequently, on 11 December 1878, the highest ministers of the Zulu realm (including John Dunn), met with a galaxy of colonial top brass on the south bank of the Tugela River, under the shade of a majestic Natal fig tree.

The ceremony opened by stipulating the awards of the Boundary Commission: a gratifying slice of the disputed territory would once again come under Zulu rule. The Zulu deputation were delighted. But they were directed not to go away as the *indaba* was not yet over. Then, with the Secretary of Native Affairs, reading from a 5,000-word document, the bombshell was dropped. The proclamation began:

Message from his Excellency the Lieutenant–Governor of Natal to Cetywayo King of the Zulus and Chief Men of the Zulu Nation.

The Lieutenant-Governor of Natal sends, in the name of the Queen's High Commissioner, these further words to the Zulu King and Nation.

Then began a strident tirade of scolding accusations and demands, that went on for half an hour, finally ending in:

It is necessary that the Zulu army shall be disbanded, and that the men shall return to their homes.

Let every man then be free to remain at his home, and let him plant and sow, and reap and tend his cattle and let him live in peace with his family.

Let him not be called out for war or fighting, or assembling in regiments, except with the permission of the great council of the nation assembled, and with the consent also of the British Government.

Let every man, when it comes to man's estate, be free to marry. Let him not wait for years before he gets permission to do this for oftentimes the King forgets to give permission and the years pass . . .

. . . in future it will be necessary that promises be kept, for the British Government holds itself bound to see that this is so, and in order that they may be kept and that the laws regarding them may be duly carried out, the Queen's High Commissioner, will appoint an officer as his deputy to reside in the Zulu country, or on its immediate borders, who will be the eyes and ears and mouth of the British Government towards the Zulu King and the Great Council of the nation . . .

If any case of dispute occurs in which any of the missionaries, or in which any European is concerned, such dispute should be heard by the King in public and in the presence of the British Resident; and no sentence of expulsion from Zululand shall be carried out until it has been communicated by the King to the Resident, and, until it has been approved by the Resident.

So there it was. The Zulu army to be disbanded and only to reassemble with the consent of a British Resident – a euphemism for governor or overlord – an official who, as can be seen, was to have considerable authority over the affairs of the Zulu kingdom. The ultimatum also reiterated that the culprits responsible for the 'outrages' be handed over for trial; that the various fines in cattle be paid; that the coronation 'laws' be obeyed; that missionaries be allowed to return; that all Zulu subjects be free to accept Christianity if they so wished.

Whether the king may or may not have accepted some of the demands is immaterial as all were insignificant in comparison to the British insistence for an all powerful colonial overlord and the disbanding of the Zulu Army. Cetshwayo could no more consider these two demands than could he contemplate destroying the national harvest. It was exactly what was expected. Had not the king emphatically stated: 'I am also a king in my own country and must be treated as such. I shall not hear dictation. I shall perish first.' War, as anticipated, was inevitable.

Chapter 12

War to the Bitter End

There is a wealth of literature on every aspect of the Anglo-Zulu War of 1879 and it need not be fought again here as a military documentary. Instead let the combatants describe the war through their own experiences.

The ultimatum that had been served on the Zulu king allowed thirty days for the disbanding of the army, thirty days during which there would be no British punitive action. In fact, thirty days grace during which Lord Chelmsford would be at liberty to deploy his troops along the Zulu border unmolested, ready to strike the moment the ultimatum expired.

The actual ultimatum had been handed to Dunn who kept it in his possession in the belief that it was pointless sending a written message to Cetshwayo; rather he rehearsed one of his trusted men to remember and then to relate its contents verbally. On the verbal receipt of the terms of the ultimatum, several days later, Cetshwayo immediately protested to Dunn at the limited time allotted for the fulfilment of its conditions. Dunn responded with a letter to the Natal Government to which the Secretary for Native Affairs replied:

Sir,

I have the honour to acknowledge the receipt of your letter of the 18th instant, which the Lieutenant-Governor has laid before his Excellency the High Commissioner for his information. I am directed to express the satisfaction of the High Commissioner at the receipt of your letter, and to inform you that the Word of the Government, as already given, cannot be altered.

26. On the expiry of the ultimatum, the British juggernaut of men, weapons, wagons and supplies, entered Zululand.

Unless the prisoners and cattle are given up within the time specified Her Majesty's troops will advance, but, in consideration of the disposition expressed in your letter, to comply with the demands of the Government, the troops will be halted at convenient posts within the Zulu border, and will await the expiration of the term of thirty days, without in the meantime taking any hostile action, unless it is provoked by the Zulus.

The die was cast and as the thirty days hastened by British forces continued to deploy while the warriors of the Zulu army, an army that would total 40,000 men, began to assemble at their barracks close to the royal residence at Ondini.

After some minor shuffling of his columns, Lord Chelmsford invaded the kingdom in a three-pronged attack, each column more or less of equal strength and size: one, commanded by Colonel Charles Pearson, entering Zululand by way of the lower Tugela Drift; one to the north, commanded by Colonel Henry Evelyn Wood, crossing the border by wading the Buffalo River; and a central column, commanded by Colonel Richard Glyn, crossing the Buffalo at Rorke's Drift.

Chelmsford and his staff accompanied Glyn's column with John Dunn joining Pearson's column after some persuasive words from Chelmsford. When Cetshwayo had received the terms of the ultimatum from Dunn's messenger, he realised at once that if it came to fighting, his white friend would be in an impossible position, torn by loyalty to both sides, so Cetshwayo graciously gave Dunn the opportunity to bow out and remain neutral, telling him to 'stand on one side'. Lord Chelmsford was less sympathetic, however. Realising what a useful fellow Dunn would be, Chelmsford, who had requested Dunn's presence only a few days after the ultimatum had been delivered, asked Dunn what course he intended to take. Dunn replied that he had no quarrel with the Zulus and intended to remain neutral but went on to 'beg' Chelmsford's advice which, when given, was for Dunn to vacate Zululand with all his followers. Chelmsford continued with the threat: 'You must either take one side or the other – Join us, or take the consequences.' Not only did Dunn hasten across the Tugela with all his followers and cattle, but within weeks had formed a highly efficient combat unit which he

27. Colonel Evelyn Wood, the most successful of the British column commanders, was knighted and promoted to brigadier general for his services in Zululand. (*John Young Collection*)

28. A regiment of the Natal Native Contingent (NNC) line up for inspection. Only one man in ten was said to be issued with a firearm. In this picture the weapons are clearly Martini-Henry rifles, the same as issued to British troops. (*Campbell Collection, Durban*)

named 'Dunn's Fighting Scouts' thus deserting Cetshwayo, his once friend and benefactor.

Chelmsford's force was a mixture of imperial troops; colonial volunteers and police, – the latter two units usually making up the cavalry element – and conscripted blacks from Natal who were, of course, of Zulu descent and who bore the title of 'The Natal Native Contingent' (NNC). As an example of Britain's premeditated intent to take over the Zulu kingdom, each of the white colonial volunteers had been offered the incentive of a free farm in Zululand on conclusion of hostilities.

The invaders' morale was high and Lord Chelmsford expressed his satisfaction with the Martini-Henry .450-calibre breech-loading rifle, with which most of his white troops and every tenth man of his native force were armed: 'I am inclined to think that the first experience of the power of the Martini-Henry will be such a surprise to the Zulus that they will not be formidable after the first effort.' Then, on further reflection, he wrote: 'I shall strive to be in a position to show the Zulu how inferior they are to us in fighting power. We may possibly induce the Zulu King to attack us which will save us a great deal of trouble.' Equally confident, one of his young officers wrote home to his mother: 'The number of troops that have gone into Zululand is thirteen thousand – a sufficient number to beat the Zulus ten times over.' Even the private soldiers believed that they were in for some high jinks and an easy time. Private Owen Ellis, from Wales, wrote: 'We are about to capture all the cattle belonging to the Zulus and also burn all their kraals', while his mate, Private Goatham, expressed the opinion that 'Zulu warriors, though big and strong, do not have the martial spirit of an Englishman'.

But first the column had to cross the Buffalo River, which meant wading chest-deep for the NNC, who were harangued and encouraged all the way by their regimental witch doctor. The crossing was described by Henry Charles Harford, a young white officer attached to the Contingent: 'In order to scare away any crocodiles that might be lurking in the vicinity, the leading company formed a double chain right across the river, leaving a pathway between for the remainder to pass through. The men forming the chain clasped hands and the moment they entered the water they started to hum a kind of war chant, which was taken up by every company as they passed over. The sound this produced was like a gigantic swarm of bees buzzing about us, and sufficient to scare crocodiles or anything else, away. Altogether, it was both a curious and grand sight.'

Having successfully crossed into Zululand on 11 January 1879, the centre column was less than five miles distant from the stronghold of none other than Chief Sihayo whose sons had killed his adulterous wives, thus partly giving rise to the British ultimatum. Sihayo's kraal would be the first of Chelmsford's targets. However, Sihayo and most of his warriors had already gone to report the king. Nevertheless, the defenders that remained put up a fight, taking full advantage of the labyrinth of caves that Sihayo's clan inhabited. Their resistance did not last for long, however, and an elated Lord Chelmsford speculated: 'I am in great hopes that the news of the storming of Sihayo's stronghold and the capture of so many of his cattle may have a salutary effect in Zululand and either bring down a large force to attack us or else produce a revolution in the country.' But the redcoat invaders were not to be so lucky and marched on to pitch camp in the shadow of a sphinx-shaped hill called Isandlwana.

Eleven days after crossing the Buffalo River Lord Chelmsford was lured by Zulu stealth and cunning into believing that the Zulu army, spoiling for a fight, had assembled ten miles north of Isandlwana, so he embarked on a wild goose chase taking with him over half the column's strength while the Zulus descended on the weakened camp.

The Zulu strategy, as the silhouettes of thousands of warriors began to appear against the skyline, was to bewilder and deceive – a game plan that was eminently successful. There were about 1,700 British troops in camp (that was later described as having been as defenceless as an English village) including 900 blacks of the NNC. The redcoats and colonials were, in the main, armed with the Martini-Henry rifle that, in the hands of a trained soldier, was capable of firing twelve aimed shots a minute. The infantry were also supported by two 7-pounder field guns. The NNC, however, were poorly armed with little more than muskets and spears.

Yet, despite the superior British weapons, the camp was taken in a bloody hand-to-hand uproar that lasted little more than an hour. One warrior, late in arriving, remembered:

> When I got in sight of Isandlwana the whole place was a twisting mass of soldiers and Zulus, the Mkankempemvu and uMbomambi were all killing and then we attacked. I heard the 'Bye-and-bye' [the Zulu word for artillery] firing . . . I carried no gun, only two throwing spears, shield and stabbing assegai . . . I prepared to stab a white man, he was holding on to an assegai held by a friend of mine with both hands . . . and I stabbed the white man in the back . . . I saw a line of soldiers, shoulder-to-shoulder and I was afraid to attack them . . . They were standing like a fence with bayonets . . . They were killed by the same two regiments . . . Some white men who had climbed on to the top of Isandlwana Hill were followed and thrown off the top of the rock . . .

Paul Brickhill, a civilian interpreter and guide, recalled: 'Men were running everywhere . . . I saw one of the field pieces brought into the camp; the men jumped off and took to their heels. Simultaneously with this, the only body of soldiers still visible rose from firing their last shot and joined in the general flight. Panic was everywhere and no shelter to fall back on.'

Durnford, now a brevet Colonel, arrived with five troops (250 men) of the Natal Native Mounted Contingent, later to become the Natal Native Horse (NNH), just as the battle began. Two of his troop commanders,

Captain Shepstone and Lieutenant Raw, had been Carbineers with him during the Langalibalele affair as had Hlubi, then a scout, now a Troop Sergeant-Major. When it was clear beyond any doubt that the battle was lost, Durnford made no effort to save himself nor did he encourage his men to save their own lives. A senior NCO, Jabez Molife, later wrote that he should have had Durnford bound and carried from the battlefield in order to save his life, while Sergeant Simeon Kambule recalled: 'I looked back and there I could see my chief [Durnford] in the centre of his square with his long moustaches and one good arm in the air. He was shouting and laughing: "Come round me, come round me …".' A trooper of the Natal Mounted Police, who escaped, reported that Durnford had shouted to the troopers: 'Now, my men, let me see what you can do!' It would seem that the Carbineers, not wishing to again be accused of cowardice, stayed: the bodies of nineteen of them, all in a heap, were found lying around Durnford's body, and their horses, on which they could have escaped, lay killed nearby.

A warrior of the uVe Regiment, later told how he had killed a red soldier who was fleeing to the river: 'As he raised his right arm that held a "volovol" [revolver] and as he was about to fire, I stabbed him in the arm pit. I pushed it in, I did not hear him cry out, I pushed it until he died.'

Sergeant-Major Nyanda, of the Natal Native Mounted Contingent, remembered:

We were then chased into the center of the camp – and saw a large number of soldiers being assegaied . . . Then the Zulus drove in the right wing and the whole of the force, white and black – foot and horse [infantry and cavalry], were mixed together and being assegaied – A rush was made for the Nek and we were met by Zulus on the other side and everyone who could save himself tried to do so.

And when it was all over a Zulu warrior remembered:

We stripped the dead of all their clothes. To my knowledge no one was made prisoner and I saw no dead bodies carried away or mutilated. If the [witch] doctors carried away any dead bodies for the purpose of afterwards doctoring the army, it was done without my knowing of it; nor did I see any prisoner taken and afterwards killed. [It was common

29. Quarter-Master William London of the Natal Carbineers, killed at the Battle of Isandlwana. (*KZN Archives, Pietermaritzburg*)

practice for the Zulu *iziNyanga* (witchdoctors and healers) to take parts from the bodies of brave adversaries and to use them in concoctions with which they would 'doctor' (anoint) the warriors both before and after battle.] I was, however, one of the men who followed the refugees down the Buffalo River, and only returned to the English camp late in the afternoon . . . The portion of our army which had remained to plunder the camp did so thoroughly, carrying off its maize, the bread stuffs, and stores of all kinds, and drinking such spirits as were in the camp. Many were drunk, and all laden with their booty; and towards sunset the whole force moved back to the encampment of the previous night, hastened by having seen another English force approaching from the south. [Lord Chelmsford and his column returning to camp at dusk having pursued an elusive foe all day.]

Those of the defenders who survived the attack on the camp fled with forlorn hope down towards the Buffalo River and Natal, remorselessly pursued by the victorious and maddened warriors who, over the broken terrain, could outrun a horse.

Brickhill, the interpreter, was one who ran the gauntlet and was brave enough to admit that he acted like a coward:

30. Lieutenant J A Roberts of the Natal Native Horse, killed at the Battle of Isandlwana. (*Ron Lock Collection*)

Our flight I shall never forget. No path, no track. Boulders everywhere – on we went, borne now into some dry torrent bed, now weaving our way amongst trees of stunted growth . . . Our way was already strewn with shields, assegais, hats, clothing of all description, guns, ammunition belts, and I don't know what not. Our stampede was composed of mules, with and without pack saddles, oxen, horses in all stages of equipment, and fleeing men all strangely intermingled – man and beast all inflicted with the danger which surrounded us. How one's bosom steels itself to pity at such a time. I came up with poor Band-Sergeant Gamble tottering and tumbling about amongst the stones. He said, 'For God's sake give me a lift'. I said, 'My dear fellow, it's a case of life and death with me', and closing my eyes I put spurs to my horse and bounded ahead.

Captain Essex, an Imperial officer, later wrote:

I had, thank God, a very good horse, and a sure-footed one, but I saw many poor fellows roll over, their horses stumbling over the rocky ground. It was now a race for dear life. The Zulus kept up with us on both sides, being able to run down the steep rocky ground quite as fast as a horse could travel.

31. John Bullock, Quarter-Master Sergeant, Natal Carbineers, killed at Isandlwana, a Pietermaritzburg chemist in civilian life. (*KZN Archives, Pietermaritzburg*)

And another young officer by the name of Smith-Dorrien: 'I was riding a broken-kneed old crock which did not belong to me and I expected it to go down on its head every minute . . . The enemy were going at a kind of very fast half-walk, half run . . . and kept killing all the way.'

It was an overwhelming Zulu victory, a victory that shook the British Empire. When finally – and still in disbelief that such a disaster could have happened – Lord Chelmsford and his column, in the gathering gloom, arrived at the stricken camp, all that they found was death and destruction: 'The dead were lying in such numbers that we constantly fell over corpses, but whether European or Zulu it was too dark to see. The gunners of the Royal Artillery had to pull bodies out of the way because the horses would not pass them.'

There were many individual descriptions of the night's ordeal:

It was a mercy that the surrounding darkness shut off from our view many ghastly sights . . .

We laid down in a square for the night literally amongst our slaughtered comrades . . .

No pen could adequately express the feelings of those who spent the night at that ghastly halting place amongst the debris of the plundered and mutilated bodies of men, horses and cattle . . .

But there were also many Zulu dead, estimated at around 1,000; so many in fact that it was as though, in King Cetshwayo's words: 'An assegai had been plunged into the belly into the Zulu nation.'

Just prior to the commencement of hostilities, a young Dutchman by the name of Cornelius Vijn, had been trading in Zululand and had been apprehended just at the time when the Zulu army was ready to depart for Isandlwana:

When the king heard how his people had treated me he was astounded, and said that this had occurred without his order or cognisance. He then agreed with his chief men and brothers that no harm must be done to me, and that all my goods must be collected and brought back to me. . . .

32. By 1880 the battlefields of Isandlwana had, to a large extent, been cleaned up. Colonel Bowker and Major Stabb, keen naturalists, take the opportunity to catch butterflies. (*KZN Archives, Pietermaritzburg*)

That no one must dare to touch me or my property, since I, and all I had, belonged from that moment to the king until the war should be over, when I might return in quiet to Natal again.

When the news of the warrior casualties reached Zululand there was lamenting for many days. Vijn observed:

> . . . a troop of people, who came back from their gardens crying and wailing. As they approached, I recognised them as persons belonging to the kraal in which I was staying. When they came into or close to the kraal, they kept wailing in front of the kraals, rolling themselves on the ground and never quietening down; Nay, in the night they wailed so as to cut through the heart of anyone. And this wailing went on, night and day, for a fortnight; the effect of it was very depressing; I wished I could not hear it.

Two other battles were fought on the same day as Isandlwana. Lord Chelmsford had left 100 men to guard the make-shift hospital and commissariat store at Rorke's Drift on the Natal bank of the Buffalo River. At 4.30 p.m. part of the Zulu army, some 3,000–4,000 strong, that had missed out on the plunder at Isandlwana, descended on the British post that, having been forewarned of the Zulu approach, had just one hour in which to throw together, helter-skelter, a flimsy barricade made of biscuit boxes and sacks of corn. The engagement that followed has become as famous a victory for the British Army as the fight at Isandlwana has become a byword for blunder and defeat. And the Zulu regiments that were eventually vanquished by the redcoats, fighting at odds of more than twenty to one, were ridiculed by their kin – but the redcoats who eventually triumphed, after twelve hours fighting – much of it hand-to-hand combat, had unstinted praise for the courage of their Zulu foe.

Let the mocking Zulu critics speak first:

> The Uthulwana Regiment was finished up at Jim's [the Zulu name for Rorke's Drift named after James Rorke: KwaJimu or Jim's Place] – shocking cowards they were too. Our people laughed at them. Some said 'You! You're not men! You're just women, seeing you ran away for no reason at all, like the wind!' Others jeered and said, 'You marched off!'

The British defenders thought differently. Lieutenant John Chard, the officer commanding Rorke's Drift, speaking of the first rush of the Zulu attack:

> ... A series of desperate assaults splendidly met by our men and repulsed by the bayonet ... Those Zulus were an enemy that it was some credit to us to have defeated. Their bravery and courage could not have been excelled, and their military organisation and their discipline might have given a lesson to more civilised nations. Cruel and savage as they were, the Zulus were a gallant enemy...

Colour Sergeant Frank Bourne:

> ... They made rush after rush, but we kept them at bay. Still they came on. There was no question of quarter. They asked for none, and they gave none ...

Sergeant Fred Milne:

> They hurled themselves on our people's defences, to be repulsed by our concentrated fire and by bayonets. Again and again they came on. Assegais clashed against rifle barrels. They shouted their war cries and we gave British cheers. At first I felt nervous, but the savage instinct, the blood thirst came up on top. So close was the conflict that one soldier felled two Zulus with his fists.

Private Frederick Hitch:

> They pushed right up to us, and not only got up to the laager but got in with us! But they seemed to have a great dread of the bayonet which stood with us from beginning to end. During the struggle there was a fine big Zulu seeing me shoot his mate down he sprang, dropping his rifle and assegai, gripping hold of the muzzle of my rifle with his left hand and with his right hand got hold of the bayonet, thinking to disarm me, he pulled and tried hard to disarm me and get the rifle from me, but I had a firm grip of my rifle with my left hand. My cartridges were on top of the mealie bags which enabled me to load my rifle with my right hand and shoot the poor wretch.

And so the fight continued into the night until, twelve hours after it had commenced, the Zulu attack finally wavered and the warriors withdrew.

The miraculous British success at Rorke's Drift together with the award of eleven Victoria Crosses to the defenders, did much to distract both military and public attention from the disaster of Isandlwana. Both engagements, each spectacular in their own way, also distracted attention from the third battle fought on 22 January 1879. The British Coastal Column, under the command of Colonel Charles Pearson, 2,800 strong, engaged and defeated a Zulu army at a crossing of the Nyezane River. Then, marching on to Eshowe and taking possession of Bishop Schreuder's deserted mission station, Pearson and his men were besieged there and would remain so for the next two months.

The British invasion of Zululand came to a sudden halt. The Colony of Natal had been indeed fortunate that a handful of redcoats had managed to deter and daunt the Zulu army at Rorke's Drift. Although Prince Dabulamanzi (he who had lost the shooting competition to the boy soldier at Cetshwayo's coronation) had specific orders not to cross into the colony, he later confessed that had he taken Rorke's Drift, he would not have restrained his rampaging warriors and believed that as he pressed on into the defenceless countryside, the local natives, to save themselves, would join him, rise up against the whites, and the holocaust that the settlers feared would come to pass.

Yet, as far as the Zulu kingdom was concerned, the threat of invasion remained. Lord Chelmsford would have to make a second attempt and reinforcements began to arrive from around the British Empire. A Captain Montague remembered the tales being told aboard the ship, each story more terrifying than the last:

Men lately returned from Zululand had talked to them freely of the terrors of the place. Defeat was a certainty. Death indeed a mercy; tortures of the most appalling nature, described with a realistic force quite convincing, were with a certain loss of those unfortunate enough to escape death. Isandlwana was an every day occurrence in wars of this kind: the names of officers who had fallen here was quoted as 'instances of fresh horrors'; their bodies had been recovered all but unrecognizable, owing to their treatment ... The listeners were young and ready of belief, and the accounts of what they had heard cost nothing in the telling, and were detailed on board as the most cheerful news to be had.

By the end of March Lord Chelmsford was ready. However, the Zulu army had not been idle and Chelmsford would have to ride the shockwaves of two further disasters before the fortunes of war swung in his favour. First a redcoat convoy, carrying amongst other things 90,000 rounds of ammunition, was ambushed in a dawn attack, suffering sixty casualties, either dead or missing, and the loss of the entire load of ammunition. This incident caused *The Graphic* to protest: 'British soldiers (officers and men alike) will persist in underrating the enemy, especially if he wears a black skin.'

The second calamity was the defeat and near-annihilation of over 200 crack colonial horsemen who were attacking the Zulu stronghold of Hlobane Mountain. But the following day, fortune finally favoured the British invaders. Following up their victory over the colonials, a Zulu army, 20,000 strong, now at the zenith of its power and success, rashly descended on the fortified encampment of No. 4 Column, commanded by Colonel Evelyn Wood, at Kambula Hill. Every precaution, over a number of weeks, had been taken against such an attack. The wagons had been converted into temporary two-tier firing platforms; shelter trenches had been dug; ammunition boxes opened; guns had been entrenched; range-markers had been positioned as far out as a thousand yards in every direction and every man knew his exact position and duty.

After the debacle of Rorke's Drift, Cetshwayo had instructed his generals that on no account must an attack be made on an entrenched enemy – the king contemptuously comparing the British to bushpigs who also burrowed in the ground. However, the headstrong young warriors, exultant and eager to re-enact the glory of Isandlwana, calling out to the redcoats as they advanced: 'Don't run away, Johnny; we want to speak to you', charged the British defences, squandering their lives, and in one futile assault sealed the fate of the Zulu kingdom. Although there was yet a final battle to be fought, Kambula was the decisive engagement of the war; a correspondent of the *Cape Argus* reported on the first phase of the battle: 'We were able to see dense masses of the enemy advancing in perfect order in four columns; their end seemed

33. The surprise dawn attack on the 80th Regiment's convoy was another Zulu victory that filled the young British troops with apprehension.

never to come and no doubt many in the camp were doubtful that they would resist the rush of such masses.'

And then they charged, into a killing ground of rifle volleys and shellfire:

> ... But still they came on, with the ferocity of tigers, never halting, never wavering, never flinching or hesitating for a moment.
>   ... A line of Zulus swept around the corner wagon at full speed and raced along our line, seeking an opportunity to enter. As they passed each wagon a sheet of flame and smoke from the Martini-Henry rifles welcomed them. They tumbled and fell, but it made not the slightest difference; they did not shear away from the wagons or abate their speed, and they still came on – an endless stream. Finding no opening, the Zulus turned and charged the whole line. Crash! – As the shields struck the wagons, and the whole line shook.

That was the recollection of young George Mossop, a seventeen-year-old volunteer of the Frontier Light Horse. Captain George Dennison of Wetherley's Border Horse had similar memories: 'Loud and continuous was the din of battle interluded with a deep base and weird battle cry added to the rattling of many thousands of shields by the Zulus as they made successive charges on one or other side of the camp.' Mehlokazulu, Sihayo's son, remembered the engagement from the Zulu side: '... So many were killed that the few not killed were lying between dead bodies so thick were the dead ... Our regiment was so anxious to distinguish itself that we disobeyed the King's orders ... Had we waited properly for supports we should have attacked the camp on both sides at once and we should have taken it ...' The battle over, the Zulu dead were so numerous that it took three days to bury them. Commandant Schermbrucker of the Kaffrarian Rifles described the scene: 'It was a ghastly ditch, 200 ft long, some 200 ft broad and 10 ft deep which received wagon load after wagon load of dead bodies of the bravest warriors of a brave people. Full military honours were accorded, as batch after batch, closely packed, they were deposited in a soldier's grave.'

On 2 April, 100 miles away, Lord Chelmsford also fought a battle, but against a smaller and less resolute Zulu army. He was victorious and went on to relieve Eshowe where, it will be remembered, men of the Coastal Column had been under siege for a number of weeks. Now

34. The Frontier Light Horse was originally raised in the Eastern Cape from the rough, tough drifters of the frontier. It followed the fortunes of Chelmsford's army but was immediately disbanded after the Battle of Ulundi.

the way was clear for an advance on the Zulu capital. But it would take another three months for the now victorious British to get there; and on the way another catastrophe that would shake the world befell the unfortunate Lord Chelmsford. Attached to his staff was a non-combatant observer, none other than Louis, Prince Imperial of France, son of Napoleon III and great-nephew of the Napoleon Bonaparte. He was an adventurous and headstrong young man who took himself off on a reconnaissance patrol, deep into Zulu territory, and was ambushed and killed. His death caused an international sensation that did nothing to enhance Chelmsford's reputation and which caused Benjamin Disraeli, (who was by then Lord Beaconsfield) the British Prime Minister, to remark: 'A very remarkable people, the Zulus: they defeat our generals; they convert our bishops and they have settled the fate of a great European dynasty.'

The Zulu taunt 'fight us in the open' – in other words, outside an entrenched position – had rankled with Lord Chelmsford, as indeed it

35. A further disaster for Lord Chelmsford: Louis Napoleon, Prince Imperial of France, is brutally killed by Zulu warriors whilst on a reconnaissance. Major Stabb stands by his handiwork of erecting a memorial while Zulu labourers give the royal salute.

36. Zulus who had left the kingdom to live in Natal were conscripted into regiments led by white officers and NCOs, many of whom lacked the necessary qualities of leadership. (*Local History Museum, Durban*)

had with the whole of the army, and Chelmsford had determined that
the final battle would be won in a manner that he and his men could
be proud of. After much hardship on the march, during which they
plundered and laid waste in an orgy of vengeful destruction everything
in their paths, the redcoats and colonials arrived at the Umfolozi River,
four miles from the Zulu capital of Ulundi. Here, the column performed
a remarkable military manoeuvre. Having waded the Umfolozi, the
whole force of 5,000 men formed a square, the size of a polo ground,
and in that formation marched on Ulundi and, in the open, awaited the
Zulu onslaught. They did not have to wait for long. 'They [the Zulus]
advanced in beautiful order, covered by skirmishers, apparently in one
continuous line about four deep, with intervals between the regiments
... it is evidently their object to surround us, with their largest force in
the rear to cut off our retreat; it was a grand sight.'

But, although the British were outnumbered four to one, they had
5,000 breech-loading rifles, twelve field guns and two Gatling guns

37. Ernest Grandier, a Frenchman serving in Weatherley's Border Horse,
was the only white man to be taken prisoner by the Zulus. A few weeks later
he escaped relatively unharmed.

38. At the battle of Ulundi the seven and nine pounder guns of the Royal
Artillery, devastated the packed ranks of the Zulu army. Total British
casualties, killed and wounded, eighty two. The Zulu killed were estimated
at 1,500.

while, by contrast, the Zulus had less than 1,000 captured breech-loaders,
spears, shields and muzzle-loading muskets. A comparison of casualties
tells the story: on the British side, thirteen killed and sixty wounded
whereas the Zulu casualties were estimated at 1,200. Fire power had
ensured that the Zulus never closed with the British square.

Captain Montague again:

> No prisoners were taken. Hours after the battle the popping of the
> Basuto's [NNH] carbines told of the horrible kind of warfare we were
> engaged in. Merciless savages are these Basutos, so brave soldiers, and
> not a few of them Christians. But 'War to the death' is their motto, one
> and all. One of them happened to hit a wretched Zulu in the legs as he
> was running away, and captured him. Sitting down beside his prize, he
> pulled out some meat and a bit of biscuit and took his lunch, conversing

all the while in a pleasant, friendly way with the Zulu, prompting him by asking all sorts of questions, and talking of old times when they might have met. Lunch over and the questions disposed of, the Basuto tightened his girth, put the bit into his pony's mouth, and nodding to his poor captive, said he must be off, as time pressed – and without more ado took up his carbine and shot him dead.

It was a British triumph. For all practical purposes the war was over. Chelmsford had not only beaten the Zulus, he had also beaten Sir Garnet Wolseley, the new commander-in-chief, who had been riding furiously in an effort to take command and direct the final battle. As it happened, he arrived a day too late and an elated Chelmsford greeted him with not only the news of his victory but also of his resignation. He would leave Wolseley to sort out the mess and to have the renown of capturing the Zulu king.

Chapter 13

The End of a Kingdom

The unjust war was over, leaving Zululand destitute. But Britain would not be satisfied until Cetshwayo was captured. What his fate would be when that was achieved was uncertain but his capture was imperative. And so, only days after the Battle of Ulundi had been fought, British patrols, often comprising of little more than a couple of officers, an interpreter and a small escort, were roaming Zululand, miles from any reinforcements, and would find themselves received with good-natured curiosity. But none, it seemed, were willing to betray their king.

An interpreter, Henry Longcast, recalled:

> We could get nothing from the Zulus. We were treated the same at every kraal. I had been a long time in Zululand, I knew the people and their habits, and, although I believed that they would be true to their king, I never expected such devotion. Nothing would move them. Neither the loss of cattle, the fear of death, nor the offering of large bribes would make them false to their king.

Lieutenant Henry Harford accompanied one of the many 'seek-search-and-capture' patrols and, on one occasion when the questioning was over and curiosity satisfied, Harford recalled:

> . . . One of Somkele's warriors came up and asked if any of us had been at Isandlwana, and on telling him that I was out with the Contingent [NNC] at Isipezi at the time of the fight, he caught hold of my hands and shook them firmly in a great state of delight, saying it was a splendid fight. 'You fought well, and we fought well', he exclaimed, and then showed me eleven wounds that he had received, bounding off with the greatest ecstasy

39. The Zulu were not alone in taking gruesome trophies. Amongst the bric-a-brac of a British officer's tent, there can be seen a human skull. (*Local History Museum, Durban*)

to show how it all happened . . . I now had a look at his wounds. One bullet had gone through his hand, three had gone through his shoulder and smashed his shoulder blade, two had cut the skin and slightly in to the flesh right down the chest and stomach, and one had gone clean to the fleshy part of the thigh. The others were mere scratches in comparison with these, but there he was as well as ever and ready for another set to. Could anything more clearly show the splendid spirit in which the Zulu fought us? No animosity, no revengeful feeling, but just sheer love of a good fight in which the courage of both sides could be tested . . .

All the warriors throughout the kingdom were required to surrender their firearms which they did reluctantly, but with good grace. Later Captain W. E. Montague, whose job it had been to collect the old muskets, wrote of his experiences:

> . . . Walking magnificently, upright and springing, with skins like satin, their faces far above the usual Negro-type and their figures pictures

of grace and activity. They came on without the slightest show of fear, straight into the camp, and were taken at once to their quarters where they all squatted in a semi-circle while their fire-arms were collected, each man in turn being called by name, when he advanced and deposited the arms he carried, he received in return a pass to secure him from being molested. One day came Mahanana, a brother of Cetshwayo's, and not unlike him in face and form. He was enormously fat, standing over six feet in stature, perfectly naked all but for the kilt he wore, and came forty miles to surrender to us, on foot. His bodyguard consisted of six rough-looking Zulus, who squatted with their master opposite the tent door, as though they were equals. But there was no mistaking the chief; his composure was intense, the indifference with which he treated everything about so delightful, and his whole attitude truly royal. An officer wishing to possess something of his as a memento, asked him to give him the rough stick he carried. Mahanana raised his eyes for a second and replied in his low, soft voice: 'That stick has touched my hand, and there may be some of my own royal sweat upon it. I am a king, and nothing of a king's can touch a stranger and not be defiled!' . . . And yet the man was a prisoner, and beaten. It was amusing to talk to the Zulus; they are so magnificent in their ignorance and so full of themselves.

And so the British army suddenly felt affection and a camaraderie for their former foe. Later, a report published by the Intelligence Division of the War Office pondered:

> There can be no doubt that the Zulu is a born soldier. No one who knows the Zulu nation can doubt their high military qualities, and it may be taken as admitted that better rough military material could scarcely be found. A Zulu by birth, by tradition and from the earliest training is a soldier. He is brave, hardy and enduring.

And a young officer speculated how with a Zulu army, Britain could have conquered much of Africa: 'With a remodelled system, and an army led by Englishmen, these men would have followed us anywhere. We might have had Southern Africa up to the Zambezi and beyond it . . .'

But as time wore on with the king still at large, it was not all 'Hail fellow well met' between the searchers and the searched. Cornelius Vijn, the young Dutch trader who it will be remembered had been caught up in Zululand at the beginning of hostilities and had remained there throughout the war, had now been eagerly employed by the British as a guide who, it was hoped, would lead them to the king. On the orders of Sir Garnet Wolseley, Vijn at first went alone, found the king and tried to persuade him to surrender. But Cetshwayo was apprehensive, believing he would be shot. Vijn returned to Wolseley who immediately ordered 500 mounted men, under the command of Major Percy Barrow, to set out in pursuit. But the king had fled. After floundering around in the bush for two days, and with tempers raw, the party approached a village. Vijn remembered: 'We off-saddled and sent out scouts, who by noon had collected forty Zulus ... Major Barrow required them to tell whither the king had gone, and said he would shoot one of them if they did not tell him but they could not or would not.'

After a further three days of fruitless search they returned to Ulundi only to sally forth again a day or so later. But now Barrow had sensibly streamlined his force to only twenty-five men. Vijn continues the tale:

The next day we went as far as the first kraal belonging to Sibebu, where we off-saddled. We found here some guns which we smashed, but no

40. After the final shots were fired, Cetshwayo evaded his enemies for over two months.

Martini-Henry's. Then we made the owners of the kraal give their stored mealies for our horses, which they did very unwillingly, being afraid of starvation, and one actually cried, saying that they 'would have nothing now to eat'. The officer took only half the mealies from the kraal, and took the rest from another kraal. He then sent for the headman of the second kraal, and sent him with a message to Sibebu, that he must surrender, and bring in his guns and royal cattle, and if he did not come in two days' time, they would burn all the kraals in his country and take all his cattle.

However, Barrow was not destined to have the kudos of capturing the king. Quite by chance, it would fall to Major Richard Marter of the 1st Dragoon Guards.

The king had now evaded capture for over two months during which time dozens and dozens of patrols had set forth with high hopes but, as was the case with Captain Barrow, the terrain, the climate and the antagonistic disdain of most Zulus saw patrol after patrol return to camp exhausted, crestfallen and empty-handed. Barrow, in fact, had handed over command of his particular search party to Captain Lord Gifford who, by diligently following every clue, was soon hot on the trail of the king. By 28 August, Gifford was confident that the king was his. Having stealthily deployed his men about the approaches to a village, Gifford was waiting for dusk before pouncing on his quarry. However, unbeknown to him, there was another hunting party approaching the village from the opposite direction. Major Marter's patrol of the Dragoon Guards were looking down on the back of the village from a mountainous ridge 2,000 feet high. Let Sergeant Smith of the Dragoons describe what happened:

> The kraal down at the bottom of the hill, about a stone's throw off to look at, but it took about three hours to get to it, having to lead our horses all the way through the forest. When we eventually got through and Major says to us, 'When I say Gallop, I want you to gallop', which we did up one hill, down another, and then on the level with stones as big as wheelbarrows to get over, through, or any way we liked. I heard one man and then another calling out 'Stop that horse' as the horse had fallen down with them, but it was every one for himself until we surrounded the kraal. The inmates were quite surprised, as none of them knew where we had sprung from. The king was a long time before he would surrender

to us, but he was told that if he did not come out, we should burn him out, so he quietly came out, and looked as stately as a General coming to review a few thousand men on parade.

Major Marter also described what happened. Having descended through the forest, the Dragoons were still faced with some rugged terrain which they had to cross as fast as they could go:

Accustomed as our horses had become to following us over very difficult ground, the sheer fall from one ledge of rock in particular so dismayed some of them that there was nothing for it but to have them pushed over and let them take their chances ... The foot was reached at 3 o'clock, two horses having fallen to rise no more, and one man's elbow having being dislocated in this part of the run. Here fortune favoured us, for on the lower edge of the forest was a little dell, hidden in which we could mount unobserved. This was a great advantage, and waiting till all were out and on their horses, I gave a low word 'Gallop, march' and gallop we did.

In no time the kraal was surrounded and finally Marter called out to the king:

I called on the king to come out which he positively declined to do, insisting that I should go in to him. Being unable to turn him from this, and at the same time quite determined that he should come out and surrender himself, I said that I was very sorry, but, having no time to waste, I was about having a match applied to the hut, when he asked the rank of the officer to whom he must yield – by whose authority I had come – and stipulated that I should not kill him. I then said that I had been especially sent by the High Commissioner to bring him in, under the authority of the Queen of England, and that I would not kill him if he came with me quietly and made no attempt to escape. At last he came out, fine fellow as he is, and throwing his mantle over his shoulder, stood in front of me, and quite 'the King'. Looking haughtily to the right and left and seeing the helmets of the mounted Dragoons surrounding the kraal he asked 'How did they get here?' And on the chief pointing to the mountain behind him, added, 'I never thought troops could come down the mountain through the forest, or I should not have been taken.' ... The king was by no means, as has been represented, 'worn to a shadow', or 'foot-sore and weary', but in splendid condition, and as fresh as could be, showing not the smallest sign of having fallen away. His weight must be enormous, but he is not over burthened with superfluous fat, or out of proportion in girth – a noble specimen of a man in form, without, a bad or cruel expression, and, as I have said before, 'the King' all over in appearance and bearing.

During the long journey back to Ulundi, Cetshwayo let it be known by word and gesture that he was king, often infuriating Marter and trying his patience to breaking point. A number of his courtiers had accompanied their king and on one occasion four attempted to escape. Having been previously warned that any attempted flight would be met by shooting, two were gunned down while the other two got away. After this incident the cavalcade moved with more alacrity, Cetshwayo completing the last leg of the journey in a mule cart that had been acquired by Marter especially for the king's comfort. But, on drawing close to Ulundi and the crowds of military spectators who had assembled to witness the spectacle of his arrival, Cetshwayo alighted:

41. The king, carefully guarded, on the way to Lord Wolseley's camp.

... The king was evidently much dejected, and just before reaching the top of the hill overlooking Ulundi, he stopped, and placing his hands upon the top of his long staff, rested his forehead upon them for about a minute – then, raising his head, he threw off all signs of depression, and marched onwards and into camp with the most perfect dignity, the troops having all turned out to see him come in.

Wolseley wasted no time and hardly had Cetshwayo set foot in the British camp than he was about-turned and marched off to the coast. On 4 September, two months to the day after the Battle of Ulundi, he was embarked upon a coasting vessel, the *Natal*, that, over an eleven day voyage, took him to the Cape and thereafter to confinement in Cape Town Castle.

So Cetshwayo had not been betrayed by the Zulu people as the white politicos had predicted; he was not, it would appear, the infamous despotic ruler, feared and hated by his people, as Sir Bartle Frere would have the world believe – nor was he a grotesque black savage as had been portrayed by more than one English pictorial. He was, as the curious white population of the Cape soon discovered as they crowded for a glimpse, not a bad-looking fellow. In fact, his description as appeared in *The Times* was positively flattering:

Cetshwayo's personal appearance is quite unlike any of the so-called portraits, which have appeared in the pictorial press. He is an exceptionally fine specimen of the noble savage, of well-proportioned and fully developed frame, a good-natured, broad, open-face, of the prominent Zulu-type.

Despite of his immense proportions I never saw a finer specimen of the races of South Africa or amongst them so intelligent a face. Those who have seen the photograph 'from a painting' are made to believe that he is monstrous in face and form – a huge carcass with a fiendish countenance. He is nothing of the sort ... The face is massive, open, and good-natured, and lights up quickly at a pleasant thought or a humorous suggestion . . . The eyes, large and lustrous, would – in the glance I had – indicate a restless energy and quickness of comprehension. All those who see the king will be astonished that one in such good condition and with so good a face, had ever been the great war-spirit of the land.

42. It was popular to portray Cetshwayo as a fearsome monster as painted 'from life'. (*Local History Museum, Durban*)

Meanwhile in Zululand, Wolseley had been busy imposing upon the Zulu people a classic example of divide and rule; and thus the reason for the unseemly haste with which Cetshwayo had been marched out of Ulundi becomes clear. On the day he was triumphantly brought into camp as a prisoner, some of the great chiefs of the nation, those specifically selected by Wolseley himself, were beginning to assemble at the British camp. They were to hear on the morrow what the future of their land would be and what part they might play in its administration; and the last thing that Wolseley wanted was the presence of the king.

The British authorities, or rather Wolseley, had decided not to annex Zululand after all as that would require direct rule and enormous expense to the government. Rather, let the Zulus get on with it themselves, with a minimum of British supervision, no more than just a Resident. There would be no influx of white settlers (those colonial soldiers to whom Lord Chelmsford had promised farms in Zululand would have to be disappointed). If the Zulus didn't like the way he had proposed to cut up the kingdom they could fight amongst themselves and being busy on that score, the bogey of a Zulu invasion would be laid once and for all. And the Colony of Natal would at last sleep soundly.

Wolseley had decided to divide the kingdom into thirteen self-ruling chiefdoms, leaving no door by which, at a later date, Cetshwayo may be able to return and enter his former realm. In addition Wolseley's choice of his thirteen rulers was not only astonishing but outrageous. Two were not Zulus at all: One was John Dunn and the other Sergeant-Major Hlubi, a former NCO of the Natal Native Horse and Durnford's chief scout at the Langalibalele affray. Nevertheless, all were required to take an oath. The *Narrative of the Field Operations Connected With the Anglo-Zulu War*, compiled by the Intelligence Branch of the War Office, records what they were required to say:

> I recognise the victory of the British Arms over the Zulu Nation, and the full right and title of her Majesty Queen Victoria, Queen of England and Empress of India, to deal as she may think fit with the Zulu chiefs and people, and with the Zulu country; and I agree, and I hereby sign my agreement, to accept from Sir Garnet Joseph Wolseley, GCMG, KCB, as the representative of Her Majesty Queen Victoria, the Chieftainship of a territory of Zululand . . .

There followed a long list of further conditions which the future rulers swore to obey, such as the banning of the Zulu military system, that men be allowed to marry at will, that no firearms be permitted, that any fugitives from British justice be arrested and delivered to the authorities, and that no British subject be brought to trial or sentenced without the approval of the British Resident.

So a Resident was duly appointed and the thirteen chiefs sworn in on the following day, 2 September 1879, then, with breathtaking haste, the British evacuation of Zululand began. The War Office Narrative records: 'The stores which had been collected in the various posts having being consumed or removed, all these posts were abandoned, and by the end of September, 1879, the last attachment of British troops had left Zululand', leaving behind a ravaged land rife for civil war. What had it all been about?

Of all these happenings, and the destruction of his kingdom, Cetshwayo knew nothing. He was accompanied to his incarceration by his head gaoler, Captain J. R. Poole of the Royal Artillery, his interpreter, Henry Longcast and nine Zulu companions. On his way to Cape Town Castle he witnessed the first instance of a strange phenomena. People of British stock, now represented by the citizens of Cape Town, always sympathetic with the underdog and quick to applaud celebrities and those unjustly vilified, now saw a mixture of all those traits in Cetshwayo and, much to his amazement, the crowds began to cheer him. Where he had expected loathing and hostility, he received acclaim and admiration. Soon everyone who was anyone was requesting permission to visit the king in his sparsely-furnished quarters which, nevertheless, commanded panoramic views of Cape Town. One such visitor who would have significant influence on his future, was a Lady Florence Dixie, who arrived in Natal in March 1881. A newly-married twenty-year-old aristocrat, richly endowed with looks, wealth and good fortune, she was also a superb horsewoman, a first-class shot and as tough as they come. In addition she had recently been appointed the London *Morning Post* Special Correspondent to cover the war that had recently broken out between Britain and the Transvaal. It was a war merely of days with Britain suffering an ignominious defeat at Majuba Hill, the like of which it had not experienced in all its long history, so the war was over before Lady Florence could put her descriptive pen to paper. Instead she began to take an interest in the affairs of Zululand, soon becoming a stalwart advocate for the release and restoration of the Zulu king.

In the meantime, while Cetshwayo was transferred to less formal confinement, a farm on the Cape Flats called Oude Moulen, Zululand was fast becoming a cauldron boiling with resentment and revenge. The royal family, Cetshwayo's brothers and kin, had been placed under the gloating authority of Zibhebhu kaMapita of the Mandhlakazi clan and it was now his pleasure to treat them as though they were serfs, robbing them of their cattle and forcing them into a state of destitution. John Dunn and Hamu, in their respective domains, were no less brutal in their dealings with their 'subjects' who might have provoked their displeasure. Such was the state of unrest throughout Zululand that by August 1881, less than two years since Cetshwayo's capture, the British thought it wise to listen to a deputation made up of notable chiefs and thousands of followers, all of whom wished to express their discontent and plea for the return of their monarch.

Colonel Sir Evelyn Wood, the victor of the Battle of Kambula, now a Brigadier-General, had been chosen as the strong man to represent the British government. His Zulu name was Kuni, which he self flatteringly wished to believe meant 'a man who was as hard as ironwood'; but it was merely a direct translation of his surname, Wood, into Zulu: *Kuni* or firewood. It had been arranged to meet the Zulu deputation at Inhlazatshe Mountain.

Foul and bitter cold weather delayed the proceedings and it was not until 31 August 1881 that the Zulu delegation began to state its case. The indefatigable Lady Florence Dixie had let neither pouring rain, nor the mud and the misery, deter her in her quest to find the true state of Zululand and its people. What she discovered that day would change her life forever. She arrived a jingoistic imperialist and left a staunch crusader for the underdog.

The delay caused by the weather had given Lady Florence the opportunity to wander freely amongst those drenched delegates who had already arrived. She was to write: 'Many a wholesome truth I learnt that day from the lips of the chiefs, indunas and common people.' Though previously she had admired Sir Bartle Frere and his handling of the Anglo-Zulu War, she now derided him: Where was the fear, the hate and the terror for this tyrant [Cetshwayo], this despotic savage, this manslaying machine of Sir Bartle Frere's, which we in England had been taught and encouraged to believe existed?' She found that the majority of those present desired above all the return of their king. But there were also the dissenting voices of John Dunn and Chief Zibhebhu (attended by his white advisor, twenty-five year-old Johannes Colenbrander) both of whom feared that the return of Cetshwayo would be the end of their own fiefdoms. And, in promoting a case for their vested interests, they were voicing exactly what the British wished to hear: that the Zulu people did not want their king back.

Wood, surrounded by a bevy of staff officers, armed troops, officials, a military band and with the damp royal standard hanging limply from a hastily-erected flagpole, opened the proceedings by describing the new demarcations of Zululand, demarcations that once again saw the former kingdom diminish in size: that portion of the Disputed Territories that two years earlier the Boundary Commission had awarded to Zululand, Wood now told the assembly Wolseley had, after all, given all of it to the Boers. Also, Wolseley had not only demarcated the borders of Swaziland, which Zululand must now recognise, but had declared that particular kingdom to be an independent state. Perhaps Wolseley's surprising generosity towards the amaSwazi was a reward for the assistance that the kingdom had given him in his recent war against the baPedi: at a crucial moment 6,000 Swazi mercenaries had tipped the scales in Wolseley's favour when it seemed that the baPedi had the upper hand.

Having described the relocation of Zululand's boundaries, Wood then revealed Britain's plans for the future administration of the former kingdom: an annual tax of ten shillings per hut was to paid to the British Resident; chiefs desiring the services of a white assistant (they would need one in order to comprehend what was going on) would require the appointment to be approved by the Resident; the Resident's expenses and those of sub-Residents would be paid from the proceeds of the hut tax as would the cost of sustaining a police force; chiefs were to establish and maintain roads and schools; white man's liquor was to be banned; and all chiefs were to unite in order to suppress rebellion and conflict.

43. All the swank and polish of a military band has gone but, nevertheless, the band played on keeping up the spirits of officers and men alike. 13th Light Infantry, Zululand 1879. (*Africana Museum, Johannesburg*)

Yes, but how about the return of our king, they asked, and the tyranny of Sibebu, Hamu and John Dunn? They were told, in so many words, that the purpose of the *indaba* was to ensure that Wolseley's stipulations were adhered to – it was not for the submission of complaints. The assembly dispersed, leaving most Zulu delegates bitterly resentful. It seemed that Zibhebhu, Hamu and Dunn had been given the nod to carry on as before which they did forthwith, with Sibebu in particular fulfilling a tyrant's role in his domain. Zululand was fast descending into a state of anarchy.

Down in the Cape prospects were improving. Robert Samuelson, whose father had been a life-long friend of Cetshwayo, had been appointed interpreter. In addition, Cetshwayo had been offered his freedom, provided he did not return to Zululand. Rather than accept such condition – and although desperate for his release – he replied: 'You warn me not to return to Zululand ... I was the King of the Zulus, had my country invaded by the Queen's troops, tried to defend my country, but was beaten, taken captive and brought down here by the Queen's orders. Here I intend to remain until the Queen restores me to Zululand.'

However, due to the efforts of, among others, Lady Florence, the Colenso family and Robert Samuelson, there were now strong political forces in England demanding that Cetshwayo be restored. So it was with great joy that Cetshwayo received the news that the Earl of Kimberley the Colonial Secretary, was to make arrangements for him to visit London in order to state his case.

There were inevitable delays and bureaucratic shilly-shallying and it was not until July 1882 that Cetshwayo sailed from Cape Town. On his arrival in London he created a sensation, not only amongst the common crowds, but amongst all classes. Lady Wolseley, whose husband had been the architect of the king's destitution, wrote:

Fancy my waiting at Grivy's balcony in Bond Street for an hour to see Cetshwayo come out of the Bassano's. The crowd was so great I was afraid to venture out into the street. I saw him capitally. He rolled majestically across the pavement ... They had to send for more police and hustled him off through Benson's shop to dodge the mob at the former's door.

A Miss Luxmore had been more bold: she gave the king a gift: 'A beautiful gold locket on a ribbon of blue velvet' which she accompanied with a compliment: 'Tell him it is the gift of an English Lady to a brave man.'

The king, in fact, received a considerable number of letters that today would be called 'fan mail'. All were addressed in the most respectful forms: 'Dear King Cetshwayo', 'Your Majesty' and 'Most Gracious Sovereign'. One or two hinted at romance; another, through a newspaper ad in *The Standard*, suggested some sort of risqué rendezvous: 'Meet me at the Grosvenor Turkish Baths, any day this week at 4 'o clock.' Sir Bartle Frere's shirtmaker asked for an appointment. Many requesting employment, professed themselves to be the King's 'most humble servant', and one lady beseeched Cetshwayo, on his return to Zululand, '. . . to be kind to all the cows and other animals'. Yet, not one letter contained any animosity.

Had there been such a thing as paparazzi, Cetshwayo would have been pursued relentlessly. H. B. Finney, an old acquaintance, who was acting as an additional interpreter and diplomatic advisor, recorded:

> Every day's occupation was all arranged for him and was, as a rule, an exhausting program to get through. He had to receive people who flocked in upon him by hundreds; receive deputations from this or that society; go here, there, and everywhere; and generally perform the arduous duties of a 'lion' of English society, and this continuous condition of excitement appeared to have paled upon him for he used to say, 'I like the scenes I have to visit well enough, but I do not care to be made a show of; if the English people have never seen a black man before, I am sorry. I am not a wild beast, I did not come here to be looked at.' It appeared to make him uncomfortable when his every action was noticed and commented upon and for this reason he refused a great many of the invitations he received.

Shortly after his arrival in London Cetshwayo had the first of three interviews with the Colonial Secretary, Lord Kimberley. The upshot of these meetings was a proposal from Kimberley that Cetshwayo be restored to his kingdom – provided he accepted conditions similar to those that Wolseley had imposed on the thirteen chiefs prior to their receiving authority: that he accept the appointment of a British

Resident and that a portion of the Zulu kingdom be reserved for those who did not wish to accept his rule, the boundaries of such reserve to be defined later, once the number of dissenting Zulus became known. Kimberley gave his assurance that no more land would be reserved than was, in the opinion of the British government, absolutely necessary. Cetshwayo formally objected to this last proposal, stating that Sir Garnet Wolseley had already considerably diminished the size of his kingdom. Nevertheless, the possibility of being re-united with his beloved Zululand was too tempting a prospect to jeopardise and, with a soaring heart, he accepted Kimberley's conditions.

A combination of the British people's adulation, the forthcoming restoration to his kingdom and a visit, only days away, to Queen Victoria at her summer residence on the Isle of Wight, caused a gush of gratitude from Cetshwayo who, through his interpreter, remarked: 'The English I know are just and they have been good to me. I shall never forget their kindness. They are a great nation and deserve to prosper.' Within a matter of months these words would be as dust in his mouth.

Queen Victoria was initially reluctant to receive Cetshwayo but the visit was a great success with the queen presenting her visitor with a large engraved three-handled silver beer mug: one handle to be held by the royal butler and the other two for the king to grasp as he imbibed deeply. The queen graciously informed Cetshwayo that she respected him as a brave enemy and that he would now be a firm friend. Cetshwayo in return remarked that Queen Victoria was '. . . a good and gracious lady and like myself born to rule men. We are alike.'

Discreetly, he enquired of his interpreter, as to how many generations Queen Victoria could trace her royal line and, on being informed, Cetshwayo smugly asserted it was not up to the standard of the House of Zulu that could name a lineage of no less than forty generations but, nevertheless, he would acknowledge her family as royalty and she as a sister royal. Thereafter, when describing or mentioning Victoria, Cetshwayo always referred to her as his *udadewethu* (sister).

There followed visits to Windsor Castle, the Woolwich Arsenal, Portsmouth Naval Dockyard and other impressive establishments. All in all, King Cetshwayo's visit, brief as it was, seemed to have been an unqualified success. His departure from Southampton was witnessed by cheering crowds with Cetshwayo, delighted as ever by the warmth of his reception, bowing to the mob in return. He took with him, in addition to a mountain of luggage, 'a little bit of England' in the form of a bulldog, two greyhounds and a spaniel.

But he did not return directly to Zululand as he had hoped. First it was back to Cape Town and another stint at Oude Moulen where the euphoria of his restoration soon began to evaporate into disillusion and despair. The commitments given by Lord Kimberley could, it seemed, be undermined and, indeed, usurped by colonial officials without rousing the British government's wrath or condemnation. It was as though, with the larger-than-life presence of Cetshwayo now far away back in Africa, the attitude of the British government had drastically changed: Zululand was a place which it would rather be rid of. Let the colonials sort it out themselves.

Having landed at Cape Town on 24 September 1882, Cetshwayo was kept waiting there until early January while one excuse after another was proffered as the reason for the delay. In the meantime, Zululand had split into two factions: those wishing Cetshwayo's return such as his uSuthu faction, those loyal to the royal family, and those like John Dunn and especially Chief Zibhebhu of the Mandhlakazi who were violently opposed. And it would soon be a fight to the finish between the uSuthu faction and the Mandhlakazi. It is easy to imagine the degree of resentment that must have been aroused amongst the rulers of Wolseley's thirteen chiefdoms when they were deposed of their short-lived fiefdoms.

Nevertheless, there was little opposition from most chiefs who, it seemed, would be happy to once again have Zululand ruled by one central power rather than the anarchy of thirteen squabbling 'barons'. It was Zibhebhu, Hamu and Dunn who were the steadfast opponents of Cetshwayo's return with Sibebu being particularly favoured by the colonial government. Overriding the agreement struck in London, it was proposed that Zibhebhu alone of the thirteen barons be allowed to retain and rule his territory. In addition, all the land south of the uMhlatuzi River was to be given up as a Reserve Territory, controlled by a British-officered police force, in which those who preferred to live there could reside. Cetshwayo now found the Governor of the Cape, Sir Hercules Robinson, holding a pistol to his head: accept the new conditions or remain in exile. There was to be no discussion.

44. While Cetshwayo was in London and the Cape, many of his senior ministers formed deputations demanding their King's return. (*KZN Archives, Pietermaritzburg*)

45. This delegation to the Natal Government was led by Ndabuko (No. 1 centre), the king's brother. (*KZN Archives, Pietermaritzburg*)

Later, in Zululand, Cetshwayo confided to W. Y. Campbell, a special correspondent for the *Natal Advertiser*, that the conditions imposed by Robinson were:

> . . . Quite new to me and I attributed them to Bulwer [the Natal Governor] acted on by Misjan [J W Shepstone] who bears no love to either me or my people. We, myself and companions, were astonished at the new proposal and we cried out to Robinson against them . . . But when Robinson told me that south of the uMhlatuzi River was taken from me and that Sibebu was confirmed in his command, I cried out and asked 'Wence these laws? They were never given in London. You say you will take all my south lands; you will also give Sibebu lands in the north. Where then is the country I am being returned to? . . . We had a long discussion about the land and Robinson eventually said 'Well we must end this matter. We must accept the conditions laid before you.' I then said I wished him clearly to understand that I protested against these conditions and if mischief arose in the country it would not be my fault.

46. Sir Hercules Robinson, Governor of the Cape

Finally, pining to return, Cetshwayo agreed, under protest, and with his retinue was put aboard a coasting vessel bound for Zululand. However, the place of disembarkation would not be the calm, safe waters of Durban harbour but a surf-pounded stretch of beach on an open bay.

What could have been the reason for subjecting the king and his aged dignitaries in his retinue to such obvious danger when it was far from necessary? One cannot help but muse it was hoped that they all – or Cetshwayo at least – would perish. For the colonial government his death would be most convenient. And it would not be the first occasion that the prospect of Cetshwayo's demise had been contemplated as a solution to the administration of Zululand. Robert Samuelson later wrote of an incident that had occurred during Cetshwayo's time in Cape Town:

> The King was invited to the Highland Sports as the guest of the Governor of the Cape, Sir Hercules Robinson, which were held on the sports ground, in the village of Rondebosch, on the 16th September 1881: part of the sports consisted of throwing the caber by the Highlanders – the King sat to my left and the Governor to my right, and I kept interpreting between the Governor and the King. We were seated very near to where the caber was being pitched, the King often remarked what fine men the Highlanders were and what fine attire they wore, and he enjoyed the sports very much; but an incident occurred which merely made the King anything but happy and satisfied. A brawny big and powerful Highlander pitched the caber so forcefully that it fell quite near to the King, whereupon the Governor remarked, 'Had it fallen on the King's head a great problem would have been settled.'

Nevertheless, the king and all his followers completed the perilous landing and on 10 January 1883, wet but safe, at last set foot in Zululand, soldiers and sailors having formed a chain out into the waves to assist them to the shore.

But the king's homecoming was far from being a triumphant spectacle. His return had been kept secret for fear that it might excite his loyal followers into punitive action. Therefore, most of the welcoming committee, to the king's great disappointment, were white men with the foremost being none other than his old enemy Sir Theophilus Shepstone, escorted by a detachment of the 6th (Inniskilling) Dragoons, who, having farcically proclaimed Cetshwayo king ten years earlier, was now about to reinstate him in that role. But now it would be Cetshwayo's lot to rule not only a vastly diminished kingdom, but one ravished by invasion and civil war, all of which had been brought about, to some degree, by the intrigue of Sir Theophilus himself.

It had been decided in advance that Cetshwayo's restoration ceremony would take place at Mthonjaneni, the very windswept location, high above the eMakhosini Valley, the ancient burial place of the Zulu kings where, ten years earlier, Shepstone had been kept waiting impatiently prior to Cetshwayo's coronation. Shepstone was equally impatient now, wanting to get on with it and hasten back to Pietermaritzburg. However, an essential and revered personage, Mnyamana, Cetshwayo's Prime Minister, had not yet arrived.

Cetshwayo was also impatient and agitated: a day or so earlier, while the cavalcade had briefly paused at St. Paul's Mission, Shepstone had reiterated the British terms permitting Cetshwayo's installation to which the king had agreed, one by one, until the final two: those of Zibhebhu's private fiefdom and of the slice of Zululand to be set aside as a British-administered reserve. To these he had objected strongly as he had done in Cape Town. But Shepstone was in no mood to either listen or compromise. However, it had been agreed between the king-in-waiting and Shepstone that no weapons of any kind would be permitted at the ceremony. It was then a provocative and flagrant gesture of contempt when Zibhebhu, accompanied by a following of armed warriors, all mounted, rode arrogantly into the Mthonjaneni camp, demonstrating his disrespect in the most public way. He and his swaggering troublemakers, having paid their respects to Shepstone, calmly rode away without receiving a single reprimand for carrying arms when all had been strictly forbidden to do so. It seemed clear to the thousands of Cetshwayo's supporters that there were rules that Zibhebhu could ignore with impunity.

While in London, Cetshwayo had been 'officially' dressed, for normal daily wear, in the informal attire reserved for British generals: blue frock-coated uniform with a low-crowned peak cap. It was dressed thus that he had come ashore, in appearance so unlike the king his subjects once knew, that it gave Zibhebhu the opportunity to start a rumour that it was not Cetshwayo at all but only a wooden doll. Consequently

47. Cetshwayo made an elegant figure and was lionised by British society during his trip to London.

many watched in awe, the strangely-attired object, discussing amongst themselves in subdued whispers, whether or not it was human.

The following morning, without further delay, Shepstone gave orders to his staff to set in motion the ceremony of installation. The 6th Dragoons were deployed and the massed crowds of supporters marshalled into a huge circle facing the dignitaries who were seated under a flagstaff flying the Union Jack.

Eventually the shuffling and hubbub subsided. Sir Theophilus rose, and began to read the terms of Cetshwayo's restoration and as he did so there began a low murmur of protest from the throng as one condition followed another, each stripping their monarch of his power and kingship. Cetshwayo attempted to rise to make his own protest but was prevented from doing so. But it was not possible to stop the assembled chiefs, all men of eloquence, and eventually they were able to establish their right to speak. Dabulamanzi, who four years earlier had led the assault against Rorke's Drift, was undoubtedly the most outspoken. He first gave thanks for the king's return:

We thank you, Sir, for bringing him back . . . Do you say that you are restoring him, this son of the Queen [Victoria] while all the time you are destroying him just as you did formerly? Sir, you are killing him still as you did before when you first made him King and then killed him. Show us these 'dissatisfied ones' for whom you are cutting off our land, who do not wish for the King. Do you say that we are to move? Where will you put us since you are eating up all Cetshwayo's land? Tell us where you will fix Sibebu's boundaries? Why do you give the land to the very people who have been killing us? Do you approve of their blood-shedding? You have come to kill him, not to restore him.

The crowd vigorously showed its support, with angry shouts and gestures and it was Cetshwayo himself who restored calm, telling his followers that no good would come of hurling abuse and that time would tell. He was no doubt firm in the hope that, in due course, the queen and Kimberley would put matters right.

Shepstone grasped the silence that followed as an opportunity to go and, wasting no time, he, his officials and the Dragoons departed, leaving the new monarch bewildered, apprehensive, unprotected and unarmed. (It is interesting that British troops in Zululand at this time were officially designated as being on active service.) Even the borders of what was left of Cetshwayo's scant realm were ill-defined. And there seemed to be enemies on all sides. To the north, the pugnacious Zibhebhu, with white mercenaries to back him up, bided his time, ready to attack; to the west, Hamu, stripped of his fiefdom and in theory once again the monarch's subject, swore he held no allegiance and to prove the point he had already massacred much of the abaQulusi, a clan fiercely loyal to the king; and to the south the newly-formed 'Nongqayi', the Zululand Native Police, protected all fugitives from Cetshwayo's territory, providing a refuge for his enemies. It was a bitter cup to drink for a king who had believed he would be restored to a realm little diminished in size and one which with authority he would unite. With the hurried departure of Shepstone, the king, accompanied by all his followers, prepared to move off to his old capital of Ulundi.

Samuelson, Cetshwayo's friend and former interpreter who had not accompanied him to London, had heard of the king's home-coming and having ridden hard for several days, arrived in time to witness Cetshwayo's procession of departure; a procession that would be the last

48. With the partition of the Zulu Kingdom, a force, given the name
Zulu Reserve Territory Carbineers, was raised to police and keep order.
Commandant Mansel, its Commander, had been at Isandlwana.
(*Campbell Collection, Durban*)

pageantry of the old Zulu kingdom; a procession in which ceremony
was still evident but of which pomp there was none: the renowned
regiments, with their great distinctive war shields were no more; the
regalia of otter and leopard skin, and of bobbing ostrich plumes, had
long since been abandoned as unnecessary clutter by refugees who
had once been warriors; and the scattering of weapons that a few had
bravely brought in defiance of Shepstone's orders, no longer gleamed
but were dull with rust. Samuelson described the scene:

> There was a very large concourse of Zulus camped round about, who
> were escorting their sovereign . . . and Mnyamana, the King's Prime
> Minister, was the head of the concourse. I had a general chat with the
> King and was introduced to a remarkably fine grey-headed Zulu, who
> had the proud position of being the chief Bard 'Imbhongi' [the praise
> singer of the King]. At about 3 am. next morning, being awake, I heard
> a heard a human voice imitating the crowing of a cock, but in such a
> way that you could just detect that it was a human voice, and not that

of a cock, and when the crowing ceased, the human cock commenced to shouting out the praises of the King and those of his ancestors, and well as those of various heroes, off and on, till nearly 7 am. A light morning meal was then partaken of, and somewhere about 8 am. the voice of Mnyamana rang out, loud and clear, giving orders to assemble and fall in for the march forward. In an incredibly short time all the concourse were in their places and ready to move. Mnyamana then ordered an advance guard to proceed, and then halt and wait for the King, while he ordered the rear guard to stand fast, and the out flankers and scouts to take their places. When the King and his staff had taken up their place for marching on, the Prime Minister gave a loud and ringing order to advance, and the whole concourse moved on, arriving and encamping near the site of the Ulundi Kraal which was razed at the time of the Battle of Ulundi in 1879. I may here mention that the above mentioned bard was named Umahlangeni, was the last royal and national bard of the Zulus ...

It was only a day's march from Mtonjaneni to the Mahlabathini Plain where stood the burnt-out ruin of the king's former residence of Ondini, destroyed by the British at the climax of their victory at Ulundi. Samuelson remembered the King's pleasure in dispensing gifts amongst his family and retainers:

The next day I called on Cetshwayo, about 9 am, and found him seated in a chair, surrounded by many of the Zulu nobility, including his Prime Minister; he was, at the time of my arrival, busy attending to his daughters, giving them presents of shawls, etc., which he had purchased in Cape Town ... The sight of the King sitting there kindly addressing his daughters and some of his wives and maids of honour, and giving them presents, he had acquired during his captivity, was very touching ...

No doubt the king's thoughts were far from magnanimous when at last he surveyed, for the first time, the charred ruin of what had once been the noblest structure in Zululand. W. H. Tomasson, a lieutenant in Baker's Horse, a colonial unit that had been raised in the Eastern Cape, remembered the excitement with which they had galloped to Ondini to be the first to loot and destroy:

Up to this we raced, and jumping off, rushed through the opening and find ourselves in a sort of labyrinth made of tall stiff wooden fences, over which it is impossible to climb. This was evidently built to guard against a surprise: it stretches all round the royal house, and might be held for a long time by a handful of resolute men against a foe who was not possessed of artillery . . . The floor was of clay hardened like cement and was swept clean. It was a low single-storey house built of mud bricks or mud and wattle. It contained eight rooms, had a steep thatched roof, that the rockets had touched but not burnt. A vigorous kick by Captain Baker to the rude unpainted door and we were inside it . . . On first entering Captain Baker stumbled over two bits of wooden-like substance and kicked them out of the way; Lord William Beresford picks them up and we see they are two elephant tusks . . . A large box or locker stand in the corner and a kick opened it; one does not stand on ceremony when looting. It is found full of old newspapers, 'Illustrated London News', 'Times', 'Standard', 'Graphics', and many colonial papers . . . All containing references to the Zulus and Ketchwayo; some where five years old, and they contained all the doings of the Boundary Commission . . . comment on the Zulu Army and war-like contentions of Ketchwayo, everything tending to give him an idea of how frightened the colonials were of him . . . Many others were found, too numerous to mention.

Leaving the house, we found a troop starting off to burn a kraal still further on. The writer was ordered by Colonel Buller to commence to burn the Royal Kraal . . . 10,000 huts which made up Ulundi [Ondini] were burnt, no one else assisting or being near. The huts were nearly a mile round, and were dry and burnt well. The burners rode from hut to hut with flaming torches of grass, and after hard work got everything in flames

Dismayed but resolved to reign, Cetshwayo soon set his subjects about the construction of a new Ondini but peaceful pursuits were soon replaced by conflict. His brothers, other royal relations and loyal subjects, now that their king was returned, sought vengeance on Sibebu and his Mandhlakazi who had treated them so harshly for the last three years. But the British had not left the king to reign unfettered. Their head man in Zululand, with the title of Resident Commissioner, was Melmoth Osborn who had held the post for close on three years and was an administrator of considerable experience but with little military muscle to back up his statutes and decrees. He was to be told in no uncertain terms that the British military presence in Natal, consisting of the 6th Dragoons and three infantry regiments, were there to impress rather than to be deployed. The Governor of Natal, Sir Henry

Bulwer, admonished Osborn: 'You will understand that the detachment of troops is intended solely to support by its presence at Eshowe [the Commissioner's Administrative Headquarters], your position of authority as Resident Commissioner and to give confidence to the loyal people of the territory, and that it is not to be in any way used for military operations.'

The British overseer of Cetshwayo's particular part of the country was a colonial-born white man whom the Zulus called 'Gwalagwala' after the feather of the Lourie bird which he sported in his cap. He held the appointment of 'British Resident with Cetshwayo'.

Gwalagwala was an acquaintance of long standing and he did his best to dissuade Cetshwayo from attacking the Mandhlakazi, knowing full well that the colonial authorities favoured Zibhebhu, seeing him as a counterbalance to the possible rebirth of Zulu imperialism influenced by the king's return. Zibhebhu was well aware of his British backing hence the recent flaunting of his armed warriors before Shepstone without reprimand. He also attired his men with red headbands, the British insignia worn by its native troops throughout the war of 1879.

Gwalagwala had a tented HQ on a hill close by Ondini and believing civil war to be inevitable, attempted to explain the difficulty of his task to his superiors. He stated how he had constantly reminded Cetshwayo that he must hold fast to the conditions of his restoration. '. . . And I am doing my duty as his friend and I tell him again and again the Government holds him personally responsible for any breach or breaking of the laws of his restoration, including any disturbance committed in or beyond his district by his adherents.' So wrote Gwalagwala shortly after Cetshwayo's return. Indeed the Resident's position was a difficult one and he was once sternly admonished by a revered chief for Britain's shortcomings. 'We thought that this king was now a child of the Queen. [It being believed that Cetshwayo would rule under British protection.] Do you mock us in saying you are restoring him?'

The old chiefs' thoughts were strangely similar to those of the Earl of Kimberley who had had the power to rectify the confusion surrounding Cetshwayo's restoration but, for the lack of will it seems, allowed colonial interests to take the helm and steer a different course: 'Had we left Cetshwayo on the throne, or annexed the country, we should in either case have taken an intelligible course. As it is, we neither control the affairs of Zululand nor or are we free from the responsibilities for them.'

Despite Gwalagwala's empathy and his friendship with Cetshwayo, one wonders whether the monstrous irony of his appointment to the position of what amounted to the 'King's Minder' had ever occurred to either Gwalagwala or the king, for Gwalagwala was none other than Henry Francis Fynn Junior, the son of he of the same name who, shipwrecked and destitute, had been the first white man to visit Shaka. At that time Shaka was the supreme power; now, fifty-nine years later, the son of the castaway held power over the king.

Nevertheless, Fynn Junior, was unable to prevent the inevitable war of vengeance against Zibhebhu that the uSuthu demanded of their king. Within days of Cetshwayo's arrival at Ondini, uSuthu elements were raiding old enemies and by late March Cetshwayo's younger brother, Ndabuko, was ready to lead an army of 5,000 warriors against the Mandhlakazi. Having marched north for fifty miles Ndabuko

49. Second from the left, back row, Henry Francis Fynn, son of the first white trader, Lord Chelmsford's political officer and interpreter. To his left Major Dartnell, who commanded the Natal Mounted Police.
(*KZN Archives, Pietermaritzburg*)

found his enemy who, though supported by several white mercenaries, fell back in confusion – or so it seemed. But it was a ruse that led the uSuthu into a well-prepared ambush. Over 1,000 warriors were slain for a loss of only ten Mandhlakazi. One uSuthu warrior recalled: 'We got mixed up in the fight, and were pursued and stabbed and shot down, only one company of the uSuthu made any resistance . . . Both forces had large numbers of guns and Sibebu got possession of the guns and assegais of the fallen men of our force.' Many of the uSuthu later recalled that their hearts were not in the battle, believing that Ndabuko had launched the raid without Cetshwayo's blessing.

For the next two months both sides set about recruiting for their armies until by late July both were ready to engage the other. Again Zibhebhu was the master tactician. On 20 July he led a night march of over thirty miles, surprising and confounding the uSuthu by the dawn appearance of his army, 3,000 strong, three miles east of Ondini. Taken completely by surprise, the uSuthu attempted to scramble

50. Ndabuko kaMpande, another royal brother who fought at Isandlwana. (*KZN Archives, Pietermaritzburg*)

their bewildered ranks into battle array and to recall 1,800 warriors, a third of their total strength, from their camp over four miles away. The Mandhlakazi advanced rapidly, burning homesteads as they came, denying the uSuthu a moment's pause in which to assemble and form ranks. Ondini that morning was host to the greatest assembly of royal personages and uSuthu chiefs that had gathered in many years. They had come at Cetshwayo's bidding to confer, advise, and, no doubt, witness an uSuthu victory over the Mandhlakazi that the king believed he would, within days, inflict upon his enemies. But the Mandhlakazi onslaught was without mercy. Old men, women and children all perished, a number of Cetshwayo's wives and offspring included. Amongst the chiefs who perished was Ntshingwayo kaMahole, one of the greatest of the Zulu commanders, he who had defeated the British at the Battle of Isandlwana. It is likely that he suffered the ignominious death of being slain by pack of young boys. A white mercenary, by the name of Grosvenor Darke, perhaps witnessing his death: 'All the principal headmen were killed ... being all fat and big bellied, they had no chance of escape; and one of them was actually run to death and stabbed to death by my little mat bearers.' Later, the war correspondent, W. A. Walton, of the *Pictorial World*, who witnessed the battle sketched the corpse of Ntshingwayo prostrate on the ground, covered in stab wounds but still clutching his shield and war club.

A few of the uSuthu found sanctuary in Fynn's hilltop camp a few miles north of Ondini, where Fynn could only protect them, as he courageously did, by his presence alone. However, the King was not amongst the refugees. Wounded in the leg, he had fled to the Nkandla Forest. Zibhebhu had scored another remarkable victory. He would be able to gloat over the 500 uSuthu dead for the loss of only five of the Mandhlakazi.

The colonial authorities, greatly alarmed, decided to send troops to Osborn at Eshowe and soon the Dragoons and five companies of infantry were on the march north. However, Cetshwayo, with his new, half-completed, Ondini having been razed to the ground again and his forces scattered, decided to remain in the sanctuary of the Nkandla Forest until, in October, Fynn persuaded him to seek Osborn's protection at Eshowe. However, before proceeding, the King begging like a castaway, sent a solicitous request to Osborn that was delivered orally by his royal messenger: 'Cetshwayo says he wants to come to you, but he cannot walk all the way, he therefore, asks you to give him a horse to ride, also a pair of trousers, a shirt, and a hat.'

Cetshwayo reached Eshowe in mid-October and there he stayed under Osborn's protection until early February when he died suddenly of what was officially described by the British military doctor who examined his body, as 'fatty degeneration of the heart'. But many disputed this diagnosis, his loyal subjects believing that he had died of a broken heart while the actual doctor who would eventually make the above diagnosis initially stated that he had been poisoned. However a case of poisoning would require a post-mortem and Cetshwayo's retainers, having been told that their master must be cut open, replied emphatically: 'If you cut our chief, we will cut you.' So said, it was enough to deter the doctor and he took a less perilous route and settled for 'degeneration of the heart'. There is considerable support for the poisoning theory, the *Natal Mercury* of 3 April 1884 stating that the

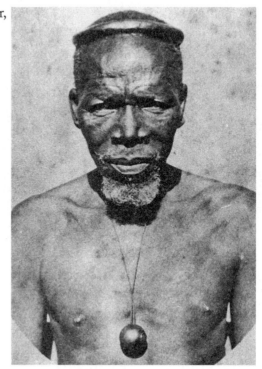

51. Mfunzi, the king's messenger, was sent to Natal in order to arrange peace discussions. He was arrested and held at Fort Buckingham for over three weeks. (*Local History Museum, Durban*)

British Medical Journal supported the hypothesis that Cetshwayo did not die of heart disease.

Those Zulus who believed that death was caused by other than a broken heart, also supported the theory that their king had been poisoned, the culprit being variously named by them as either Osborn or Zibhebhu. Cetshwayo's body was eventually loaded onto what was probably little more than a farm cart, drawn by a couple of oxen, and was taken to the Nkandla Forest where, seventy-four days after his death, he was ceremoniously buried in a sitting position accompanied by his ceremonial assegai, sleeping mat and other personal belongings.

With Cetshwayo's death and the earlier slaughter at Ondini of so many members of the royal family and royal chiefs, the old order of the Zulu nation was gone forever. Cetshwayo's sixteen-year-old son, Dinuzulu, supported by his royal uncles, now assumed kingship of a defeated realm. Nevertheless, the young monarch was determined to fight for what remained of his kingdom and, perhaps, regain that

52. Dinuzulu, son of King Cetshwayo. (*KZN Archives, Pietermaritzburg*)

which had been lost. So civil war continued and while the fortunes of both the uSuthu and the Mandhlakazi rose and fell, Osborn, alarmed at the escalating violence, reinforced the 6th Dragoons stationed in the Reserve Territory with additional British redcoats, their purpose being to support the Mandhlakazi as much as to oppose the uSuthu.

Dinuzulu, aware that the odds against his faction were overwhelming, decided to approach an enemy of old, the Boers, for assistance and in so doing traded away yet more of his diminished kingdom. However, in June 1884, the combined forces of Dinuzulu and the Boers completely routed the Mandhlakazi, sending them fleeing to find refuge with Osborn in the Reserve Territory.

The Boers, ever-hungry for more land and grazing, encroached still further into what was left of the Zulu kingdom and having done so proclaimed an independent state which they grandly named the New Republic. Furthermore they extended their domain by declaring a protectorate over the remnant of Dinuzulu's territory. The British government, perhaps wishing to believe that the Boers had solved the Zulu problem, at first acknowledged the Boer proclamation. But Britain quickly changed its mind when it became aware of German aspirations concerning St. Lucia Bay, on the coast of northern Zululand, and the possibility of a future German alliance with the Boers. Britain, therefore, agreed to acknowledge the New Republic subject to Boer renunciation of its protectorate. Thus, the fate of the diminished Kingdom was temporarily decided but, as was inevitable, in May 1887, Britain proclaimed Zululand to be a colony in which missionaries and traders would be freely permitted to pursue their vocations and which, in one area of approximately 275 square miles, white settlement would be permitted:

WHEREAS Zululand came under the Paramount Authority of Her Majesty the Queen as a consequence of the war of 1879:

AND WHEREAS, in the interests of peace, order and good government, it has been deemed expedient that Her Majesty's Sovereignty should be proclaimed over Zululand as is hereinafter defined:

AND WHEREAS, Her Majesty has been pleased to authorise me to take the necessary steps for giving effect to Her pleasure in the matter:'

And so, in the same pompous language, the Governor of Natal and Special Commissioner, ordered 'all Her Majesty's subjects in South Africa to take notice . . . that the whole of Zululand . . . shall be taken to be a British possession.'

Of course, those most affected by the imperious proclamation, the uSuthu, were unable to immediately comprehend what was afoot and aggressively resented the sudden influx of white government officials who diminished traditional authority. And in many areas the establishment of British control was crudely and inimically applied. On 2 June 1888 Dinuzulu attacked a combined punitive force of British cavalry and redcoats accompanied by a contingent of Zululand Police, and put it to flight. It was the last occasion that a Zulu army would do battle with a British force and defeat it.

Further battles and skirmishes between Dinuzulu and colonial forces would follow but, inevitably, the uSuthu were defeated and the

53. The conclusion of the war brought about a time of civil strife and poverty for Zululand. (*Local History Museum, Durban*)

young king, like his father before him, was sent into exile. Again, like his father, he would be permitted to return but it was to a Zululand that would have been unrecognisable compared to the realm in which Henry Francis Fynn Snr, fearful and vulnerable, had once found succour and hospitality. There would, of course, continue to be encounters with the Zulu people but they would never again embrace the honour, the kindness, the cruelty, the courage and the spectacle of those early days which, like the old Zulu order, would never return to stir and inspire the spirit of lesser men.

Bibliography

Published Sources

Angus, George French, *The Kaffirs Illustrated*, Cape Town: 1849.

Barter, Catherine, *Alone Among the Zulus*, edited by Patricia L. Merrett, Pietermaritzburg: Killie Campbell Africana Library Publication, 1995.

Bell, William, *Entrance of the Conch at Port Natal*. Durban: 1869.

Binns, C. T., *The Warrior People*, London: Robert Hale & Company, 1975.

Brookes, E. H. and Webb, C. de B., *A History of Natal*, Pietermaritzburg: University of Natal Press, 1965.

Bryant, T., *Olden Times in Zululand and Natal*, reprinted Capetown: C. Struik, 1965.

Buchan, John, *Prester John*, London: Thomas Nelson & Sons, 1938.

Bulpin, T. V., *To the Shores of Natal*, Cape Town: Howard Timmins, 1953.

Burman, J., *Great Shipwrecks off the Coast of Southern Africa*, Cape Town: 1967.

Champion, Rev. George, *The Journal of the Rev. George Champion*, reprinted Cape Town: Rustica Press, 1967.

Chase, J. C., *The Natal Papers*, Cape Town: Struik (Pty.) Ltd., 1968.

Delegorgue, Adulphe, *Travels in Southern Africa*, Volumes I and II, translated by Fleur Webb, Pietermaritzburg: Killie Campbell Africana Library Publications, 1990–1997.

Dunn, John, *Cetshwayo and the Three Generals*, edited by D. C. F. Moodie, Pietermaritzburg: The Natal Printing and Publishing Company, 1886.

Eyre, C. J., *Dick King, Savior of Natal*, Durban: Durban Publicity Association, 1932.

Fynn, Henry Francis, *The Diary of Henry Francis Fynn*, reprinted Pietermaritzburg: Shuter and Shooter, 1951.

Fynney, F. B., *The Zulu Army*, m/s compiled at the request of the C.- in- C., Southern Africa, Pietermaritzburg: 1878.

Gardiner, A., *Narrative of a Journey to the Zoolu Country*, London: 1836.

Guy, Jeff, *The Destruction of the Zulu Kingdom*, Johannesburg: 1979, and London: 1982.

Herd, N., *The Bent Pine*, Johannesburg: Ravan Press, 1976.

Isaacs, Nathaniel, *Travels and Adventures in Eastern Africa*, London: 1836, and reprinted Cape Town: 1970.

Knight, Ian, *Great Zulu Commanders*, London: Arms and Armour Press, 1999.

Krige, Eileen Jensen, *The Social Systems of the Zulus*, Pietermaritzburg: 1957.

Laband, John, *The Atlas of the Later Zulu Wars, 1883-1888*, Pietermaritzburg: University of Natal Press, 2001.

Laband, J. P. and Thompson P. S., *Kingdom and Colony at War*, Pietermaritzburg: University of Natal Press, 1990.

Laband, J.P. and Thompson, P.S., with Sheila Henderson, *The Buffalo Border Guard*, Durban: University of Natal Press, 1983.

Laband, J.P., *Rope of Sand*, Johannesburg: Jonathan Ball Publishers, 1995.

Ladysmith Historical Society, Editorial Committee, *Langalibalele and the Natal Carbineers*, Ladysmith: Westcott Printing Company Ltd., 1973.

Lock, Ron and Quantrill, Peter, *The Red Book, Natal Newspaper reports on the Anglo-Zulu War, 1879: a compilation*, Pinetown: Pinetown Printers, 2002.

MacClean, Charles Rawdon, *The Natal Papers of John Ross*, edited by S. Gray, Pietermaritzburg: Killie Campbell Library Publications, 1992.

MacKeurtan, G., *The Cradle Days of Natal*, Pietermaritzburg; Shuter and Shooter, 1948.

Meintjies, Johannes, *The Voortrekkers*, London: 1973.

Milton, John, *The Edges of War*, Cape Town: Juta & Co Ltd., 1983.

Mitford, Bertram, *Through the Zulu Country*, London: 1883; reprinted London: Greenhill Books, 1988.

Molyneux, W. C. F., *Campaigning in South Africa and Egypt*, London: 1896.

Montague, W. E., *Campaigning in South Africa*, London: 1880.

Nathan, Manfred, *The Voortrekkers of South Africa*, London: 1937.

Pearse, R. O., *Barrier of Spears*, Cape Town: Howard Timmins, 1978.

Posselt, Wilhelm, *The Story of His Labours Among Xhosa and Zulu 1815-1885*, translated and edited by S. Bourquin, Westville: Bergtheil Museum, 1994.

Ransford, Oliver, *The Great Trek*, London: 1974.

Roberts, Brian, *The Zulu Kings*, London: 1974.

Samuelson, L. H., *Zululand in Transition, Legends, Customs and Folklore*, Durban: 1974.

Samuelson, R. C., *Long, Long Ago*, Durban: 1929.

Stalker, The Rev. John, *The Natal Carbineers*, Pietermaritzburg: 1912.

Struthers, R. B., *Hunting Journal, 1852-1856*, Durban: 1991.

Stuart, James and Malcolm, D., *The Diary of Henry Francis Fynn*, Pietermaritzburg: Schuter and Shooter, 1986.

Stuart, James, *The James Stuart Archives*, edited by C. de B. Webb and J. B. Wright, Durban: University Press, 1976.

Tomasson, W. H., *With the Irregulars*, Pietermaritzburg: Remington and Co., 1881.

Turner, Malcolm, *Shipwrecks and Salvage in South Africa – 1505 to the Present*, Cape Town: C. Struik, 1988.

Vijn, Cornelius, *Cetshwayo's Dutchman*, London: 1880; reprinted London: Greenhill Books, 1988.

Webb, C. de B. and Wright, J. B., *A Zulu King Speaks*, Pietermaritzburg: 1978.

Willcox, A. R., *Shipwreck and Survival*, Natal: Winterton, 1984.

Newspapers, Journal and Periodicals

Chadwick, G.A., *Veglaer*, National Monuments Council, Durban: 1982.

Thompson, P.S., 'Isandlwana to Mome, Zulu Experience in Overt Resistance to Colonial Rule', *Soldiers of the Queen*, Vol. 77, 1994.

Legg, Philip, *The Mfecane Debate*, Anglo-Zulu War Historical Society: 2005.

Smail, J. L., *Monuments and Trails of the Voortrekkers*, Cape Town, 1968.

Tucker, A. R., 'The Congella Incident', *Soldiers of the Queen*, Vol. 74, 1993.

Wood, Jack, *The Huskar Pit Disaster*. An undated pamphlet.

Unpublished Sources and Printed Information

Fynn, Henry Francis, *My Recollections of a Famous Campaign and a Great Disaster*, M/S Campbell Collection, Durban.

Correspondence, April — August 1842 between: Captain T. C. Smith/Sir Charles Napier; Major Goodman/Sir Benjamin D'Urban; Captain William D'Urban/Sir Benjamin D'Urban;Lt. Col. A. J. Cloete/Sir Benjamin D'Urban.

All Campbell Collection, Durban.

A letter, concerning the Battle of Congella, from Capt. Durnford to Mr. Fawkes, date August 7th 1842. Campbell Collection, Durban.

Manuscript papers of Henry Francis Fynn, Jnr.; Sir Evelyn Wood; Rev. Francis Owen; Richard Hulley; Tpr. Blamey and J.A. Brickhill, Campbell Collection, Durban.

Chadwick, G., *The Life of Alexander Biggar*. An undated pamphlet.

Dominy, G. *Thomas Baines and the Langalibalele Rebellion*, Pietermaritzburg: Natal Museum, 1991.

Index